The Metaphysics of Modern Existence

This book is the eleventh in Harper & Row's Native American Publishing Program. All profits from this program are used to support projects designed to aid the Native American People.

Other Books in the program

Seven Arrows, by Hyemeyohsts Storm
Ascending Red Cedar Moon, by Duane Niatum
Winter in the Blood, by James Welch
Indians' Summer, by Nas'Naga
Carriers of the Dream Wheel, edited by Duane Niatum
Riding the Earthboy 40, by James Welch
Going for the Rain, by Simon Ortiz
The Blood People, by Adolf Hungry Wolf
Digging Out the Roots, by Duane Niatum
Wind from an Enemy Sky, by D'Arcy McNickle

The Metaphysics of Modern Existence

Vine Deloria, Jr.

Published in San Francisco by
HARPER & ROW, PUBLISHERS

New York   Hagerstown   San Francisco   London

FIRST EDITION

Designed by Patricia Dunbar

Library of Congress Cataloging in Publication Data

Deloria, Vine.
  The metaphysics of modern existence.
  Bibliography: p. 218
  1. Religions (Proposed, universal, etc.)
2. Religion and culture. 3. Indians of
North America—Religion and mythology.
4. Civilization, Modern—Moral and religious
aspects. I. Title.
BL390.D43   291.2   76-8708
ISBN 0-06-450250-3

78 79 80 81 82 10 9 8 7 6 5 4 3 2 1

Contents

Introduction

The subject matter of this book may seem strange to people who have read my previous books. Outlining the treatment of the American Indian by the United States government, suggesting new ways of solving perennial Indian problems, and developing new theories for understanding Indians are hardly a prelude to a book on metaphysics. There is a consistent thread throughout, however, if one pierces to the central theme of the issues that separate Indians from the rest of American society. In every area in which Indians have had to relate to Western European concepts, policies, and programs, there has been dreadful misunderstanding, which the years and the changes of administrations and Congresses have done little to resolve.

The fundamental factor that keeps Indians and non-Indians from communicating is that they are speaking about two entirely different perceptions of the world. Growing up on an Indian reservation makes one acutely aware of the mysteries of the universe. Medicine men practicing their ancient ceremonies perform feats that amaze and puzzle the rational mind. The sense of contentment enjoyed by older Indians in the face of a lifetime's experience of betrayal, humiliation, and paternalism stuns the astute observer. It often appears that Indians are immune to the values which foreign institutions have forced them to confront. Their minds remain fixed on other realities.

Attending school away from the reservation is a traumatic experience for most Indian people. In the white man's world knowledge is a matter of memorizing theories, dates, lists of kings and presidents, the table of chemical elements, and many other things not encountered in the course of a day's work. Knowledge seems to be divorced from experience. Even religion is a process of memorizing creeds, catechisms, doctrines and dogmas—general principles that never seem to catch the essence of human existence.

No matter how well educated an Indian may become, he or she always suspects that Western culture is not an adequate representation of reality. Life therefore becomes a schizophrenic balancing act wherein one holds that the creation, migration, and ceremonial stories of the tribe are true and that the Western European view of the world is also true. Obviously this situation is impossible although just how it becomes impossible remains a mystery to most Indians. The trick is somehow to relate what one *feels* to what one is taught to *think*. Western peoples seem to have little difficulty doing this since accumulating knowledge is for them an initiatory act that admits them to higher status employment. They do not seem concerned with the ultimate truth of what they are taught. Indians, for the most part, fail to comprehend the sanity of this attitude at all.

Perhaps a generation ago there was little chance that the schizophrenia would ever be resolved. Aside from some friendly anthropologists like Paul Radin and an occasional folklorist who might suggest a literal and historical basis for Indian traditions—and thereby gain a suspicious reputation among his colleagues—few scholars in any discipline gave the Indian traditions any credence. Indian customs and beliefs were regarded as primitive superstitions unworthy of serious attention. In recent decades non-Indians have finally come to recognize that many Indian ideas were ecologically and scientifically sound and only seemed primitive. The U.S. Forest Service, after nearly a century of frantically extinguishing forest fires, has come to realize that many fires act to eliminate tree-choking plants and that the Indian method of forestry with its periodic burnings was a rather sophisticated means of ensuring proper tree growth. The Army Corps of Engineers, in its massive dam building programs, has destroyed fish runs that Indians cherished and preserved for many centuries and is only in recent times recognizing the damage it has caused by thoughtless construction. Examples of Indian traditions that have been verified to be scientifically correct are numerous.

At any rate, the Indian traditions were discredited by definition. Evolutionary interpretations of the experiences of our species viewed tribal peoples as a more primitive stage of social development than the industrial cultures of the West because these peoples lacked a mechanical technology. So the question of the validity of knowledge contained in the Indian traditions was eliminated before any discussions of reality began.

The natural response of Indians, including myself, has been to accept those dissident and heretical theories of Western culture that seem to correlate and support the Indian interpretation of the meaning of life. In recent years this has not been a difficult task. Modern physicists, incapable of expressing space-time perceptions in the English language, now often refer to the Zuni or Hopi conception of space-time as the more accurate rendering of what they are finding at the subatomic level of experiments. Psychoanalysts, working with dream theories, are now more inclined to view the dream-interpretation systems of the Cherokee and the Iroquois as consistent and highly significant methods of handling certain types of mental and emotional problems. Geologists, attempting to understand the history of rivers and volcanoes, are now turning to Indian legends in an effort to gain some perspective on the problems.

The movement is not merely of scientific significance. Marshall McLuhan, describing the effects of the electronic media on human behavior, continually applauds the tribal peoples and the manner in which they handle experiences. Alvin Toffler, working with basically the same material, sees generalists as capable of surviving the impact of future shock. Christopher Stone, a brilliant attorney, suggests that according natural objects legal rights may be the first step to ecological sanity—a conclusion inherent in the Indian view of the world.

In the fields of scientific knowledge and social reform we see a gradual and irreversible movement away from the sterility of the traditional Western European formulas and doctrines into a more flexible and broader awareness of the manifold experiences of life. This movement has been so fragmented that few people have perceived it as a comprehensive change. The young people of this generation, and a few poets like Gary Snyder, have seen intuitively that the view of the world which formerly dominated Western peoples and which currently dominates Western science is being transformed into an ancient and all-encompassing attitude toward life, best characterized by the American Indian cultures and traditions.

Over a period of time it became increasingly clear that the trend in modern thought was approaching the Indian conception of the universe; the work of synthesizing ideas became more urgent. Dissident and heretical views became more important and seemed to stand out as unresolved questions that demanded proper answers. For nearly a decade, then, I have entertained heretical thoughts with respect to the Western structure of knowledge. The theory of evolution, for example, has seemed less and less compelling, and the majesty of some Indian ways of classifying life-forms has seemed much more satisfying from an emotional point of view since they incorporate psychological factors that modern biology fails to consider. The same could be said for other areas of knowledge.

Faced with this irresistible urge to attempt to outline an alternative way of conceiving reality, I became aware of a phenomenon of modern life that continually astounds me. People seem to look for *the* single, simple answer to all of life's questions. In recent decades innumerable books have been written by very astute thinkers who felt a burning desire to translate some of their insights into a new, unified world-view. Alvin Toffler, Robert Ardrey, Carl Jung, Immanuel Velikovsky, Werner Heisenberg, Charles Reich, Philip Slater, Gregory Bateson, Pierre Teilhard de Chardin, and Ian Barbour seem to have grasped some of this vision. For the most part they have been given a brief time onstage, and the public has moved on to new books and thinkers, as if making sense out of the world were a matter of intellectual supermarket shopping and as if the slickness and glitter of slogans were sufficient.

Writers, as a whole, are serious people and do not spend their time dreaming up fantasy-pictures of the world. Yet, as far as I can discern at present, many of the best ideas of our time have been given perfunctory examination and have then been discarded because people seemed incapable of relating a great many ideas in one comprehensive interpretation. No person can claim to have pierced the veil of reality and properly articulated what he or she has found. Yet some better picture of what we know and what we perceive can be devised for our times, and certainly the world, which we experience as a unity, should be capable of being described in a unified fashion.

The question then becomes: In what manner could such a synthesis be achieved? Obviously the collective insights of the American Indian tradition, while helpful, derive from a radically different period of history and therefore cannot be translated into a comprehensive understanding that would include the sophisticated theories of modern science. Does modern science, however, rest upon such solid foundations that reconciliation with nonscientific traditions is impossible? An examination of the foundations of modern science reveals that although we are taught Newtonian mechanics, with its absolute space and time, such a system is useful only for certain-sized phenomena. Although we are taught evolutionary theories in biology and social science, the evidence for the absolute validity of evolutionary principles is slim indeed. And although we are taught that Christianity incorporates the best teaching of all the world religions, the great need for psychoanalysts in predominantly Christian countries obviously indicates that all is not well.

In a more concrete sense, if an Indian tells other Indians that he or she has seen a ghost, describes the experience, and asks others for advice, he or she is taken to be a serious person with a serious problem. However if a non-Indian tells another non-Indian that he or she has seen a ghost, it is another matter entirely. Scientists will give the person a suspicious look and recommend a psychiatrist. The priest or minister will take great pains to reassure the person that he or she in fact did *not* see a ghost. The average listener may or may not believe the person depending upon the listener's orientation toward the supernatural.

Therein lies the difference. The Indian confronts the reality of the experience, and while he or she may not make immediate sense of it, it is not rejected as an invalid experience. In the Indian world, experience is not limited by mental considerations and assumptions regarding the universe. For the non-Indian the teachings of a lifetime come thundering down. Such things do not occur in time and space. Reality is basically physical. No one sees ghosts. Reality, in a certain sense, is what you allow your mind to accept, not what you experience. And a host of other beliefs rush in to cover up, confuse, and eventually eliminate the experience itself.

This attitude goes far back in Western tradition. Pasteur had immense difficulty convincing his peers that there were tiny organisms in the world.

Western medicine has reluctantly dealt with psychosomatic illnesses, unable for a considerable period of time to reconcile the unity of spirit and body with what they had been taught to believe. That a reality exists which we cannot measure is difficult for non-Indian peoples to believe, or at least to believe emotionally rather than intellectually.

So the problem became one of tracing the origin and scope of the peculiar beliefs of the non-Indian rather than finding a way to express the reality of the Indian experience in Western European scientific and religious terms. The nature of this inquiry, therefore, was what Western peoples formerly called *metaphysics*—a search for the structure and meaning of reality. This quest was not, in any abstract sense, a search for a first principle that would unlock the mysteries of the universe. It was simply a survey of what serious writers and thinkers had suggested was important to see if they were converging in the direction of a new view of the world or diverging and making the task of unifying one's view of reality more difficult. Fortunately, as I hope this book demonstrates, they are converging and describing a new vision of reality.

A final technical problem existed. Western society, and particularly its educational and academic establishments, did not like the nonspecialist intruding into already sanctified domains that had been allocated to the respective professions. The heretical amateur had upset too many apple carts for the professional theologian, scientist, and scholar to welcome any new voices into the discussion. Cries of "credentials" and "authority" would ring out every time a synthesizer appeared, and there was no reason to believe that a layman's book on metaphysics would receive any kinder greeting. This problem bothered me considerably, but discourse with respected social scientists soon calmed my concern. Quizzing some about evolution, I was informed that while it did not explain very much it was better than any other theory. Questions about the so-called Indian migration across the Bering Straits produced the same response. It was not a good theory, in fact linguistic studies might indicate that it was faulty, but it was better than any other theory, and, most important, it was acceptable to scholars who had not seriously considered the question for some time!

I soon came to realize that theories are not accepted because they are true. They are accepted because they are accepted by the authority figures in each field! Being accepted does not mean that a theory explains phenomena satisfactorily, although modern physics would seem to indicate that phenomena and theory can closely correspond, but it really means that a theory is accepted because it is accepted. I decided, therefore, to quote only those serious thinkers who impressed me with their ability to handle the data and give interpretations of that data that were not overladen with abstractions but had general importance.

The use of quotations of other thinkers in this book, therefore, is extensive by design. To my knowledge no one has tried to place the collective thoughts of these people into one consistent exposition of an alternative way of conceiving reality. Rather than paraphrase what they might have said or what I would have liked them to say, wherever possible I have used what they actually said. Friends reading the various drafts of this manuscript have asked disgustedly where my own thinking is going in comparison to the scholars, scientists, and theologians I have quoted. The answer, of course, is that the idea of bringing their collective thoughts together in this manner is my contribution, not any startlingly new revelations on the nature of reality and not some esoteric Indian doctrines that have not yet been revealed to the Western world.

The contribution this book might make is therefore to be understood in terms of searching. Making sense out of the mass of information available to us today is a process of continual search and the hope that by being astute we can form, re-form, and continue to re-form a cohesive vision of reality. If we go far back into the Western tradition, we discover Socrates spending a lifetime looking for a cohesive explanation of knowledge and experience and conducting his search in a practical and synthetic manner. That is probably the only sane and human way of doing business. Truth becomes the criterion, not authority and not credentials.

There is no guarantee, however, that many unnecessary twists and turns have not been taken. Who can walk into an unknown woods and head directly for the other side? Wandering for a spell sometimes makes the journey even more exciting. Thus occasional overemphasis on points or a hurried rush through other points should indicate little more than a fascination with some things and an inclination to be off on more important business at other times. On the whole I believe that this sketch of where we should look for a new vision of reality makes sense. This book thus forms the first part of a two-part effort, since it ends with a recommendation that we consider a new unity of perception in determining what elements of knowledge can make up an alternative under-standing. The second part of the effort will be to reinterpret how we look at specific fields of knowledge when that knowledge is cast in a planetary context and the witnesses of all peoples are considered. This new unity of human knowledge will be built around the emerging theory of catastrophe as the proper manner for understanding planetary history. As such it will challenge the assumptions we use to approach our data, and not the data itself.

Finally, at least part of the motivation for this book comes from the reception that some young Indians gave to *God Is Red,* a previous book that attempted to outline the areas of difference between Western religious conceptions and a generalized theory of Indian beliefs. In the years since *God Is Red* was published, a number of young Indians have thanked me for writing it, saying they always believed the migration, creation, or revelation stories of their tribe but were unable to defend the reality they experienced in the face of disbelieving non-Indians. That a catastrophic theory of interpretation could be used to verify their tribe's traditions and, in some instances, could show them how to relate their traditions to modern developments in physics, medicine, psychology, and religion encouraged me to attempt a more thorough outline of the differences that exist between traditional Newtonian and Darwinian interpretations of the world and the new ideas now surfacing. I thus firmly believe that the newly emerging view of the world will support and illuminate Indian traditions and that Indian traditions will prove extremely useful and accurate when cast in a new and more respectful light.

The book is thus an effort to break new trails in thinking, perceptually and conceptually; it is not a technical effort to establish any orthodoxy or to articulate an Indian alternative to Western thought in quasi-scientific terms. I hope it will encourage others to give the thinkers quoted in these pages a great deal more respect. If considered as prophetic voices attempting to describe other ways of thinking and perceiving, they are a significant group of people.

I. A Planet in Transition

Throughout most of human history people have lived as tribal groups in small villages in relatively isolated areas. They have been born, have married, given birth, grown old, and died unaffected by events, beliefs, and developments of other groups of human beings on other parts of the planet. Even the great empires of ancient times—Chinese, Assyrian, Egyptian, Persian, and Roman—hailed as magnificent and world encompassing in their heyday, did not affect a significant number of human societies, and they enjoyed decades of prosperity without exploiting more than a tiny percentage of Earth's natural wealth. There was no concept of world history aside from the local interpretations of small nation-empires, which saw in their origin and rise to prominence a paradigm for understanding the meaning of human existence. But each in turn suffered a decline and collapse, leaving little more than exotic pottery and massive ruins.

A radical transformation of all human societies occurred when the European explorers discovered the Western Hemisphere. Suddenly the scope of planetary existence began to take shape, and the people of Western Europe spread over the globe exploring, colonizing, and finally exploiting the lands and peoples that had formerly lived in relative isolation. European languages replaced tribal languages in many lands, and first French and then English became the tongue of the civilized world, of diplomacy and trade, and finally of the accepted expressions of civilized values. Through the establishment of colonial administrations, Western European political forms were thrust upon non-Western peoples, and Western economic interests came to dominate the economies of other continents. By the beginning of the twentieth century, Earth was conceived as a gigantic garden designed exclusively for the benefit and entertainment of Europeans. Other peoples existed as much for the sake of European tourist visitations as for themselves, and the quaint and exotic seemed to be the only acceptable characterizations of non-Western societies.

Because the business of Western Europeans was business, their technology and industrial capabilities became the dominating influences in social and political change throughout the world. Their standard of living became the goal toward which the other peoples of the globe aspired, and their forms of entertainment and relaxation became universally accepted as expressions of luxury. European political ideas were thrust upon non-Western nations in varying degrees, and while democracy was extolled as the ultimate human virtue, European nations were reluctant to grant any measure of self-government, even in a democratic sense, to the colonized nations they controlled. In those areas where the European nations became weak and lost colonies, particularly in South America, the former colonies instituted their own brand of European economic and political forms, which were as oppressive and dominating as any European institutions.

The Second World War brought an end to the period of colonization. It was the first truly planetary struggle, and although it began as a quarrel among European neighbors over the expansion of German "living-room," it soon embroiled the colonies and trust lands controlled by European nations. The alliance between Germany and Italy, when expanded to an Axis coalition to include Japan, ensured that the struggle would be waged from pole to pole and in all continents. Calling on their colonial peoples to resist Axis domination, the Allied forces justified their military expeditions and atrocities on their alleged support of four basic human freedoms, which Axis totalitarian theories seemed to deny. And with the assistance of colonial armies the Allied forces were victorious, forcing the total collapse of the Axis powers and their surrender.

Following the war, the victorious Allied powers attempted to rejuvenate their faltering colonial empires, but with little success. The cry for freedom that had inspired diverse peoples to resist the German and Japanese armies now inspired them to seek political and economic freedom from their colonial masters. For many smaller nations the Second World War was not a struggle to keep from learning German or Japanese but the beginning of a long and bitter effort to free their lands from all foreign domination. In some instances the European nations saw little to be gained by continued colonization of remote lands. Pretending that independence was a reward for faithful services rendered during the war, they granted a form of freedom that ensured strong economic ties but allowed a measure of political independence.

Not all nations received such a gratuity, however, and particularly in Southeast Asia and Africa, the European nations made every effort to retain their colonial possessions. Thus France, Belgium, and Portugal struggled with wars of liberation conducted by patriots in their colonies in the decades following the war, and these powers surrendered their claims only when the war became so costly as to threaten the collapse of the Mother Country's economy. The decolonization process is hardly concluded, but at present it seems inevitable that European political control over all lands will be eliminated, except in those where European immigrants have totally settled, such as New Zealand and Australia.

In three decades of decolonization, eighty new nations were established from the ruins of old colonial empires. For the most part this was a peaceful process in which the European nation assisted in founding a democratic form of government often modeled on its own. Today only eleven of those democracies survive; the rest have fallen victim to revolutions and political coups, often choosing some form of dictatorship that guaranteed social and economic stability over the chaos of a democracy in which the basic economic foundations were still controlled by foreign interests. Seven of the eleven are today little more than island republics, isolated for the most part from important developments in world affairs and content in their limited relationships with larger powers. This transitional process from democracy to totalitarian governments has been interpreted by Western leaders as an indication of the decline of Western humanistic traditions, and some American political leaders *have privately admitted that their goal for foreign policy is to secure a guaranteed second-best status for* Western nations in a world increasingly hostile to the Western way of life.

The United States emerged from the Second World War as the leading nation on the planet and as the sole possessor of atomic weapons. But American governmental officials understood the world as a Western possession, and postwar American foreign policy was designed to prevent the decline of colonial empires by the strange device of seeing liberation movements as part of a gigantic planetary Communist conspiracy. Regarding European culture, values, and institutions as the highest expression of human civilization, American governmental leaders saw in divergent movements for political freedom a threat to the very existence of civilization itself. The United States frequently found itself supporting puppet governments that sought neither political freedom nor justice for their people but simply their continuation in power. Acting as a global policeman, the United States became embroiled in *a substantial number of military adventures* as it attempted to bolster the institutions of a world which had long since vanished.

The drive for liberation was a planetary phenomenon, however, and manifested itself inside nations as well as within their colonial possessions. Dissident racial and ethnic groups within the Western nations saw the movement of Third World countries as being similar to their own aspirations for more social, political, and economic freedom, and reform movements began to express these concerns. The most important domestic movement within the Western democracies was the Civil Rights movement in the United States, which had strong ideological links with new political crusades around the globe. During the

Second World War, Nazi theorists had advocated racial supremacy, which was not ideologically different from the racial theories held by most Americans. In opposing Nazism on egalitarian grounds the United States had undercut the ideological basis for its own racial practices. The Allied triumph over the Axis powers was thus a direct motivation for internal reform in race relations in the Western countries. It seemed unreasonable to deny one's own citizens those rights the Axis powers had tried to deny to all humanity.

But internal reforms were not initiated by U.S. political leaders. The representatives in Congress were a timid lot who acted only after the rest of society had long since adopted new forms of understanding. Reforms became necessary when protesting groups had so disrupted the tranquility of the domestic scene that to do otherwise seemed disastrous. Protests and demonstrations thereby became the format for social and political change in the United States. In the mid-1960s, when the energies of the reform-minded were directed toward American participation in the Southeast Asian war, American foreign policy became a function of internal debate and protests, indicating that even American institutions had become outmoded in the postwar world. The antiwar movement persisted for nearly a decade as Americans of all persuasions attempted to change the course of their nation's foreign policy. And the antiwar energies soon found themselves directed to peripheral but related fields of reform such as women's rights, consumers' rights, and conservation and ecological concerns.

In the early 1970s the antiwar movement reached a fever pitch. Demonstrators, frustrated by their inability to change the direction of foreign policy, began predicting a violent revolution in the United States unless basic reforms were instituted. Such rhetoric seemed to confirm the worst fears of the conservatives who saw every demand for change as a Communist plot. When Martha Mitchell interpreted the May Day demonstrations against the Cambodia invasion as similar in intensity and design to the Russian Revolution, the nation braced for a violent confrontation with the forces of change.

Among the many voices predicting such a fundamental change was the French Marxist philosopher Jean-François Revel. His book *Without Marx or Jesus* was translated into English and published in 1971, with the subtitle "The New American Revolution Has Begun." Rather than advocating a violent revolution in American society, Revel described a process of planetary transformation. According to his analysis, the United States was the nation with the most beneficial aspects to assume a role of planetary leadership. Unfortunately Revel used the word *revolution* to describe the process of change he detected. The important insights he offered were thereby lost in general fear over the possibility of violent revolution that Americans felt might engulf them. The book did not receive the serious attention it merited. American critics, cynical over the left's failure to influence American foreign policy, chided Revel for his optimism, and Mary McCarthy, noted social critic, in an afterword to his book, wrote that "his 'revolution' is only a metaphor." [1]

The failure of American thinkers to come to grips with Revel's thesis was predictable. Americans seem to visualize things in a practical, concrete sense. Discussions of revolution evoke images of farmers grabbing guns and pitchforks to rush to Concord Bridge or French peasants storming the Bastille rather than the radical transformation of the manner in which people view the world. Insofar as some Americans were expecting a violent exchange of ruling classes to occur as an empirical validation of Revel's concept, they were disappointed. But insofar as his analysis records the passage of understanding from one view of reality to another, his thesis remains valid and prophetic.

Revel suggests that a first revolution had occurred in Western culture in the fundamental changes of the eighteenth and nineteenth centuries, during which a shift in viewpoint rather than a replacement of social classes took place. This reorientation of ways of understanding reality, according to Revel, while not fundamental, kept more promises than it broke, and became irreversible. It was, in this sense, profoundly revolutionary. Describing this shift in outlook Revel noted:

> Authority henceforth found its source in those subject to authority, or rather in those who delegated authority; the contractual concept replaced that of divine right, or of the right of the strongest; the power of the law took the place of personal power; an egalitarian society replaced a hierarchical society; a separation was effected between state and church; knowledge and, in general, culture were freed from political and ecclesiastical control.[2]

This fundamental change from inherited authority, no matter how derived, to inherent democratic rights gathered to create and allocate authority has become so commonplace to us today that it is regarded as a natural condition of human society and not the revolutionary change it really was. That it should have occurred so recently remains a shock to many people who accept these propositions as part of the reasonable structure of human existence. We wonder why it was so difficult for such self-evident truths to achieve universal acceptance. That they are not yet acceptable to most human societies indicates the rate of change we are experiencing.

The collapse of embryo democracies hastily devised as an answer to demands of decolonization, when seen from a more comprehensive historical perspective, is not as disastrous as one would initially suppose since democracy is itself such a relatively new concept. The flirtation with totalitarian forms of government now indulged in around the globe may be an even more transitional form to a new universal conception of human existence that transcends all previous forms of political, social, and economic organization. Revel pointed out that "just as the first world revolution consisted in substituting institutions for the despotism of rulers in the domestic affairs of the state, so, too, the second world revolution must consist in replacing despotism with institutions in the area of international relations; or, more accurately, it must consist in the abolition of international relations."[3] The two revolutions, therefore, taken together, must be understood as a centuries-long process of fundamental change in which the triumphant

Western world view of colonial days is replaced by a planetary understanding of the meaning of human existence that so transcends particular national differences as to enable the human species to create a planetary peace in the absence of an imperial power to enforce its particular institutions on anyone. In short, a coming to maturity of the human species.

A transformation of this profound a depth must necessarily take form in the actions of the most capable nation on the planet, and Revel, after surveying the various claimants to leadership, decided that the United States fulfilled the basic requirements such a role entailed. He acclaimed the United States as the prototype nation in a process of world transformation. He cited many factors present in the United States but absent or improperly developed in other nations as justification for his choice. The United States had a continuing pattern of growth and economic prosperity unmatched by any other nation, a technological excellence not rivaled by anyone else, and a high level of basic research that would continue to provide increasingly sophisticated insights into the nature of basic scientific and social problems. Revel also felt that the United States was culturally oriented toward the future, whereas the European countries were directed toward the past, and the Communists were mired in theoretical and doctrinal considerations, rendering them incapable of confronting rapid and continued change.

The multiple and dissident life styles emerging in the 1960s also indicated to Revel that the United States had more internal flexibility to tolerate change than did any other country and that this diversity would produce sufficient human vitality to make the United States a society of experimentation in new expressions of human experience. But the most important quality Revel found in Americans was their willingness to admit collective guilt in the treatment of racial minorities. Pointing out that the educational system of the Western nations from the time of the Greeks until the present had been designed to justify crimes committed against humanity in the name of national honor or religion, Revel noted that "the Germans refused to admit the crimes of the Nazi; and the English, the French, and the Italians all refused to admit the atrocities committed during their colonial wars." [4] The United States, as Revel saw it, was the first nation in history to confront seriously its own misdeeds and to make some effort to change national policy to make amends for acknowledged wrongs. This manifestation of a collective conscience indicated a greater sensitivity to human needs and an ability to empathetically deal with foreign cultures and values. This was the vital characteristic needed to provide a stance of moral leadership to support a planetary transformation of cultures.

Rather than dwelling on the series of political upheavals then plaguing Western societies, Revel transcended the traditional Cold War ideology to interpret the world situation as planetary transformation in five basic areas. He listed essential conditions under which the human species could achieve a form of maturity necessary to bring stability to the planet:

In order for this revolutionary process to exist in reality, five basic conditions must be met; that is, critical work must have been done in five distinct, but complementary and convergent areas. . . . Those conditions and areas are as follows:

1. . . . a critique on the *injustice* existing in economic, social, and racial relationships.
2. . . . a critique of *management,* directed against the waste of material and human resources. . . .
3. . . . a critique of *political power,* directed against its source and principles as well as against its exercise, . . .
4. . . . a critique of *culture:* of morality, religion, accepted beliefs, customs, philosophy, literature, art; of the ideological attitudes which underlie these things; . . .
5. . . . a critique of the old *civilization-as-sanction,* or a vindication of individual freedom.[5]

Recent events indicate that many countries are experiencing radical changes in some of these areas. The collapse of the postcolonial democracies signifies a process of transforming political power from its middle-class colonial base to a different ideological stance even though the transitional form becomes oppressive in order to achieve independence from older institutional forms. But certainly no other nation is proceeding in all five areas with the intensity and novelty of the United States. American domestic movements of the past two decades were all aimed at fundamental reforms in social, economic, and racial relationships. Therefore, in the first area of concern, redressing injustices, the United States has already been engaged in a revolutionary undertaking.

Because we are speaking of a process of transformation that unfolds over the course of centuries, it is difficult if not foolish to ascribe to any recent changes in political institutions or management of resources the fundamental characteristics that Revel sees necessary in the second and third areas. With the energy crisis, the consumer movement, and the post-Watergate demand for more responsible government we are certainly in the process of beginning a critique of those parts of our society that have merged in recent centuries—political and economic institutions. Whether an increased concern by the average citizen in the United States will make the reforms now being discussed permanent remains to be seen, but all indications seem to point toward a prolonged period of reform in these areas.

The fourth and fifth areas of revolutionary concern, the critiques of culture and civilization-as-sanction, are qualitatively different from the first three. They largely involve the transformation of attitudes and beliefs, and in this sense Revel is asking us to critique our own individual and social identities rather than describing a process already underway. He writes that these critiques "are relevant only if they are, for the most part, expressed by the governing class itself." [6] That is, the beneficiaries of our society must themselves undertake to identify and transform those attitudes and beliefs that provide the justification for our behavior and values. As examples, Revel refers to the participation of aristocrats in previous revolutionary situations, to the acceptance of divorce when practiced by those in power, and to the transformation of attitudes when models of a society push beyond commonly accepted patterns of behavior, indicating their acceptance of fundamental changes.

This process may be either deliberate or unconscious, depending upon the nature of the emerging change. When we look back several decades at the sexual attitudes that dominated our society and compare those times with the present, we see how much we have already transformed our understanding of human needs with a minimum of articulated theoretical change. We have simply cast aside attitudes that we felt were irrelevant and adopted more flexible patterns of behavior without any enforced prescription for action. The same process has been operative in our attitudes toward work, recreation, art and literature, religion, and morality and ethics as practiced both privately and publicly. Not all the changes have been beneficial, but they have nearly all been spontaneous expressions without much authoritarian direction.

Changes in culture and conceptions of civilization can be compared with the gradual change in the pieces of a mosaic. At a certain point in the process of replacing one piece with another, we no longer have a clear picture of what we had, and we do not yet have a clear picture of the new pattern we are creating. There is a dreadful middle ground in this process of transformation in which we simply substitute meaningless pieces over and over again. Change, even transformation of attitudes, is not an end in itself unless it leads to a more profound and comprehensive idea of the meaning of existence. We always run the risk of lapsing into a new and more sophisticated barbarism.

The task, therefore, of examining culture and civilization-as-sanction is not one of rejecting or reinforcing the traditions that have come down to us; it is one of pursuing a new course of inquiry that will render additional areas of knowledge and experience intelligible and meaningful. "Revolution," Revel declares, "consists in transforming reality." [7] In a practical sense it is not reality we transform but those aspects of our lives that define the boundaries of reality. In this sense a critique of Revel's fourth and fifth areas of concern involves two specific tasks: (1) a challenge to the attitudes that compose our belief in what constitutes civilization, and (2) a survey of our present state of knowledge concerning the world and ourselves that can determine the most reliable and comprehensive scheme for interpreting present and future experiences.

Culture underlies and defines civilization, and a civilization is dependent upon the elements of knowledge, experience, and behavior that are commonly shared and supported by the people concerned. What we know and how we act upon what we know seem to constitute the ongoing process of cultural change and the stability that a civilization finds. But unless we can discover a basis for examining our attitudes and knowledge about the world, we cannot determine a realistic position from which we can bring about systematic and fundamental change that is self-sustaining and continuing in the face of future insights and acquisitions of knowledge and experience.

Attitudes about Western culture and civilization seem to revolve about two poles: (1) a defense of the Western tradition in the subjective sense, and (2) a willingness to examine that tradition as if it were an objective process with which we have little or no relationship. We might characterize these two approaches as internal and external critiques. Such an analytical framework is not without usefulness, but we must remember that we are dealing with attitudes toward human experience and not with the data of human experience itself. To illustrate these internal and external dimensions, we might cite two thinkers. Pierre Teilhard de Chardin (1881–1955), the great French philosopher and paleontologist, stood fully within the Western tradition as a champion of European culture and wrote with considerable ethnocentric arrogance in *The Phenomenon of Man:*

> . . . we would be allowing sentiment to falsify the facts if we failed to recognise that during historic times the principle axis of anthrogenesis has passed through the West. It is in this ardent zone of growth and universal recasting that all that goes to make man today has been discovered, or at any rate must have been rediscovered. *For even that which had long been elsewhere only took on its definitive human value in becoming incorporated in the system of European ideas and activities.*[8]

This attitude carefully avoids criticizing Western culture and substitutes evidence and arguments that are designed to bolster belief in the Western way of life. As such it hardly qualifies as a process of transforming Western culture into a planetary understanding, which Revel finds necessary. It rather seeks to defend its appropriation of the insights and experiences of other cultures on the basis that Western peoples made such knowledge relevant. The difficulty with such an attitude is that it understands Western culture, which it admits is an amalgam of insights, as the final expression of human experiences, thus dismissing many thousands of years of history and the collective wisdom of non-Western societies. When confronted with evidence of the subsequent erosion of the Western world view it responds after the fashion of German physicist Werner Heisenberg, (1901–1976), who became famous for his studies in theoretical atomic physics. Writing in *The Physicist's Conception of Nature*, Heisenberg assures us that "what alone matters is our unshakable faith in the West."[9]

The objective or external point of view regarding Western culture is best expressed by Philip Slater, a contemporary cultural analyst. In *Earthwalk*, he remarks:

> The kind of growth Western culture has experienced over the past three hundred years would be considered a sign of gross malfunction in any other context. Healthy

growth is paced differently—it does not absorb or destroy everything living around it.[10]

Considered as another phenomenon and not as the highest expression of human values, Western civilization has a cancerous appearance; rather than transforming values it seems intent on destroying them. The objective viewpoint transcends the need for unexamined faith in the West, for it seeks a critical evaluation of those characteristics of all cultures that produce destructive results. As such, it more closely approaches both a search for truth and Revel's requirement of critical workings that must be accomplished in the areas of culture and civilization-as-sanction.

Thus if we are to embark on a quest for understanding, which must mark the fourth and fifth areas of revolutionary concern, we should consider an objective, not a subjective, view of Western culture. But unless we make one aspect of such an evaluation clear at the beginning, we will only tread an already familiar path. It is not necessary to dwell on the mistakes of Western peoples in order to examine the basis upon which they have built both their civilization and their cultural traditions. Such an approach would only produce propaganda or would review the collective guilt of one society of the human species, perhaps implying that other societies are blameless. Our task is to examine the present state of knowledge produced by Western society and accepted throughout the world in order to determine if this culture and its civilization can truly assume leadership of the human species on the planet with the maturity and insight such a role requires. Casting aside belief in Western civilization as the ultimate value, we face the task of examining the components of Western culture to determine their relevance and validity.

II. Transforming Reality

Culture, as conceived by Revel, included morality, religion, accepted beliefs, customs, philosophy, literature, and art. A process of revolutionary transformation occurring within all these fields simultaneously would involve a complete reorientation in how we conceive our heritage and in the way we assign values to our lives. The scope of such a transformation transcends the specific truths inherent in each subject field and leads to a new realm of inquiry when we begin to critique the culture itself. We leave behind the individual pieces of the mosaic and concentrate on the meaning to be found in the emerging picture. Our task is to discern from the continuous introduction of new elements of knowledge and experience a coherent interpretation of the scheme of things.

Traditionally, Western people have called an inquiry of this kind *metaphysics,* and its task has been to discover the structure and meaning of what was real. The word itself has become somewhat frightening to Western peoples because of their inclination to make metaphysical conclusions an absolute canon of faith, thus imposing abstract principles on their practical understandings of the world around them. Preferring immensely simple explanations of universal processes, Western societies have often scoffed at efforts to derive philosophical understandings from the mass of data available to them. Such an attitude has done violence to efforts to clarify the meaning of human existence that emerges when the particularities of specific fields of knowledge are transcended. And thinkers have been discouraged from attempting to synthesize the respective fields of knowledge into a coherent whole. For many centuries, Western peoples held tenaciously to the picture of the world described by Aristotle and rejected new understandings. Today Western society seems content to make a popular version of Newtonian physics its practical and accepted metaphysics, refusing to allow the discoveries of Einstein and other contemporary thinkers to affect its world view.

Metaphysics is not frightening if we cast aside the old connotations of impractical abstraction and reconsider what the process itself means. Ian Barbour is a physicist-theologian who has devoted himself to the study of the relationship between science and religion. His book *Issues in Science and Religion* is a comprehensive discussion of the intellectual development of the important issues separating science and religion. In *Myths, Models and Paradigms* Barbour attempts to establish a theory of complementary models that would enable science and religion to exchange insights.

Although Barbour is exploring subject areas that demand a high level of professional expertise, his definition of metaphysics is hardly beyond the comprehension of the interested, concerned lay person. He says simply that metaphysics is "the search for a coherent set of categories for the interpretation of all experience." [1] Confronting the massive amount of information thrust upon us, our task is to discover a meaningful pattern for interpreting what we know. The goals of a metaphysical search, as understood by Barbour, are simple and practical:

> Systematic connectedness is sought among areas of inquiry usually considered in isolation. Insofar as it succeeds, the power of such a conceptual synthesis lies in its ability to integrate and illuminate a wide range of experience—in science, history, art, ethics, religion and so forth. [2]

The process of synthesizing a wide range of cultural experience is precisely the revolutionary transformation that Revel feels is necessary if the reforms in other areas of modern life are to be permanent and effective. So it would appear that the creation of a new metaphysical description of experience would be one way to bring some order to the revolutionary processes now emerging.

Western peoples have been accustomed to drawing their descriptions of the world from more than one source, however, and if metaphysics can lay claim to the task of articulating the structure and meaning of reality, so can science and religion. One might better characterize the history of Western thought as a continuous struggle between religion and science, with metaphysics occasionally attempting to provide a systematic ordering of the doctrines and beliefs of both. But this struggle is so fundamental that few people consciously understand that it characterizes Western thinking, and even the best thinkers see no inconsistency in simultaneously advocating the truths of science and religion. Werner Heisenberg, for example, in discussing the state of knowledge in the world, remarked that "in every sphere of modern life examination of the root of things, whether methodological, historical, or philosophical, brings us up against the concepts of antiquity and Christianity." [3] By antiquity, Heisenberg means Greek philosophy and science, and he is apparently content to maintain a dualism of truth rather than seek a reconciliation of two basic views of reality.

The attitude that science and religion each produce a set of truths about the nature of reality is difficult to overcome because in pretending that each covers a distinct and complementary area of human experience one is relieved of the need to make sense out of the wealth of information and beliefs that inhabit the modern world. Ian Barbour has raised the most consistent voice against the continued separation of science and religion, maintaining that the two disciplines are complementary and yet each is a "perspective on a single world." Barbour even finds their methods of interpreting experiences to be similar:

> Both scientific and religious language are realistic and referential in intent; in neither case can one remain satisfied with "useful fictions." The two sets of statements must contribute to a coherent interpretation of all experience, rather than remain as unrelated languages.[4]

But the problem of coordinating two complementary languages to explain one reality is that the logic of each division precludes the integration of facts with doctrines, and the two fields of knowledge relate to each other by providing paradigms instead of coalescing their respective insights into one unified interpretation.

It is difficult to bring together science and religion without using metaphysics as an arena of unification because the methodological assumptions of Western knowledge are designed to maintain this isolation. Leon Brunschvicg (1869–1944), a French idealist philosopher, typifies this attitude when he writes:

> Whether we consider the expanding universe, or humanity divided at any moment between the weight of primitive traditions and the need for spiritual progress, we find that both and each after its own fashion, are proceeding towards a destiny where even the immediate future cannot necessarily be defined by simply continuing the curve which has already been described.[5]

On the one hand, we seem to recognize that the logic used by science and religion, which depends on a linear progression of terms, is inadequate because the future cannot be simply an extension of what is already known. On the other hand, the unexamined assumption exemplified by Brunschvicg's statement is that a gulf exists between the expanding universe and humanity and that this gulf is incapable of being bridged. A gulf also exists between the parochial traditions of the human species and the need for spiritual progress. As long as Western thinkers fail to see the necessity of discovering the hidden relationships between these respective factors, no revolutionary transformation of either Western attitudes or culture can take place.

Yet today both scientists and theologians are searching for a framework of interpretation that can provide a unified vision of knowledge and the meaning of human existence. Werner Heisenberg hinted at the probability of undiscovered relationships in the field of knowledge when he discussed the manner in which the sciences presently appear to be connected:

Chemical structure is explained on the basis of atomic physics. Modern astronomy is connected with it most closely, and can hardly make any progress without it. Even in biology, many bridges are being built towards atomic physics. The connections between the different branches of science have become much more obvious in the last decades than at any previous time. There are many signs of their common origin, which, in the final analysis must be sought somewhere in the thought of antiquity.[6]

The connections that seem to exist among the respective branches of human knowledge suggest a common historical origin, but they must certainly also suggest a basic unity of the universe. We can easily trace their historical roots, but discovering a new manner of conceiving their unity would suggest the need for a transcending system of interpretation independent of the insights of any particular branch of knowledge but intimately related to all of them.

Religious knowledge stands at the same crossroads as does science with respect to interpreting reality. Theologians have avoided alliances with the sciences for many decades because of the bitter conflict over evolution of the last century, a battle not quite concluded on the popular level where Christian fundamentalists continue to maintain the literal truth of the Bible against the discoveries of science. But thinkers such as Paul Tillich (1886–1965) have long since pushed their analysis beyond the literal truths of religion in an effort to refine the basis upon which theological and religious truth can be apprehended and articulated. According to Tillich, who was a German-American theologian-philosopher, religious knowledge has some of the same characteristics as scientific truth because of its persistence in pursuing meaning. Religious knowledge is:

> ...a turning toward reality, a questioning of reality, a penetrating into existence, a driving to the level where the world points beyond itself to its ground and ultimate meaning. *If, out of such a penetration into reality, concepts and words grow which are its genuine expression, they may become keys to an understanding and a new interpretation of the tradition.*[7]

Theological insights into the nature of reality must therefore themselves originate new concepts and structures for describing reality if the process of developing religious languages is proceeding in accordance with Tillich's understanding. Yet within Western religious circles, theology is not making significant progress because, unlike science, theology has hitherto concentrated, as Tillich has pointed out, on new interpretations of "the tradition." In other words, no significant new data is used in theology's driving to the level where the world points beyond itself. Rather the elements of the tradition are arranged and rearranged in accordance with new methods of viewing data, and aspects of the world not previously intuited in a religious sense are almost always shunted aside by adherence to tradition as the raw material for consideration.

If Western religious thinking were not intimately tied to the Christian tradition but included religious experiences of all human societies, then we could assume that the concepts and words, which Tillich found grow out of a penetration into existence, might be comparable or even identical with the words and concepts that emerge from the scientific quest for understanding. Unless these concepts and words begin to merge in some basic areas, it is doubtful whether a reconciliation can be effected. Ian Barbour recognizes this problem but seems to avoid its obvious solution in the creation of a new metaphysics:

> ... *communication* between paradigm communities is impossible unless they partially share a common language. If there is no core of shared terms and no experiences common to both communities, their assertions are "incommensurable" and no genuine discussion can occur. The further presence of shared criteria greatly enhances the fruitfulness of the interaction.[8]

The basic recognition that science and religion view a single world provides both disciplines with a core of shared experiences, but it is uncertain whether shared criteria can produce a common language that can fundamentally effect communication.

The solution to this problem is, of course, the creation of a new metaphysics transcending and encompassing both science and religion that permits the transposing of concepts and values. Paul Tillich hinted at this prospect but did not carry the argument into its logical mooring. He suggested that the objects of metaphysics "are not separate things, lying beyond experience, but the qualities of the world of experience in which answers to the radical inquiries of philosophy can be found." [9] Insofar as philosophy can achieve a radical inquiry that intrudes into the domains of science and religion and synthesizes the content of these subjects, we escape the present division inherent in our understanding of the world. We need not be radical in a disruptive sense. The transformation of the manner in which any culture interprets its heritage of remembered human experiences and knowledge cannot be radical if it is to have any effect on the respective human societies. Rather it must relate to the various human traditions at as many points as possible so that continuity and identity of traditions can be understood. Without this natural development, any new metaphysics would appear abstract and unrelated to people. Thus it is not the radical inquiries that are important but the systematic ordering of the qualities of the world of experience. Once we have clarified this aspect of metaphysics, the quest does not seem abstract and difficult but appears to be a natural process in which the average person has an interest.

The average person in Western society has been excluded from understanding the deliberations of philosophy, religion, and science because of the increasing complexity of the issues. Educational institutions have assumed that excerpts of philosophical and theological writings can illustrate the basic principles and that introducing students to general principles will give them a familiarity with areas of knowledge that they will later expand upon in their adult leisure. The result has been to create the need for a personal philosophy for each individual based upon his or her sketchy memory of ideas summarized in capsule courses on religion and the history of Western thought.

Undergraduates continue their education facing professors who assume that fundamental principles have already been thoroughly discussed and digested. The final result of this process is college graduates who are sufficiently familiar with Western thought to assume that the fundamental religious or philosophic questions have already been solved, insofar as they can be solved, by previous Western philosophers and theologians. Western religious and philosophical heritages thus suffer an increasing dilution of meaning and sophistication.

When such a societal attitude becomes the norm, the creation of new patterns of interpretation does not take into account the continual discovery of new means of apprehending the basic structure of the universe, but lapses into a justification of what has already become partially familiar to a limited number of people. Heinz Heimsoeth, professor of philosophy at Königsberg and Cologne, Germany, recognizes the ultimate conclusion to the Western attitude toward philosophy and religion. He points out that:

> . . . most of the leading metaphysicians of the modern period are also dominated by a conscious and explicit tendency to work out a conceptual understanding of the structure of reality in accordance with the basic truths of Christianity. But their starting point has changed from the divine and supra-sensible to the structure of the world as it is given in space and time, and the reality provided by man himself.[10]

Yet even this shift in viewpoint is insufficient because it is based upon concepts—space, time, and the reality provided by man himself—which themselves have little relationship to the scientific discoveries concerning the probable reality of the world. Since the development of Christian theology coincided with the elaboration of many philosophical and scientific theories of the West and depended upon them for its knowledge of the world, a metaphysical system attempting to work out a conceptual understanding of the structure of reality that justifies and supports the basic truths of Christianity is merely recycling outmoded concepts and is not deriving new means of interpreting reality.

The proper way to embark on Revel's suggested critique of culture and civilization, therefore, is not to repeat the traditional pattern of metaphysical system-building that has prevailed in Western society. That is, the fundamentals of Western cultural and religious traditions should not be given any more credence than the data gathered from any other source; nor should an effort be made to reconcile basic truths accepted by Western peoples with other information concerning the nature of reality that may be available to us. The search must once again be one of seeking truth in a supracultural sense, examining the insights of many traditions, gathering what appear to be reasonable and reliable data from all fields of knowledge, and bringing about a systematic understanding of the total picture that emerges from such a quest. Without such a search, all societies will simply proceed to replace the pieces of the mosaic without discovering the meaning of the process of change or the possible new patterns that can be emerging.

Change in itself is not sufficient to determine the meaning of human existence, and if we have only change initiated by the governing class, we march in a parade of meaningless fads rather than participating in meaningful change. Thus it is vitally important to discover the nature of the pieces we are replacing in our mosaic of meaning. This discovery means that we must be as concerned with the facts of metaphysics as we are with the process of deriving meaning. Frederick Ferré, contemporary philosopher and theologian, notes that the facts of metaphysics are not entirely arbitrary; they are not . . . " 'given' independent of the creative powers of intelligence. On the contrary, the 'facts' of metaphysics are supremely dependent on the conceptual activity of mind." [11] But this selection of facts from which meaning is to be derived presumes that the conceptualization process is already well under way so that inclusion and exclusion of data is predetermined before the search for reality begins. This process of preselection is characteristic of Western thinking and reduces the choice of data to familiar ground that has already been covered. "A metaphysical 'fact,' " Ferré concludes, "is a concept which plays a key role within the system, without which the system would flounder." [12]

It is fortunate that we are not seeking to establish a new system to replace outmoded conceptions but desire mainly to use metaphysics as a bridge between science and religion in order to determine if Western culture and civilization have sufficient universality to provide a meaningful vision of human existence on a planetary basis. That is, given the decline of the West, the rejection of its social and political institutions, and the need for a transformation of human cultures, our task is to discover a possible means of interpreting human knowledge and experience that does not depend on any particular tradition.

We do not need a system of metaphysics as much as we need some procedure by which we can evaluate what is already present in our lives and draw conclusions from the data. A metaphysical fact in the traditional Western sense of establishing concepts that play key roles in a system of thought is completely outmoded because we have no predetermined system of thought into which data must fit. Concepts in themselves are culturally determined, and if we seek to elicit facts of experience on the basis of conceptual activity of the mind, we must certainly choose from the multitude of facts available those that appear familiar to some cultures, thus precluding the understanding of those same facts as conceptualized by other cultures. This precise error, with respect to political institutions, has produced the domino effect on democracies over the past three decades, for not all peoples have conceived political institutions or their processes according to Western standards.

Before we can embark on a meaningful search for data from which we can determine a pattern of meaning for human existence, we shall have to examine the manner in which Western peoples have categorized the data provided for them by the phenomenal world. We must ask whether, in looking at the world and attempting to make sense out of its phenomena, Western people have not chosen to see certain patterns while excluding others, and whether Western science is not simply a verification of expectations which have already been assumed to exist in nature. The exclusionary nature of the scientific enterprise which suggests that by isolating individual entities ultimate reality can be discovered is by its very nature incomplete and narrow, avoiding a confrontation with the complexity of phenomena.

We seek to secure the facts of metaphysical information but we are required to reject, insofar as possible, the conceptual synthesis that has already ordered those facts in a predetermined set of values and structural relationships. We look beyond concepts to the immediate experiences that gave rise to them and hope to exclude the interpretation that has divided the world into two parallel systems of thought which never coalesce. From the raw data of experience we must seek a familiarity with intensity and content that characterizes events so as to allow experience to reorder itself in a more flexible and universal manner. In the process of moving beyond interpretations dependent wholly upon intellectual concepts, we may well discover that many cherished Western beliefs are no more than figments of the imagination. The first question to be asked of the Western mind, therefore, is: "How did this particular viewpoint come into being?" Does it reflect a process of thought sufficiently universal to serve as a planetary paradigm for understanding?

III. A Divided Vision

More than we would like to admit, our understanding of reality depends upon what we want to believe is true. The most sophisticated insights of physical science and the most intense religious experiences count for nothing in the popular mind if they do not conform to a general belief in what the reality of the world is. Thus our understanding of Western culture and civilization depends upon the manner in which we examine the general conceptions of reality held by Western peoples rather than upon a precise knowledge of what the most advanced thinkers have intuited. In approaching the Western conception of reality, therefore, we must fall back upon the religious and philosophical beliefs traditionally held in Western civilization.

One of the chief distinguishing characteristics of Western peoples in these fields has been the belief that ultimate reality exists over and above the transitory experiences of daily life. Arthur O. Lovejoy (1873–1962), American philosopher and historian of ideas, in his classic *The Great Chain of Being*, traces this belief to the Platonic dilemma of ensuring the validity of human knowledge and Plato's subsequent division of the world into otherworldly and this-worldly realms. Lovejoy says that the otherworldly attitude that originated most concretely with Platonic thinking is characterized by "the belief that both the genuinely 'real' and the truly good are radically antithetic in their essential characteristics to anything to be found in man's natural life, in the ordinary course of human experience, however normal, however intelligent, and however fortunate." [1] Divinity, reality, and eternity existed above and beyond the passing parade of life which we experience, and thus knowledge of the world was not an ultimate understanding but merely hinted at a more permanent structure to the moral and physical universe. The task of Greek philosophy, before and after Plato, was to divine from the welter of phenomena the ultimate constituent of the universe.

When this dualism was merged with Christian theology in the controversies over the status of Jesus, the meaning of historical revelation, and the fear of the last judgment, Greek thought was considered capable of articulating the philosophical aspects of the Christian religion and was welcomed. God existed in the Heavenly City where the faithful would be rewarded by eternal life, and all values of importance became those of the other world. Anthropologist Gregory Bateson describes the attitudes toward the world that form when this picture of reality dominates:

> If you put God outside and set him vis-à-vis his creation and if you have the idea that you are created in his image, you will logically and naturally see yourself as outside and against the things around you. And you will arrogate all mind to yourself, you will see the world around you as mindless and therefore not entitled to moral or ethical consideration. The environment will seem to be yours to exploit. Your survival unit will be you and your folks or conspecifics against the environment of other social units, other races and the brutes and vegetables.[2]

It is this precise attitude toward the world that has characterized Western peoples and that today is crumbling before the realities of the present situation in which we cannot continue to exploit the brutes and vegetables and in which the non-Western peoples reject Western exclusivity.

But the phenomena of *this-world* still had to make sense to Western peoples because these experiences and events affected them and determined their lives. One could not exist within human society believing it had no ultimate value and that life had no value. Two beliefs arose to fill this vacuum: a strong nationalism and a reliance on history as a repository of human values. History became not simply a record of past events but a record of *our* past events, a justification of the present by reference to its chronological antecedents with the evidence amassed indicating that contemporary men and women had transcended their ancestors in many important ways.

History became such a dominant form of interpreting the human experience that Western peoples ascribed a reality to it in itself, particularly when it was expressed in Christian theological concepts. All human existence had meaning because a divine plan was coordinating each and every event preparatory to a grand climactic judgment. Thus rather than negate daily existence, Western peoples became frantically concerned that every human act had cosmic significance that would be revealed at the Last Judgment. Rigid rules and regulations arose to guide the individual through his or her period of testing in order to escape eternal damnation.

Perhaps the ultimate expression of this concern for historical reality can be found in Paul Tillich's *The Protestant Era.* In an effort to distinguish the comparative interpretations of reality that have influenced human societies, he divided the religious traditions of humanity into historical and nonhistorical interpretations. The logic of such a scheme is self-defeating, for it presumes an ultimate value to history that does not exist. Yet it is important to review the characteristics of the two categories in order to see the lengths to which Western peoples have gone in their efforts to bring order to daily experiences.

According to Tillich the nonhistorical interpretation of history has the following characteristics:

1. Nature (or supernature) is the highest category of interpreting reality.

2. Space is predominant against time; time is considered to be circular or repeating itself infinitely.

3. The temporal world has a lesser reality and no ultimate value.

4. The true being and the ultimate good are eternal, immovable, above becoming, genesis, and decay.

5. Salvation is the salvation of individuals from time and history, not the salvation of a community through time and history.

6. History is interpreted as a process of deterioration, leading to the inescapable self-destruction of a world era.

7. The religious correlate to the nonhistorical interpretation of history is either polytheism (the deification of special spaces) or pantheism (the deification of a transcendent "One," negating space as well as time).[3]

In contrast to these characteristics are the characteristics of what Tillich called the historical interpretation of history:

1. History is an independent and, finally, the outstanding category of interpreting reality.

2. Time is predominant against space. The movement of time is direct, has a definite beginning and end, and is moving toward an ultimate fulfillment.

3. The temporal world is a battlefield between good and evil powers (expressed in mythological or in rational terms). Ontologically, or as creation, the world is good.

4. The true being, or the ultimate good, is in a dynamic process of self-realization within and above temporal existence.

5. Salvation is the salvation of a community from the evil powers *in* history *through* history. History is essentially "history of salvation."

6. History has a turning-point or a center in which the meaning of history appears, overcoming the self-destructive trend of the historical process and creating something *new* which cannot be frustrated by the circular motion of nature.

7. The religious correlate to the historical interpretation of history is exclusive monotheism: God as Lord of time controlling the universal history of mankind, acting in history and through history.[4]

The two lists involve innumerable difficulties in understanding because of Tillich's insistence that history occupies a place of ultimate reality, transcending even the reality of the physical world. Thus an extra dimension of interpretation is entrenched within the two lists that involves redundancy. What is the "historical interpretation of history" really but a needless repetition of the word history that unnecessarily complicates our task?

We do far better to reject complicated language and move to the basic distinction. Human societies have traditionally made either nature or history determinative of reality, and that is the point of debate in seeking an understanding, not the "historical" and "nonhistorical" approaches to history, which are themselves constructs and not realities. But it is important to examine each of the seven categories, for they seem to converge and complement one another in a basic view of the world. They indicate, perhaps better than any other available listing, the dimensions of attitude that have separated human societies over the centuries.

Tillich placed nature and history in opposition as the highest categories for interpreting reality. The distinction between nature and history entails, not simply a way of looking at reality, but also and more importantly an analysis of *how* we receive information about reality. In discussing the so-called primitive societies, Tillich remarked that "the primitive magical interpretation of reality is based on an experience of the intrinsic power of things," adding that "for primitive man things have a kind of numinous or sacral quality." [5] It is the apprehension of reality emerging from an experience of the power of things, therefore, that encourages some human societies to interpret reality through nature. A key to understanding this reliance on nature may be to ask whether the "magical interpretation of reality," which Tillich found present in the primitive, is the same process of thought that produces the concept of history. It would seem that primitive peoples report directly on their experiences without interpreting what such experiences mean. The "numinous" or "sacral" quality of reality is thus not a logical conclusion but an experiential report.

Ernst Cassirer (1874–1945), a German philosopher, supported this interpretation and said of the manner in which they conceive the reality of existence:

> To mythical and religious feeling nature becomes one great society, the *society of life*. Man is not endowed with outstanding rank in this society. He is a part of it but he is in no respect higher than any other member. Life possesses the same religious dignity in its humblest and in its highest forms. Men and animals, animals and plants are all on the same level.[6]

In other words, a community of experience is created through an encounter with the numinous quality of life that is manifested in all life-forms, and humans are seen as another species rather than as an exalted, alienated species unrelated to the rest of creation. Immediate involvement in nature and natural processes orients humans to the reality of existence as it is experienced.

On the other hand, interpreting reality through the use of history as the highest category involves a determination that the recorded experiences of the human species, and only the human species, is sufficient to interpret the meaning of the rest of creation. Nonhuman life-forms and the passage of time itself become processes that exist for the benefit of the human species rather than as ends in themselves. But what meaning of history emerges through the process of elevating human experiences above those of the rest of the universe? Johan Huizinga (1872–1945), the noted Dutch historian, said that "history is always an imposition of form upon the past and cannot claim to be more. It is always the comprehension and interpretation of a meaning which we look for in the past." [7] To determine reality according to its history, therefore, is to turn one's attention and identity toward the past rather than toward the immediate apprehension of present events and environment. When we talk of using history to interpret reality, we speak mostly of the use of fading memories to discover meaning in the past, not of using history as a tool to understand the immediate reality.

The transition from the immediate apprehension of power in the universe to memories of particular demonstrative events of that power, as must occur when we shift our attention from nature to history, is a slight development that occurs mostly in the selection process of the human mind. We do not reject nature, but we select from the plentitude of events those that seem to emphasize most clearly the power inherent in the universe. Thus it cannot be said that historical religions are devoid of contact with the natural world, but the process of establishing a relationship with the natural world now takes on a new emphasis. Ernst Cassirer described this process:

> No religion could ever think of cutting or even loosening the bond between nature and man. But in the great ethical religions this bond is tied and fastened in a new sense. The sympathetic connection that we find in magic and in primitive mythology is not denied or destroyed; *but nature is now approached from the rational instead of from the emotional side.* If nature contains a divine element it appears not in the abundance of its life but in the simplicity of its order. Nature is not, as in polytheistic religion, the great and benign mother, the divine lap from which all life originates. It is conceived as the sphere of law and lawfulness. [8]

In this transition from understanding nature as the source of life to the arena of law and order, we see the activity of the human mind transforming the immediate human perceptions of reality to different patterns of abstraction in which a factor of predictability emerges. The human species gains, in its estimation, some measure of control over nature. The attitude toward nature thus becomes anticipatory with overtones of a desire to control nature rather than to commune with it. Religion becomes more concerned about apprehending the structure of reality and less concerned about communing with the power of reality. In short, the process of bringing historical patterns out of the wealth of human experience is destructive of religious experience, not supportive of religious sentiments and realities.

If we take any human society in its infancy and introduce a process of intuiting historical patterns, we could expect with a reasonable certainty that over a course of centuries the history of this group would involve a recitation of those incidents that affected the group most intensely in an emotional sense. This recitation of memorable past events would constitute the history of the group. But would those memories adequately describe the reality of existence? Or would the memories simply record that society's chronological response to its environment? In other words, when we deal with history as the final determinant of reality, we eventually confront the problem of evaluating which memories should be used to establish the patterns of interpretation. The problem becomes extraordinarily difficult when we expand our horizon beyond the simple and isolated human society and attempt to grapple with a history of any extensive region or any significant period of time in which humans have lived. Frederick Ferré notes the difficulty in determining the relative importance of historical facts, pointing out the temporary and, finally, illusionary result of this enterprise:

> Ordinary "facts" of our everyday life are accepted as such because of their coherent place within the conceptual schema with which modern man relates himself to the world of common experience, though we usually ignore the vital role of mind in organizing even sense-experience into meaningful patterns of facts out of the "buzzing, blooming confusion" of bare sensation. *What are judged "the facts" today are by no means identical to what were "the facts" a century, five centuries, three millennia ago.* And we may expect that "the facts" of our generation will gradually and piecemeal give place to "the facts" of the future. Both "internal" conceptual refinement and "external" confrontation with experience that is difficult to deal with in terms of old concepts result in changes as to what are taken to be "the facts." [9]

Rather that eliciting a pattern of reality from history, we are constantly evaluating our memories, accepting and rejecting our own conception of events, and placing and replacing meanings, without any certainty that we have pierced the veil of reality. We remain isolated from the power of reality as it is experienced in nature because our attention is directed toward apprehending previous patterns in present events, thus precluding any novelty that might emerge in the present.

The corollary of the controversy between history and nature as the ultimate category for interpreting reality manifests itself in the philosophical problem of determining whether time or space is the dominant form of existence. Western peoples have been unique in their insistence that time has an absolute quality. We cannot doubt that the passage of time which occurs in human life has an irreversible aspect to it. We are born, mature, and die, and this process cannot be shunted aside as irrelevant. But making it an absolute value by imposing a structure on it whereby its chronology is understood as ultimate seems to be a uniquely Western attribute. Non-Western, particularly nonliterate, peoples have taken the opposite tack, treating time as qualitative rather than quantitative, reducing chronology sometimes to the vanishing point. Of more importance to non-Western peoples is the particular place in which they live where qualitative experiences keep them centered.

Christian theology has made a fetish of distinguishing between two modes of time, traditionally characterized as *kairos,* the fulness of time when qualitative experiences are present, and *chronos,* the mathematical time of clocks, seasons, and sequences. The contention of Christianity is that revelation is a particular function to be discerned within a *kairos* event in that it fills the event with significance. Apart from revelation, Christian theologians would argue, our species is trapped within a chronology that makes little sense and is ultimately demonic. Most Christian theologians forget that chronology is a construct of the human mind whereas the qualitative nature of time is an experience of the whole person.

When we compare religious traditions that make space a more dominant value than time, we discover that the society orients itself around geographical phenomena, making land the important value and restricting the memories of the group to a tradition in which the chronology of events is not as important as the intensity with which they are remembered. It is more important for such groups to be able to say that certain events happened *here* and *there* rather than *when.* Perhaps the best conclusion we can draw from this tension between time and space is that they would seem to function in relationship to each other and that no tradition has totally escaped confronting the manner in which human beings respond to times and places. A society can always return to the place where something happened, but recreating the event itself, which historical religions claim to be doing, would seem fraught with possibilities for misunderstanding.

Tillich's third set of oppositions concerned the ultimate reality of the temporal world, and he found those traditions that orient themselves toward nature as believing the temporal world to have no significance. Those following a historical interpretation conceive the world as a battlefield between the powers of good and evil. Here Tillich badly stumbled in correlating facts and theory. A great mass of data derived from the Western tradition would indicate that Western peoples have often believed the world to be evil, regardless of their intuition of any divine plan for its redemption. A considerable amount of material would also indicate that non-Western peoples, for the most part, have not evaluated the world as being either good or evil in the same way that Western peoples have posed the question.

But is the world in fact a battlefield between good and evil? Historical religions have tended to project their own mythology upon the temporal process instead of deriving from that process an understanding of reality that manifests itself as either good or evil. We have no indication whatsoever that the ultimate meaning of temporal existence can be understood as a cosmic conflict between good and evil. This interpretation of the temporal process must certainly collapse because its cultural particularity eliminates it as an explanation of universal human experience.

The fourth category of opposition concerns the nature of the "true being." Again Tillich forced his interpretation of the two distinct ways of conceiving reality. Most primitive traditions, including the early Hebrew, had an immediate apprehension of the presence of deity and had such respect for the power of deity that uttering the deity's name or attaching conceptual attributes to deity was considered impious. Those traditions relying upon nature as the interpretive factor in determining reality were generally reluctant to ascribe to themselves much precise information concerning the ultimate being of the universe. But Westerners insisted upon the *omni* descriptions of God—omnipotent, omnipresent, omniscient, and so on—thus placing true being beyond the scope of natural processes through the creation of logical contradictions. Thus Tillich's characterization of the nonhistorical tradition conceiving of true being as "eternal, immovable, above becoming, genesis and decay" is inaccurate but must follow logically from his initial premise that history is the ultimate means of interpreting reality. If anything can be said of these concepts with respect to nonhistorical traditions, it is that they indicate a continual presence rather than an existence beyond the ability of concepts to describe.

Perhaps what Tillich was attempting to convey in making this distinction is that historical religions have tended to conceive of deity as personal; nonhistorical religions have not always reached the same conclusion. But even this proposition does not stand the test, for one of the chief characteristics of the nonhistorical tradition is its conception of deity as a personality, albeit with an arbitrary inclination toward the human species, and hence unpredictable, but not radically distinct from other forms of personality. Karl Heim (1874–1958), a German Protestant theologian who attempted to bring together the fields of science and religion, commented on this problem of describing the personal attributes of deity, remarking that:

> . . . whatever theological statement we may adopt, we are in no case entitled to speak in the religious field of the personal nature of God so long as in all other fields of knowledge our conception of the universe is one which excludes this religious proposition. This is the case so long as the human personality, which after all we always have in view when we speak of a person, is for us an *indivisible* whole, a psychophysical organism in which body and soul form an indissoluble unity.[10]

The two traditions seem to divide when the problem of representing divinity is reached. Must the experience of personality always be represented by a model based on our species? Gregory Bateson's idea that isolating God and the human species as special forms of existence is important in the sense that it warns us of conceptual problems inherent in the separation from nature. Of more importance, considering the broad scope of nonhistorical traditions, is that the refusal to limit representations of personality enables a much more comprehensive range of experience to be included. Nature then becomes a subject capable of personal involvement with our species and escapes artificial restrictions which we make at our peril.

Tillich's fifth comparison concerns the salvation of the individual and the community. This category is made possible by extending the Near Eastern mythology in which salvation-from-evil plays a determinative role. It has no significance outside the Western tradition, with the important exception of Buddhism, in which salvation from the cosmic process forms the backbone of the teachings. Perhaps the more important question to be asked concerns the nature of religion. Does religion universally concern itself with salvation from natural and historical processes? If so, it would seem possible to determine the means of salvation equally well from nature or from history. But if not, salvation would appear to be simply an element of those human traditions that conceive the cosmos as a battlefield. This conclusion is hardly universal.

If we accept salvation as a universal category of religious reality, it does not necessarily follow that historical religions provide salvation for communities while nonhistorical religions in effect eliminate the individual from time and history. Joachim Wach (1898–1955) a noted German scholar in the history of religions who taught in the United States and in Germany, wrote that "whatever the prevailing mood, the religious association takes precedence over all other forms of fellowship. *Religious loyalty, in theory at least, outranks any other loyalty everywhere except in the modern Western world.*"[11] Although Tillich maintained that historical religions, which are primarily Western, deal with the community, Wach noted that the influence of the religious community was in fact weakest in the West. Wach in fact noted further that "modern Western man is all too prone to think of the solitary individual first and last, yet *the study of primitive religions shows that, individual experiences notwithstanding, religion is generally a group affair.*"[12] Tillich's interpretation of ultimate reality as a function of history breaks completely apart when confronted with the facts of human existence, for dealing with history tends to tear groups apart, not bind them together.

We come now to the real substance of Western secular thinking about history and progress in Tillich's sixth category of distinction between the two interpretations of reality. He understood the nonhistorical interpretations to view the world as being in a state of deterioration; historical traditions, he said, understand history as containing a center in which the whole meaning becomes apparent and takes direction. Tillich and other Western thinkers generally find the center of history in the life of Jesus, and the most agnostic Western thinker still classifies time according to the A.D.–B.C. scheme. Only recently in scientific circles have people begun to use the appelation B.P. (before the present) as a means of establishing dates in world history.

We can look for alternative interpretations of the center of history once we transcend the Western religious tradition and the center can be said to occur almost any time within the respective human cultural traditions as each might perceive it. Only if we restrict history to the specific events of tradition can we justify Tillich's analysis. Otherwise the possibilities are endless. We do not yet understand the origins of our species, the derivation of culture and technology, or the relationship of our planet to the rest of the universe, so it is at least premature to categorize history as having a center with its geographical roots in the activities and events of a specific region and people.

If, however, we must seek a center for history, then it would seem that we must choose a time when there was such a movement in all societies and institutions that from the total scope of change new means of understanding the world emerged. Nathan Söderblum (1866–1931), the Swedish theologian prominent in the field of comparative religion who received the Nobel peace prize in 1930, writing in his famous book on the history of religions, *The Living God,* described one of the most fruitful periods of human experience, the seventh century B.C.

> The time was a remarkable one. Great things occurred in the world of the Spirit during those centuries. Kon-fu-tse summarized the wisdom of China in reverence towards Heaven and antiquity. His older contemporary Lao-Tse showed the way to quiet goodness and peace of mind. On the banks of the Neranjara there rose up in the soul of Siddhartha the way of deliverance from the woe of existence and the attainment of Nirvana. Before him Vardhamana had sought to "overcome" by means of a severe ascetic life. From other mysterious sources came salvation by Bhakti, devotion to a personal divinity. Among the Jews appeared the great prophets and their writings. The gloomy solitary at Ephesus, Heraclitus, expounded his doctrine. In southern Italy, Pythagoras gathered an intimate band of hearers to hear his speculations and his ascetic ideals. There also the bold rhapsodist, Xenophanes, spent the greater part of his life. In Sicily the seer Empedocles proclaimed his own divinity; he was himself a god.[13]

We have inadequate knowledge of events in the western hemisphere and Australia during those centuries, but if we are speaking of discovering a time when a substantial number of human societies were undergoing transformation in their understanding of the reality of the world, the seventh century B.C. would seem to provide a broader historical and geographical perspective than any other period of human existence.

If we take a fully naturalistic approach to reality, then the world does seem to be deteriorating physically. This insight is incorporated into the world view of modern physics in the second law of thermodynamics, the law of entropy, which finds an increasing sense of randomness present in the physical world. But this law applies primarily to the phenomenon of heat dissipation and carries no ultimate message concerning human affairs. Nature does seem to move in a great cycle of renewal, occasional violent destruction, and additional renewal.

But articulating this cycle of change is not so much an article of faith as a generalization based upon the collective experiences of generations of human beings. In a relatively practical sense that natural cycles simply exist without transcendental meaning. Chief Seattle of the Duwamish Tribe acknowledged this process in a memorable speech given in 1854:

> But why should I mourn at the untimely fate of my people? Tribe follows tribe, and nation follows nation, like the waves of the sea. It is the order of nature, and regret is useless. Your time of decay may be distant—but it will surely come . . . [14]

Thus, if some religious traditions view the cycles of nature as an inevitable process to which all are subject, their insight is hardly pessimism or religion lacking salvation. It is most probably a mark of sanity.

Tillich's final category of interpretation placed monotheism (the belief that there is only one God) in opposition to polytheism (the belief in more than one God) and pantheism (the belief that all manifestations of the self-existing universe are God). The great tradition of Western countries is the affirmation of monotheism, with the corresponding rejection of polytheistic or pantheistic conceptions of deity. Polytheism and pantheism most probably represent a Western effort to describe non-Western thought-forms rather than any insights that non-Western peoples have derived from their own experiences. One of the most common assumptions made by the popular mind is that monotheism evolves out of polytheism or pantheism as superstitious people become enlightened. This explanation serves to justify the Western concept of monotheism as a "higher" religious tradition than any other.

Scholars in the history of religion are not certain that the concept of monotheism is really a religious development, however, since it always seems to be connected with political or philosophical social upheavals that are fundamentally unrelated to the religious tradition of the society. Thus Raffaele Pettazzoni (1883–1959), Italian professor of history of religion, author of several books on comparative religion, rejected the idea that monotheism comes from understanding the nature of reality. He asked:

> In such a case, how shall it be explained that ancient Greece, with all its magnificent development of philosophical thought, never embraced a monotheistic religion. *It is far more a question of some particular event, which has occurred but a very few times in the history of the world* (the great majority of the peoples have not become monotheistic by evolution, but by conversion, i.e., when they embraced a new and foreign religion which was monotheistic) and this was always connected with the life and work of a great religious personality. The four great monotheistic religions of history are "founded" religions, in contrast to the religions of polytheism. [15]

Monotheism, rather than being a self-evident proposition of human experience, seems to have been the result of teaching and conversion, making it a learned and not an experienced proposition, a logical conclusion and not an immediate revelation. And Nathan Söderblum, describing genius, history, and spiritual personality as the most important factors in the history of religion, remarks that *"they do not apply to monotheism, which is often a theoretical or political ground of unity."* [16] Rather than serving as the final and compelling argument on behalf of the historical interpretation of reality that Tillich hoped to use, monotheism seems to originate in political and theoretical expediency and not in religious experience at all, indicating the uncertainty that is created when we divide our interpretation of reality into opposing categories, or nature and history.

Tillich's effort to distinguish between nature and history is inadequate. The seven characteristics that Tillich feels illustrate the two approaches either fade into generalizations upon preliminary inquiry or demonstrate Tillich's failure to correlate data and theory. The proper approach to interpreting reality is most probably a combination of nature and history that recognizes the value in the ongoing processes and life-forms of nature while making a serious effort to derive meaning from the passage of time directed in an irreversible forward sequence. Ian Barbour raises this question in a much better format:

> Discussions of providence, for example, refer extensively to God's activity in history but are silent about his activity in nature. What, then, was God's role in the long stretches of cosmic time before man's appearance? Is a sharp distinction between history and nature tenable, if nature itself has a history and if man is rooted in nature?[17]

The impossibility of making one concept dominate the other would seem to indicate that the proper approach is to combine both in a new scheme of interpretation, recognizing both the passage of time and the existence of natural places and species. In the same way that we cannot clearly and finally separate culture and civilization, we cannot distinguish between nature and history, and we must develop a cohesive vision of reality that transcends any particular human tradition.

Rejecting the traditional Western belief in the existence of two distinct realms—the eternal and ultimate in opposition to the transitory and immediate—we escape Western particularism insofar as we are able to confront the immediacy of experience without either denying it any ultimate validity or bowing to its ultimate value. But we are still left with the great legacy of Western thought, and the totality of this material, as seen in Western scientific achievements, cannot be lightly cast aside. A critique of Western culture and society must therefore admit the discoveries of the Western mind while transforming its conclusions to a broader planetary scheme of interpretation.

A more natural division of human experiences than the Platonic scheme can be seen in the Western tradition, again among the Greeks, and this format may give us the tools to examine the world view of Western culture. R. G. Collingwood (1889—1943), who was a Professor of Philosophy at Oxford concerned with the relation of philosophy and history, in writing about the development of history as a Western science, noted that the Greeks were aware of the distinctions between the events of the physical world and the incidents of the world of human affairs. As early as the fifth century B.C., Collingwood noted, the Greeks were aware that:

> ... there was such a thing as the human world, the totality of all particular social units; they called it *n'o'ikoumene,* as distinct from *o' kosmos,* the natural world. But the unity of this human world was for them only a geographical, not a historical, unity. The consciousness of that unity was not a historical consciousness. The idea of oecumenical history, world-history, was still non-existent.[18]

We need precisely this type of distinction if we are to initiate a critique of culture and civilization-as-sanction, for we seek to bring the disparate human traditions from all parts of the planet into a geographical unity of human experiences, into a system of interpretation in which a world history becomes possible. But following Ian Barbour's suggestion, we do not distinguish sharply between nature and history since each complements and converges into the other at crucial points. If we therefore deliberately divide our inquiry into two complementary searches, surveying our present knowledge of the world of human affairs and examining the present state of knowledge concerning the physical world, we will have covered the totality of possible experience without recreating the division between history and nature that Tillich described and without downgrading daily, normal human existence in favor of the belief in a realm of certitude containing eternal essences that describe the truly good.

We must recognize, it would appear, that nature and history are inseparably related, that the human species is simply one of the possible life-forms on the planet, but a life-form that is able to preserve an incredible collection of memories. We must not allow the reality of those memories to suggest a predetermined pattern of interpretation that justifies belief in the religious or philosophical doctrines of any particular cultural tradition. Teilhard de Chardin's assertion that discoveries do not take on importance until and unless they are adopted by Western societies cannot be allowed to dominate our attitude toward data or systems of interpretation. Rather we must relate the genius and insights of every society to the new pattern of interpretation.

We will turn first to the *kosmos,* the physical world in which we live as a species, the world from which we devise mechanical power and whose secrets we probe in countless laboratories, and attempt to determine what insights our knowledge of that world can give us concerning the meaning of human existence. What boundaries inhibit our understanding of that world? What limitations does nature impose on our species? What do we have in common with other species? What are the important discoveries about the probable structure of the universe, and how are these presently being communicated?

Then we shall examine some aspects of change that are occurring in the world of human affairs, the *oikumenē.* How are human beings responding to their institutions, and how are those institutions generating or inhibiting changes in the way we conduct our lives? Assuming the erosion of Western institutions as described by Revel, what transcendent forms are emerging that would indicate the nature of revolutionary change? And finally, how must we conceive the world of human affairs, its values, and the possibility for human growth within it? If culture and civilization express the collective knowledge and experience of human society, with religion forming the central core of cultural expression, what form must religion take in the future?

We transcend, therefore, the traditional Western division of experience into otherworldly and this-worldly reality by recognizing that the proper interpretation of experience is a combination of information concerning nature and history, wisely arranged, that systematically investigates the physical world and the world of human affairs. This new division of experiences does not give us a divided vision of reality but allocates according to two points of reference, nature and man, everything we have known or can know. We can, therefore, in the next chapter, survey the present state of scientific theories, hoping to discover the nature of reality as scientific theories are presently capable of expressing it.

IV. Space-Time

The most prominent division existing among members of our species is in the approach to the *kosmos*. Two major attitudes can be distinctly outlined, and they conflict in both theory and practice. The *kosmos* can be viewed on the basis of its manifestation of energy and personality, which can be explained as spiritual activity; or the *kosmos* can be seen as a complicated structure, devoid of personality, and operating as a relentless machine, uncompromising toward human efforts to find meaning. Non-Western peoples have generally tended to follow the path of spiritual investigation, and their efforts to explain natural processes have often involved models that incorporated organic-activity experience in nature. Western scholars have characterized this approach as *animism,* and the word has assumed a negative connotation as primitive and superstitious because no abstract knowledge that is immediately useful in a theoretical sense has derived from this tradition.

Western peoples, particularly the early Greeks, concentrated their efforts to explain the physical universe on determining the ultimate constituent from which all phenomena were derived. Democritus, an early Greek philosopher, concluded that the atom, a tiny irreducible particle of matter, formed the basis for the physical world. He pictured the ultimate natural process as one in which these tiny entities conflict and combine. Plato and Pythagoras took the conclusions of their Greek predecessors and suggested that mathematics and structural forms had ultimate status, for without determinable forms into which these mindless atoms might coalesce, there would be no knowledge or identity of physical entities. Western peoples have never forsaken this tradition of searching for the understanding of forms that provide shape and meaning to physical reality.

The major accomplishment of Western thought was the ability to discern from the wealth of phenomena certain general concepts and principles that could be applied to the natural world in a predictive sense, providing additional knowledge and enabling thinkers to refine their theoretical understanding of both structure and process. Perhaps the greatest single contribution made by early Western thinkers in this respect was the belief of Pythagoras that knowledge could be achieved by understanding harmonies and proportions. Once an objective standard of comparison became possible, scientific knowledge as we know it today began to emerge. The history of Western scientific and philosophical thought records the twists and turns that the refining process took. Out of this history emerged certain basic concepts—space, time, matter, energy, and causality—that have dominated and shaped the Western understanding of the *kosmos*.

Even though abstract thought has characterized Western culture as distinct among human traditions, philosophy and science were not always respected by Western peoples. Being immensely practical, they tended to deride any system of thought that did not make use of examples easily understood by the common person. Western philosophy continually faced the practical requirement of presenting its ideas in picturable form. The most popular and influential philosophies were those that made use of models immediately familiar to people, ones they could understand without much further thought. With an immediate correspondence between the manner in which the Western thinkers pictured the universe and the practical knowledge people had of the physical world, the increasing success of Western technology made it appear that our species was finally grasping a firm knowledge of the universe.

The great representation of the *kosmos* in Western history was that of Sir Isaac Newton. His mechanics established as a precondition for discussion of the absolute status of space, time, and causality. His model of the universe—a giant, self-operating clock—proved immensely popular with intellectuals and lay people alike. The success of Newtonian mechanics in predicting phenomena in the physical world proved incredibly accurate, and Newtonian formulas were considered the ultimate description of natural processes for several centuries after the system of thought became known. Newtonian mechanics connected directly with the religious beliefs of its time, which saw the rise of deism and theism as alternatives to Christian theology. Picturing the world as a secular machine, devoid of religious overtones, yet created by a benign watchmaker who enjoyed human efforts to discern universal secrets meant the enthronement of Newtonian views in Western society.

Western thinkers accepted Newton's theories with such gusto that they committed, in the eyes of Alfred North Whitehead, the British philosopher and mathematician (1861–1947), the intellectual error of believing that they had finally captured ultimate reality. Whitehead labeled this belief the "fallacy of misplaced concreteness," and he contended that it was responsible for the periodic roadblocks that science had experienced in the course of its development. Misplaced concreteness, to be more specific, entails the elimination of a great deal of phenomena from consideration in the formulation of theory and the consequent belief that because the theory as constituted seems to work, the neglected data is not critical to the understanding and may thereafter be excluded. When Newtonian physics established *a priori* that space, time, matter, energy, and causality were inherent in the structure of the universe, and when Newtonian formulas proved immensely successful in exploring the solar system, Western thinkers forgot that these concepts were definitions generated in Newton's mind, and they came to believe that they were accurate descriptions of ultimate physical processes.

Newtonian concepts worked as long as scientists had crude instruments capable of measuring distances and forces in a relatively unsophisticated manner. As scientists expanded their knowledge of the universe, experiments called for an increasingly sophisticated set of instruments and for additional precision in interpreting the results. Gradually scientists became aware that their measurements did not precisely conform to Newtonian formulas, and immense conceptual problems began to emerge in formulating experiments and interpreting results. Questions began to arise regarding the ultimate nature of space, time, matter, and other concepts that once had enjoyed absolute status. Eventually the idea of a static, intelligible nature, waiting patiently for human examination, began to give way. According to Heisenberg, nature became:

> a collective concept for all those realms of experience into which man could penetrate by means of science and technology, regardless of whether or not they appeared as "nature" to his immediate perception.[1]

This expansion of nature to include experiences not directly perceived by ordinary means was a radical break with traditional Western beliefs about the world and seemed more compatible with non-Western intuitions, although few thinkers could see the relationship inherent in the situation.

At the subatomic levels of experimentation the clear picture of the world began to blur rapidly, and new formulations of theory became imperative. Modern science, particularly theoretical physics, began to embark on an avenue of development that abandoned the easy explanations of Newtonian mechanics and sought increasingly sophisticated theories combining space, time, matter, energy, and causality into a synthesis in which no concept could be considered without precisely articulating its relationship to the other concepts that were used. Scientific knowledge took on an esoteric aspect in that scientists used an increasingly technical language that could not be represented in simple pictures and models for the lay person. Most of Western society remained Newtonian in outlook while thinkers and philosophers abandoned the belief that nature existed "out there." In effect, Western science was having to take into account the perceptions it had earlier eliminated from consideration. The difficulty in perception and understanding that physicists and philosophers encountered did not exist in nature but in the fact that they had been trained to view phenomena in Newtonian terms, which had proven capable of explaining phenomena only on a severely limited basis.

The importance of this shift in emphasis and outlook cannot be understated because it meant that scientific knowledge had to be understood as a limited and incomplete rendering of cosmic process in the face of unusually successful practical achievements. The atomic bomb, for example, was a fact of human economic and political life; yet the theoretical steps required to produce the process of atomic fission and fusion involved conceptual changes of immense importance. Western thinkers were deeply puzzled by this change. "The abandonment of picturability is one of the striking features of modern physics," Ian Barbour commented. "Micro-nature seems to be a different kind of reality from the world of everyday experience." [2] Micro-nature, the *kosmos* on the most minute scale, was understood as different from everyday experience only because thinkers had assumed the absolute status of everyday experiences as they had been explained in Newtonian philosophy.

We are presently in the midst of the process of casting off this misplaced belief that Newtonian mechanics is capable of describing universal processes on every level of complexity. "We know from the stability of matter that Newtonian physics does not apply to the interior of the atom," Heisenberg wrote, concluding that "at best it can occasionally offer us a guideline." The implication of this change, according to Heisenberg, was that "there can be no descriptive account of the structure of the atom." [3] The situation clearly calls for the construction of new theory that encompasses both Newtonian physics and the new discoveries. Although physicists insist that this task calls for new language and immensely complicated theoretical conceptions, in fact the requirement is simply that we banish predetermined ideas about space, time, and the other concepts we have used in science and philosophy. Poetry has once again entered the field as a means of communicating experience, and perceptions of reality demand primacy over conceptions of the mind. Mathematics continues to play an important role in discussing the experiments to be considered, but an adequate explanation of things cannot depend upon the ultimate status of traditional concepts.

Scientists now recognize that they have become a part of any experiment they undertake because the instruments they use are intruding into the functioning of nature in new and unexpected ways. We no longer stand outside the atom observing it. Today we enter into its ongoing life and become a part of its history. This new development, brought about by the use of sophisticated instruments, is part of nature and history also. Heisenberg described the new technology's effect on how scientists today conceive their experiments:

> Here technology no longer appears as the result of conscious human effort to extend man's material powers, but rather as a large-scale biological process in which man's organic functions are increasingly transferred to his environment. In other words, we

have here a biological process which, as such, is removed from man's control: for *while man can do what he wishes, he cannot will what he wishes.*[4]

There can be, under present conceptions of the scientific enterprise, an objective experiment as Newton would have conceived it. Scientific inquiry has now become part of a larger process of interaction that can only be described as incorporating relationships of personal quality with nature to produce knowledge. Western science has thus arrived at precisely the starting point of non-Western peoples in apprehending more than physical and mechanical activities in nature. As the primitve peoples believed that they were personally involved in the processes of nature, so modern scientists have concluded that they are personally involved and are an important factor in the processes of nature when they attempt to learn the secrets of the *kosmos.*

The change of conception that this shift involves seems to be immense, but on reflection it proves to be more in tune with our emotions and experiences and less in tune with abstract conceptions we have learned in school. Thus Ian Barbour, in describing the new manner of understanding the physical universe, explains:

> time and space are indissolubly united in a space-time continuum. Matter and energy must be taken together as matter-energy, and according to relativity matter-energy is simply a distortion in the structure of space. In quantum theory, separate particles seem to be temporary and partial manifestations of a shifting pattern of waves that combine at one point, dissolve again, and recombine elsewhere; a particle begins to look like a local outcropping of a continuous substratum of vibratory energy. *As more complex systems are built up, new properties appear that were not foreshadowed in the parts alone.*[5]

These conceptions are complicated only if we still cling to the belief that we can discover the ultimate secret of the universe by isolating phenomena until we have uncovered the basic constituent and then assume that by rigorous formulas we can describe every subsequent event or combination that this constituent may experience. When Barbour suggests that "new properties appear that were not foreshadowed in the parts alone," he is saying that scientists are returning to a more general and less mechanical apprehension of nature, one that we can all find familiar in our experiences as sensitive personalities. The properties are new only in the sense that we eliminated them as factors before we understood the role they played in nature. They are now returning to demand respect from us.

We can best understand this transformation being experienced by the scientific mind if we refer once again to an insight of Alfred North Whitehead. "Modern physics has abandoned the doctrine of Simple Location," Whitehead contended. "The physical things which we term stars, planets, lumps of matter, molecules, electrons, protons, quanta of energy, are each to be conceived as modifications of conditions within space-time, extending throughout its whole range." [6] As long as thinkers held fast to beliefs that space, time, and other concepts were inherent in the nature of things rather than being useful ways of describing experiences, they had to insist that within absolute space and time entities had a definite location and that this location could be dtermined quite simply by measuring it. In rejecting this belief in absolute status for space and time, scientists eliminated any suggestion of simple location and came to see that location was dependent upon numerous relationships, some of which could not be described mathematically or understood, except emotionally.

When we consider this change, we discover that it conforms more to our experience than to our former beliefs. We never experience things in complete isolation, which would be expected if absolute space and time were really operative in the world. Rather we experience a conglomerate of things, and out of these things we remember with some degree of clarity those that have impressed themselves upon our emotions and personality. The vast majority of our experiences consist of infinitely complex situations that combine all elements of our environment. Common people, poets, and painters have always understood this aspect of human experience, but only recently have scientists and philosophers rediscovered it and begun to approach more closely the world in which we live.

This shift in viewpoint brings us back to the origins of the Western scientific tradition. The Greeks had developed sophisticated analytical tools for exploring the *kosmos,* but, as Tillich pointed out, they used these concepts "for aesthetic intuition of the world, for ethical resignation from it, or the mystical elevation above it." [7] Not until Christian humanists began to reconsider the physical world as an arena of investigation in its own right were the command of Genesis to "subdue the earth" and the Greek conceptualizations of the structure of the universe welded together to form the Western scientific spirit of inquiry. If, as Tillich maintained, "Christian humanism employed Greek concepts for the technical control and the revolutionary transformation of reality," [8] modern introduction of the scientist-observer as participant in a process transcending mechanical experimentation simply returns us to an understanding of nature consonant with Greek thinking and heals part of the division that centuries of speculation have introduced into our system of knowledge.

The reintroduction of the observer into the process of acquiring scientific knowledge implies, not simply the healing of an ancient breach, but the possibility of bringing theology and science together again. During the centuries in which Western science believed that nature stood apart and inert and was capable of being completely known by the human mind, scientists pursued their task with a religious fervor, considering their work as evidence of the deity but consistently eliminating the insights of theology regarding the nature of reality. Thus Werner Heisenberg, in discussing the contributions of Johannes Kepler (1571–1630), the first professional astronomer to uphold Copernicus' theories, noted that for Kepler science was not a means of procuring material benefits for human society but "a means of elevating the mind, a way of finding peace and solace in the contemplation of the eternal perfection of the Creation." [9] Karl

Heim described the separation of the sciences during the Reformation as a logical and natural part of the Western religious tradition. He suggested that restricting theological inquiry to a single area of human experience was compatible with the general spirit of the times:

> for at that time the remaining part of the world-picture, the part with which the profane sciences were concerned, was simply a further development of the central content of the faith, which was the subject-matter of theology.[10]

This underlying belief that science testifies to the existence and genius of deity remains with us, and Einstein's insistence that God does not play dice reflects this unconscious and rarely articulated tie between Western science and religion.

Western thinking has thus moved a considerable distance from its belief in the ultimate status of scientific concepts, and the explanations given by physicists about the world reflect this progress. Heisenberg wrote that "when we speak of the picture of nature in the exact science of our age, we do not mean a picture of nature so much as a *picture of our relationships with nature*."[11] He warned quite emphatically that "the old division of the world into objective processes in space and time and the mind in which these processes are mirrored—in other words, the Cartesian difference between *res cogitans* and *res extensa*—is no longer a suitable starting point for our understanding of modern science."[12] So we begin our scientific inquiry at precisely the point where the non-Western peoples began. We refuse to allow artificial divisions of subject-object, mind-matter, and space-time to lead us astray. Heisenberg was thus correct in insisting that *"the scientific worldview has ceased to be a scientific view in the true sense of the word."*[13] Experimentation is participation; knowledge is an expansion of our ability to formulate and comprehend our relationships with the *kosmos*.

Perhaps the major remaining assumption that science retains while experiencing this transformation in its understanding is the belief that nature is orderly, that is, that it can be described in fairly precise mathematical terms. This idea originates in theological beliefs yet undergirds scientific inquiry. "Clearly it is not a formal presupposition or a logical premise," Ian Barbour notes, "and it is never mentioned in scientific research itself; it is simply taken for granted in the scientific community and in the culture of which it is a part."[14] This assumption continues to control the manner in which scientists interpret their data and postulate the expansion of theories. Thus Werner Heisenberg, identifying two common constant factors that all physicists use to interpret their data—the speed of light and the quantum of action—assumed the orderliness of nature as the basis for suggesting that yet a third constant could be discovered:

> This is obvious for purely dimensional reasons. The universal constants determine the scale of nature, the characteristic quantities that cannot be reduced to other quantities. One needs at least three fundamental units for a complete set of units.[15]

We need not concern ourselves with the technical description of the universal constants. The assumption that orderliness requires an additional constant to be discovered is sufficient to illustrate the scientific reliance on orderliness in nature as an article of faith. Even this belief, however, is subject to abuse if it becomes a dogmatic article of faith rather than a presupposition that can be adapted to fit new circumstances.

The arguments reviewed in the previous chapter concerning the nature of reality when conceived in a religious and historical format are meaningless aside from an understanding of space, time, matter, causality, and the place they currently occupy in our understanding. Therefore, while modern conceptions of these ideas are somewhat complicated, it will serve us well to examine them more closely.

SPACE

Space has traditionally been confused with distance in the popular mind. Newtonian physics measured forces and masses at distances and conceived space to be an absolute element in the structure of the universe. For events and forces of human size, the Newtonian formulas are still valid, and perhaps it is this continued appeal to our powers of observation that enables Newtonian space to dominate our consciousness whenever we deal with this concept. But with increasing sophistication in our ability to measure, two developments made scientists suspect Newton's definition of space. On the macrocosmic level where we examine stars, solar systems, and galaxies, light seemed to bend when approaching and leaving large masses of material, indicating some undiscovered property of either light or space that Newton's idea of empty absolute space could not predict. On the microcosmic level where we investigate the structure of the atom and its constituent parts, distances became so infinitesimal that it was no longer possible to use space to denote distances between points. So scientists recognized that the idea of absolute space had to give way to a more sophisticated idea.

Not all scientists were uncritical advocates of Newtonian space even at the zenith of its popularity. "The possibility of empty space has always been a controversial problem in philosophy," [16] Heisenberg noted, and increasingly physicists had to assume that space was littered with various kinds of entities and energies in order to explain the results of their experiments. Newtonian mechanics relied exclusively upon Euclidian geometry, which assumed a constant and homogenous nature of straight lines and curves for its validity. Euclid, a Greek mathematician, dominated Western conceptions of geometry because his system was most useful in surveying distances and because it assumed certain principles (that parallel lines never meet) that appeared to be common sense propositions about the world. When mathematicians began to derive non-Euclidian geometries that were totally consistent within themselves but violated the propositions of Euclid, and physicists found them useful in describing the experiments they were conducting, traditional concepts of space changed to account for this new application. Geometry became an intimate part of both macrocosmic and microcosmic theories in a non-Euclidian sense while Euclidian theorems continued to be used to solve problems occurring in daily life on our scale of existence.

Einstein's use of non-Euclidian geometries to explain the relativity of time and space made these systems of thought as important as the older geometric system had been. "In the theory of general relativity," Heisenberg explained, "the answer is given that geometry is produced by matter or matter by geometry." [17] This apparent equivalency meant that neither the geometric shape nor the matter inhabiting the region under consideration could be discussed as an ultimate and isolated phenomenon. Space is thus not empty. It cannot be conceived apart from matter exhibiting itself in particular ways. Karl Heim expressed the situation well when he wrote that "the structure of space has its origin neither in the subject nor in the object but always in the *relation* which arises between a particular subject and a particular object whenever they encounter one another." [18] This conception is fully within our emotional experiences since even distance in our practical lives is a distance between points and cannot be conceived apart from things we experience.

TIME

Time suffered a similar fate as space in the development of modern scientific thought. Popular concepts of time saw it as an irreversible, linear progression that had a beginning and worked toward a known conclusion. When this idea of time merged with the religious beliefs of Western peoples, particularly with respect to the doctrine of creation, time came to be conceived as an absolute element of the universe. The *kosmos* was thought to have a definite and identifiable beginning and was expected to come to some final conclusion. Time was divided into absolute uniform units that could be measured and recorded. The most common verification of time as an absolute element of reality made by the popular mind was the aging process experienced by our species. Time does pass, seasons move into each other continually, and change of an irreversible nature does occur. The average lay person today still clings to this idea.

If there were absolute time, or if time formed an absolute aspect of reality, then it would be reasonable to suppose that the *kosmos* experiences everything simultaneously. In other words, at any moment, something is happening contemporaneously with everything else in the universe; there is universal time that can be recorded and measured. Einstein upset this belief when he suggested that there really were no simultaneous events and that observations of events depended upon the observer and his or her position with respect to them. "In the theory of relativity we have learned that the situation is different," Heisenberg explained, from former conceptions of time. "Future and past are separated by a finite time interval the length of which depends on the distance from the observer." [19] This conception of time is precisely that which we experience in our emotional lives, discovering that sometimes hours take forever and sometimes that they slip easily past us. Modern science, in devising a new and more complicated explanation of time, is really bringing its conception back into line with our practical daily experiences.

"In the new physics," Ian Barbour suggests, "time is constitutive of the being of atoms as *vibratory patterns;* a wave or a musical note requires time in order to exist—a note is nothing at an instant." [20] This idea of time is more in the order of recognizing a duration or growth of things as distinct from the inexorable workings of a homogenous chronology that relentlessly proceeds on its way. We can perhaps project a different passage of time according to the scope of our considerations, suggesting a radically different sense of time for subatomic events that happen almost simultaneously and a more profound and leisurely sense of time for events of a galactic nature. In any sense we wish to use the idea of time, we must recognize that we are restricted to the immediate physical environment. Modern developments have thus freed us from a bondage to the fear of time that has plagued Western culture for several millenniums.

MATTER

Nothing seems more certain to the popular mind than the fact that matter exists. We live in a world of hard physical reality where automobiles and airplanes crash, knees and elbows get skinned, and most of us do hard physical labor. To the common person, then, the idea of physical matter at some level of universal existence is an emotional belief verified in everything we experience. For centuries the goal of science was to locate and identify the smallest particle of matter that composed the *kosmos.* In the twentieth century this desire led to concentrated investigations of the interior of the atom that considerably changed our conception of the reality of matter. The initial debate early in the century centered on the question of whether physical reality was a *wave* of substance or a *particle* of energy. Equally good reasons existed for believing either conclusion, and the compromise that was finally accepted involved an admission, at least with respect to light, that the nature of the experiment would determine how scientists would conceive of matter. If they needed to believe it acted in waves, they could do so; if they needed to conceive matter as individual particles, that was also permissible.

This flexibility in conceptualizing matter meant that science could no longer attempt to discover what matter was "in itself," and one of the traditionally important philosophical questions of Western peoples was foreclosed. "We can no longer consider 'in themselves' those building-stones of matter which we originally held to be the last objective reality," [21] Heisenberg concluded. The definition of this problem had to cease at the boundaries of thought since there was no conceivable way that scientists could finally decide which alternative interpretation should receive primary status. Werner Heisenberg described the phenomena observed by physicists at the subatomic level where explanations ceased to explain anything:

> If two elementary particles collide with extremely high energy, they actually fall to pieces, as a rule, and often into many pieces, but the pieces are no smaller than the particles that were split. Independently of the energy available (if only this is large enough), we always obtain from such a collision the same sorts of particle that we have been familiar with for a number of years. Even in cosmic radiation, where the available energy of a particle can in some cases be a thousand times larger than in the biggest existing accelerator, no other or smaller particles have been found.[22]

With this situation being encountered in experiments, it becomes possible to describe matter as energy and energy as matter. Indeed, this possibility of transposition seems characteristic of the new discoveries in science. Heisenberg himself used the two ideas, energy and matter, as nearly equivalent concepts. *"There is only one kind of matter,"* he wrote in *The Physicist's Conception of Nature, "but it can exist in different stationary conditions."* [23] And in *Physics and Philosophy* he suggested the converse of this definition: "Energy is in fact the substance from which all elementary particles, all atoms and therefore all things are made, and energy is that which moves. Energy is substance, since its total amount does not change and the elementary particles can actually be made from this substance as is seen in many experiments on the creation of elementary particles." [24]

We do not have a precise equivalency here since science chooses neither energy nor matter but prefers to stop its analysis at the process that is being observed. In place of the traditional belief that matter is irreducible, modern science is substituting a transformation process whereby energy and matter take on aspects of the other and cannot properly be separated. "The elementary particles of modern physics can be transformed into each other exactly as in the philosophy of Plato," Heisenberg explained. "They do not themselves consist of matter, but they are the only possible forms of matter. Energy becomes matter by taking on the form of an elementary particle, by manifesting itself in this form." [25] Again this change is not as radical as some thinkers would have us suppose. If we drop the curious belief that we can discern the ultimate physical building-block of the *kosmos* and simply report what has been observed, no problems in conception arise. Only if we insist on preserving the ancient belief that one single entity undergirds and composes everything in the universe do we have conceptual difficulties.

CAUSALITY

Western peoples have relied on the idea of causality in nearly every sphere of intellectual endeavor. Not simply in scientific experiments and theories but in social sciences, humanities, religion, and law, causality has been a major tool in arranging data in a comprehensible format. Generally, Western peoples have understood causality in simple terms of antecedents and sequences. *A* always comes before *B* and is understood as a major cause creating *B,* and *C* is naturally expected to follow in succession. In religion we often remark that because of sin in the world God had to enter history and balance the scales of cosmic justice. In law we derive a series of causes to explain the accidents and injuries that are the subject of lawsuits. Historians go to great lengths to explain incidents, events, and policies as the products of antecedent causative factors.

Modern science arose in the Newtonian context in which causality played an important and determinative role. Within absolute time and space, events could be rigidly linked one to another so that causality itself became an example of misplaced concreteness. In recent decades the concept of causality has been partially abandoned because the novelty of results in some experiments seemed to indicate that *B* did not always follow *A.* It became necessary to expand the concept of the phenomena that formerly indicated causality so that the activities occurring within the context of space-time would be properly explained. Heisenberg contrasted the new meaning of causality with the meaning that the popular mind has often attributed to the idea of cause. "Whereas the layman tends to think of causality as a relation between two objects, the scientist thinks of it as a relation between different states of the same object or the same system of objects at different times." [26] Scientific causality has a much more intimate and restricted use than does the popular tendency to simply locate antecedent events.

In large measure, however, causality has been abandoned as a useful tool for interpreting experiences and experiments. "The law of causality is no longer applied in quantum theory, and the law of conservation of matter is no longer true for the elementary particles," Heisenberg argued. In fact, he warned, "We must bear in mind the possibility that experiment may well prove that small-scale space-time processes may run in reverse to the causal sequence." [27] Like absolute time and space, causality in the new scheme is restricted to the immediate experiment in which it is useful as a tool of interpretation; it is not considered as an ultimate process of the *kosmos.* The modern understanding of causality is thus more akin to Immanuel Kant's contention that it is a form of understanding we impose on sensory data than it is to more popular interpretations found in Plato, Aristotle, and Newton, which border on determinism located in natural processes and independent of our minds.

Elimination of causality as an ultimate factor in universal existence enables us to transcend many problems that have originated by applying causality to phenomena. Predestination, free will, the belief in the inexorable march of technological progress, and proximate causes in legal theory can all be recast in the light of the reduction of causality to an occasional tool rather than a vital factor in universal existence.

The most common characteristic of the new interpretations modern science gives concerning the *kosmos* is the willingness to abandon the old belief that truth could be discovered by isolating phenomena and reducing knowledge to measurable quantities. A much more cohesive picture of the world emerges when we include rather than exclude, and the inclusionary aspect of modern science, while seeming strange at the beginning, is actually more in line with our experiences than with our previous efforts to understand things. Ian Barbour gives a clear and concise summary of the physical world as conceived by modern science when he explains that "time and space are indissolubly united in a space-time continuum. Matter and energy must be taken together as matter-energy, and according to relativity matter-energy is simply a distortion in the structure of space." [28] All concepts merge into one another and quite properly appear now as inseparable elements of experience.

Science, at least with respect to the *kosmos*, is rapidly approaching the area of metaphysics because it needs an increasingly complex interpretation of phenomena that demands synthesis and depends ultimately on intuition as much as experimentation. Barbour defines science as a *"search for pattern:* scientific theories order experience intelligibly," [29] and it is precisely this task that metaphysics seeks to accomplish. Heisenberg, writing of the scientific endeavor, argued that:

> From the very start we are involved in the argument between nature and man in which science plays only a part, so that the common division of the world into subject and object, inner world and outer world, body and soul, is no longer adequate and leads us into difficulties.[30]

The argument between nature and our species is certainly not restricted to measurements of the physical universe. It includes the great variety of possible human reactions and responses to nature that the social sciences and humanities have also described. The manner in which the argument is now being conducted is less a struggle for control and more a desire for participation.

Western peoples have previously believed that scientific knowledge could indefinitely provide them with techniques to control and understand nature. They partially accomplished this goal by reducing the phenomena of nature to objects valuable only because they could be measured and modified. Even while technological progress continues, scientists are retreating from an absolute stance that purports to explain everything in theoretical terms. "The primary significance of modern physics lies not in any disclosure of the fundamental nature of reality," Ian Barbour writes, "but in the recognition of the *limitations of science.*" [31] If we have a knowledge of nature at all, we must conceive it as a *"modest, sharply delimited sector of, and extract from, the multiplicity of phenomena* observed by our senses," [32] Heisenberg argued. Complete knowledge of the world, either in the scientific or philosophical sense, would require the reintroduction of factors previously omitted from consideration. The metaphysical task that brings together all facets of human knowledge in one major synthesis would seem to be the next major step in understanding that our species must take.

V. The Process of Life

The Greek conception of the *kosmos* was not simply that of a world of atoms, metaphysical ideas and numbers, and random energies. It also consisted of plants and animals, the life-forms of the biological world, including the human species, considered as observable phenomena. We would be remiss if we based any critique of culture and civilization on the discoveries and theories of modern physics alone. Of more importance to the layman are the principles that seem to describe and govern activities in the world of which they are a part. Therefore we must investigate other fields of knowledge to see if some of contemporary interpretations of the world can be made compatible with the discoveries in the field of physics, thereby extending the possibility of our metaphysical search into a broader perspective.

The world of plants and animals is the field of biological and botanical sciences insofar as knowledge is concerned. The traditional Western view of plants and animals is best expressed by the ancient Hebrew psalmist who, centuries before Christ, described man as little lower than the angels, adding in his hymn of praise:

> Thou madest him to have dominion over the works of thy hands; thou has put all things under his feet:
> All sheep and oxen, yea, and the beasts of the field;
> The fowl of the air, and the fish of the sea, and whatsoever passeth through the paths of the sea.[1]

The central theme of this concept of the human species as dominating nature and occupying a place in the universe next to the celestial beings was illustrated in the creation story in Genesis when God allowed Adam to name the animals. In the Hebrew tradition, knowing the name of another being placed that other being in one's control and under one's power. The earliest religious conception of the status of the human species, which has continuously endured in the West, thus separated our species from the other life-forms and asserted our superiority and mastery over them.

The Greek philosophers took a more abstract and intellectual view of the status of the human species and concerned themselves with the primary philosophical question of how we know what we know. From their fascination with the theory of knowledge the Greeks derived their conception and understanding of the biological world—plants, animals, and the human species. Beginning with Socrates and Plato and culminating in the thought of Aristotle, the Greek philosophical tradition understood the world of senses as a pale and imperfect representation of a realm of eternal ideas and essences. Various individuals of any species were thought to share imperfectly in an eternal idea that transcended temporal existence and gave meaning to any particular manifestation of itself in the world of human experience. Knowledge of the biological world was a knowledge of the eternal ideas that had participated in the creation of the world of senses.

The tendency of Greek thought, seen particularly in the philosophical system of Aristotle, was to classify species and to discern distinguishing attributes that transcended individual expressions of the essence of an idea. Thus in addition to the many breeds of dogs existing in the everyday world, the Greeks felt that an ideal form of "dog" existed in an absolute sense as the ultimate reality and gave meaning to any particular dog insofar as that eternal idea provided a goal and structure within which the individual dog could be said to exist. Becoming what an entity was intended to become represented the highest expression of organic life. In this manner the biological world was seen to have purpose and human ethics was understood as an operative principle that existed in and shaped the process of life in the universe.

Greek and Christian thought moved toward each other in the centuries following the spread of the Christian religion in the Roman Empire, and the great chain of being that Greek philosophy had devised to explain the gradations of the biological world became infused with Christian doctrines of salvation. The alien feeling that Christians expressed toward the *oikumenē* of their day became somewhat alleviated with the vision of the human species at the apex of a great biological hierarchy, each member of which was striving to fulfill itself by becoming what the eternal forms or ideas had intended. The origin of these eternal forms or ideas became, eventually, the Christian God, and with this identification Western philosophical and theological traditions merged to produce a Graeco-Hebraic vision of the biological world. The combination of these two traditions gave an additional interpretation to plant and animal existence that had not been objectively articulated before. "Man was the *center of the created order,*" Ian Barbour commented about this new view. "Nature was subordinate to man. The functions of creatures below him in the scale were explained mainly by their role in human purposes, for the world was designed to subserve man's interests." [2]

Later refinements did not radically alter this conception. The purpose of other species and organic entities was oriented toward the needs and enjoyment of humans, or so Western peoples believed for many centuries. Gregory Bateson maintains that as late as the "mid-eighteenth century the biological world looked like this: there was a supreme mind at the top of the ladder, which was the basic explanation of everything downwards from that—the supreme mind being, in Christianity, God." [3] But considered in practical terms, the biological world was held to have been created in the same forms in which it was then being observed, according to the theological speculations based upon the creation story of Genesis, which was considered a historical description of the creation event.

Because the origin of species was a theological doctrine as much as a scientific doctrine, which understood the biological world as a product of instantaneous creation at a specific time in the past, few thinkers saw any possibility of species being other than what they were observed to be. All species were regarded as having their respective niches, and as each species approached human characteristics, it was felt to be higher on the great hierarchy of being. When scientists began discovering the skeletons and remains of plants and animals that did not then exist, such evidences were interpreted as debris from the planetary Flood described in the Old Testament, whole species and genera having perished in that deluge. Although philosophers may have argued that all possible forms could have existed at one time through the benevolence of God, no one suspected that species could become something other than what God had intended.

Then came Darwin. From numerous questions that arose from his observations of plants, animals, and birds on his several journeys on the ship *Beagle,* Darwin was led to question the rigid interpretation of the origin of species that saw plant and animal life as a stable product of creation week. Darwin thought he detected intermediate and transitional steps of development between closely related species, which seemed to indicate that the species themselves had in some peculiar manner initiated changes in their body structure. If either the environment or the organism could produce morphological, cr overall structural, change in species, Darwin felt, then the traditional interpretation of the origin of life, particularly the traditional explanation of the variety of life, had to give way to a new interpretation that was more in line with observable facts. He thus developed the theory of evolution, which maintained that far from an instantaneous creation of a variety of life-forms, the biological world was the result of an incredibly slow process of development in which simpler organisms gave way to more complicated ones by evolving new bodily structures that enabled them to survive more efficiently in their environment.

Darwin supported his theory with three major principles, which have since become almost self-evident to Western peoples. In the first place, he saw random variations in species that followed no predetermined course of development and could therefore be regarded as spontaneous. Such random changes could not occur in the old religious interpretation of the creation of species, but they seemed to point to a new understanding when placed in a context of gradual change to accommodate survival in a changing environment, because such random changes could be understood as efforts to transcend the finitude of existence. If the random variations could be transmitted from one generation to another, and Darwin believed they could be and probably were, then new species could evolve from old ones over a prolonged period of time.

Second, the random distribution of new characteristics would shortly produce chaos in the biological world if every change that originated within a species were transmitted over the generations. Some limiting principle was needed to explain why some characteristics had endured while others had represented only individual mutations that perished with the individuals possessing them. Darwin needed a model which could demonstrate that the variations which occurred were intimately tied to the organism's effort to extend its life. He found his model in the jungle, where the weaker members perished and the stronger and more clever members survived. The production of new species through a process of natural selection became Darwin's second major evolutionary conception. This doctrine asserted that only those characteristics that enabled organisms to survive continued, and adaptations that did not give the organism adequate capability to deal with its environment were not passed down from one generation to another. Nature selected what was useful and rejected what was useless.

Darwin's third major thesis was a logical extension of the second. Only the fittest members of each species would survive, and only those species that made the proper adaptations would continue to exist. The jungle was not simply a testing ground for new characteristics. It was the terminal point of existence for many species that could not develop sufficient protective devices or behavior patterns to survive. The strong preyed upon the weak, and the species which Darwin and other scientists observed were those that had successfully transcended difficulties from both environment and other species.

Peculiar characteristics of organisms were interpreted as if they had specifically developed unique organs and patterns of behavior to survive. Some organisms had hard shells, others developed poisons, others developed strong and powerful bodies, incredible speed afoot, or unique eyesight and hearing. The human species had developed a brain and the ability to make and use tools. But each species had ensured its survival by entering the jungle of life and developing a specialty that prevented its extinction by other species or by sudden climatic changes.

Darwin's theory of evolution was revolutionary for its day and provoked considerable controversy. It clashed directly with the religious beliefs of the

Western tradition because it eliminated the special creation of life by the Western deity and replaced such a benevolent act with an endless process of organic change, stretching backward for thousands of centuries. The human species lost its exalted place in creation and became simply another species of organic existence, the highest expression of the evolutionary process to be sure, but hardly a special creature made in the image of God. A heated controversy began between evolutionists, who maintained that the human species was descended from a long line of vertebrates and was undoubtedly closely related to simian, or apelike, cousins of the present, and the religious conservatives, who refused to believe that the divine truth revealed in the Bible should be interpreted in a symbolic and not literal sense. In many places in the modern world this battle between science and religion over the origin of species still rages, and the major contentions of each group have changed little since the controversy started, the arguments being endlessly repeated with each genera- tion of combatants.

Ian Barbour said that Darwin's theory of evolution burst the bounds of the rigid classifications that had frozen the great chain of being, and that Darwin did to Aristotle's biology what Newton did to Aristotle's physics.[4] But the revolution in thought triggered by the theory of evolution was more profound than simply loosening the categories of organic existence to allow a gradual transformation of organisms. Ernst Cassirer summarized this revolution as having "destroyed the arbitrary limits between the different forms of organic life. There are no separate species; there is just one continuous and uninterrupt- ed stream of life."[5] Western thinkers have not yet absorbed the meaning of this change in viewpoint in any fundamental way. If there is simply a continuous and uninterrupted stream of life-classification by morphology according to species, genera and other familiar biological categories are only one of a variety of ways that the biological world can be understood. The similarity that appears to exist between closely related species, families, classes, orders, genera, phyla, and kingdoms in a physical sense may speak more comprehensibly to our understanding when viewed in a spiritual sense. And evolution, once loosening the bounds of our conceptions, may have to discard its most cherished tenets of belief in the same manner that modern physics has reluctantly had to surrender such concepts as space, time, matter, and causality.

The importance of evolution in our daily lives cannot be underestimated. The concept of the survival of the fittest, which had the most practical appeal to common people, has been applied indiscriminately in a great many nonbiologi- cal areas of human life. As a slogan it fit perfectly with the religious maxim that "God helps those that help themselves" and was used to justify individual adventures in politics and commerce almost from the beginning of the controver- sy over evolution. We speak about the self-made man and attribute individual financial and social success to the inexorable workings of the principle of evolutionary change. The estimates we make of our accomplishments are couched in terms of "progress," and we judge the vitality of our societies, not on the number of wise and compassionate people we produce, but on our Gross National Product and a constantly expanding economy.

Evolution became controversial because it attempted to interpret scientific data without relying on theological certainty, which had supported previous explanations of the origin of species. In the decades when evolutionary thought was being hotly debated by the learned people of Western societies, other sciences were being born. The great seminal years of anthropology, sociology, psychology, and comparative religions coincided with the evolution controversy, and the pioneer thinkers in these social sciences saw in evolution a means of interpreting their data that seemed both reasonable and adequate. They came to believe that societies, groups of people within societies, and the beliefs and values of individuals in societies had all evolved from simple, primitve, and superstitious fears into the complicated and sophisticated organizations, attitudes, and beliefs we see today.

The respective human cultural traditions were understood by the social sciences as representing stages of growth in the human adventure, and the impressive technology of Western societies was understood as the ultimate refinement of social and technical evolution in the same way that highly sophisticated organisms represented a biological perfection. Claude Levi-Strauss, the French structural anthropologist, traced the development of this cultural attitude toward the non-Western human societies in the field of anthropology, explaining:

> The evolutionist interpretation in anthropology clearly derives from evolutionism in biology. Western civilization thus appears to be the most advanced expression of the evolution of societies, while primitive groups are "survivals" of earlier stages, whose logical classification reflects their order of appearance in time.[6]

We have already seen this attitude translated into a cultural arrogance toward the traditions of non-Western societies in Teilhard's assertion that things had no value apart from the Western European use of them. If we are to offer a critique of civilization-as-sanction as part of our metaphysical search for universal meaning, we shall have to find an alternative interpretation of evolutionary processes that avoids the predetermined conclusion that Western peoples represent the highest human accomplishment.

Evolution as an interpretive theory did not radically change the orientation of Western culture, which saw the human species as the center of creation, but it did create two major problems for the partially educated Westerner who understood the theory emotionally but could not understand its possible logical implications when applied without careful analysis to other fields of human life. If the human species were simply a part of nature and if all life-forms were in the process of becoming more complicated and sophisticated, there was really no need to attach a deity to the final phase of the evolutionary process. People could accept the suggestion that evolution explained every aspect of human affairs, and accepting such a conclusion precluded many people from considering the emergence of religion, art, music, and other intangible expressions of the human spirit as things of substance and reality. Evolutionary doctrines thus helped to justify the already present desire of people to free themselves from the restrictions placed upon their lives by organized religion without presenting them with the equally important demand to account for such feelings and beliefs in an intelligent and realistic manner.

The other problem that evolution created was the heartfelt need of religious people to attach their theological beliefs to an evolutionary framework without critically examining the validity of the theory. Theologians and historians, particuarly, made the evolutionary framework serve their own purposes by attaching their beliefs to the final term of the evolutionary process. Thus Christianity was felt to represent the highest of human religions, and other societies were seen evolving toward Christian tenets. The rise and fall of civilizations was understood as an evolutionary process of growth and decay that seemed to transcend the problems and particularities of any of the great civilizations. The uncritical assumption that evolutionary tenets represented the ultimate processes of the natural world and the reception of this assumption in nonbiological fields resulted in a foreclosure of creative thinking in many areas and an interpretation of data to fit foregone conclusions.

Because these two alternatives, an atheistic universe and the evolutionary process as divine revelation, seemed so opposed to each other in the popular mind, major figures in philosophy in this century attempted to harmonize the two interpretations, which are really alternating theological positions, into one comprehensive philosophical system. Henri Bergson developed a philosophy of creative evolution, and Jan Christian Smuts developed a similar system of philosophy in the early decades of this century. The great English thinker Alfred North Whitehead offered process philosophy, which was based upon a model closely associated with organic processes. All these philosophies grappled with the implications of evolutionary doctrines while attempting to maintain the traditional Western point of view. But each failed to incorporate a sufficient selection of interpretations from the body of knowledge available to them in biology and paleontology; so the resulting systems were vaguely articulated and difficult to comprehend.

The most recent effort to develop a philosophy based upon the findings of biology and paleontology that accepts as an operative principle the major premises of evolution is that of Pierre Teilhard de Chardin. His work is worth examining in the context of our discussion of evolution because he made a maximum effort to approach modern physics and psychology from a practical point of view, avoiding the mathematical orientation of Whitehead and deliberately introducing once again the theological dimension as a means of bringing human knowledge back to its original Western roots. An examination of Teilhard's thought will therefore enable us to discuss evolutionary processes and the manner in which they relate to other aspects of Western cultural and religious tradition.

Teilhard's philosophy is built upon three major concepts, which, taken together, trace out the possible connections that all elements of the universe must have. These concepts must hold true whether we talk of organic or inorganic, societies, nations, or mere associations. As such they provide simple tools for analyzing every phenomenon we should wish to examine. The three concepts are: *cosmogenesis,*[7] *noogenesis,*[8] and *ultra-hominisation.*[9] While the words are new and devised by Teilhard to have specific meanings, if we keep concepts in mind when we explore the specific points of his philosophy, we will be able to understand much better the implications of his thinking for our present quest. And we will be able to evaluate the relevance of the theory of evolution for interpreting the biological world today.

Cosmogenesis denotes the process of universal evolution in which all parts of the universe—atoms, minerals, plants, animals, and humans—participate. Everything is subject to this process, and any activity that can be found at any level of existence can be found in some recognizable form at any other level. If we are to describe life at all, we can use *cosmogenesis* as that single word that covers everything. It is the process by which the seemingly infinite number of entities come into being and through which the universe exists.

Within the process of cosmogenesis a radical change occurs at a certain level of complexity of organization in which mind or mental properties emerge as a novel production of the process. These properties appear to be inherent in the universe from its simplest expression. They are not predictable from their predecessor events and entities and therefore represent a qualitatively novel expression of cosmogenesis, although logically comprehensible upon careful consideration. This process of emergence of mental or mind properties is called *noogenesis.* It marks organic life at a sophisticated level from the far more simple forms of organic life and the inanimate level of cosmic existence.

The process of cosmogenesis eventually produces the human species, and human history becomes a nonphysical expression of the cosmic process. But the human species is not the final product of the evolutionary process any more than a vertebrate is the final expression of it. Teilhard believes that the immediate future will unveil another qualitative leap in the cosmogenesis—*ultra-hominisation*—which will transcend the human species as radically as the human species transcended the other vertebrates and as radically as the first emergence of mental properties in the expression of noogenesis transcended the general process of cosmogenesis. In terms which the ordinary person can understand, the combination of these three aspects of evolutionary change indicates that the universe is transforming itself over the stretches of cosmic time from predominantly physical and material existence and forms into predominantly spiritual and mental existence and forms. Ultra-hominisation is not simply the production of superhumans but the emergence of a new species altogether, a quantum leap from the human species to a new species.

Modern physics concludes its experimentations with the rather enigmatic statement that the probable constituent of the universe is energy-matter transformation, which can be understood only as a process involving the combined appearances of space-time and matter-energy in an observed event. Teilhard began his system with this conclusion and introduces a structural redefinition of energy into two forms—radial and tangential. *Tangential energy* "links the element with all others of the same order (that is to say, of the same complexity and same centricity) as itself in the universe." [10] Tangential energy allows individual units or entities to relate to each other in the objective world and thus appears to be comparable to the energy we see expended in Newtonian terms in our daily lives, a largely mechanical energy manifesting itself in physical relationships.

Radial energy, on the other hand, Teilhard described as that "which draws it towards ever greater complexity and centricity—in other words forwards." [11] Radial energy can only be compared in our ordinary language to what we have formerly called "psychic" energy, and its manifestation is in the realm of what we have traditionally acclaimed as accomplishments of the spirit. Implied in the distinction between these two forms of energy is Teilhard's insistence that both have always existed and work in complementary fashion. The implication of this dualistic definition of energy is that the physical world is a living organism, not a giant machine, a conception that now seems to dominate the thinking of modern biologists and which is occasionally suggested by physicists and astronomers as well. [12]

The concern with "centricity" [13] that characterizes Teilhard's definition of energy is important. Suggesting that the universe is composed of energy alone is a meaningless statement because it is impossible to conceive of pure energy. One thinks of an inertial mass of potential or a blinding demonstration of power. Neither picture is accurate or relevant for our understanding. But with two forms of energy that are working at cross-purposes to each other carefully and continually desiring to enclose itself about a center, we have a focus of tension in which developments can occur. The continual tension expressed by the interplay of these contradictory forces Teilhard calls *convergence,* and he sees it as the tendency within the evolutionary process to balance energy as it is manifested in radial and tangential forms. The universe, while expanding, still has a tendency to fold in upon itself, producing entities of infinite variety.

Centricity is thus a state of being in which centripetal trends are superimposed on centrifugal trends. The interaction of the two prevents ultimate fragmentation of the system because each force limits the self-destructing tendencies of the other. Novel and unpredictable arrangements arise as the forces influence each other. The emergence of new species, new patterns of action and behavior, and increasingly sophisticated mental capabilities depends upon the operation of the convergence principle with respect to the two forms of energy. Insofar as we can determine the universe to have a direction, we can explain our conclusion by suggesting that radial energy is lightly dominant in the process of growth and is producing a movement toward spiritual qualities by the gradual accumulation of intensity and complexity at the center of each entity.

Basing his system upon energy does not mean that Teilhard abandons the reality of matter or denies to physical existence any relevance as a means of interpreting the cosmogenetic or universe–creating process. He understands the physical world as consisting of matter but insists that matter has three faces: plurality, unity, and energy.[14] We thus have structure as well as an accelerative principle precluding any accusation that cosmogenesis is either purely mental or purely material. An example of the treatment of how these faces of matter interact is Teilhard's insistence that "the more we split and pulverize matter artificially, the more insistently it proclaims its *fundamental unity,*"[15] giving, perhaps, the biologist's equivalent statement to Heisenberg's puzzling observation that when we split the smallest bit of matter we produce identical bits of matter and that we have in effect transformed the structure in which the ultimate universal constituent appears.

Teilhard treated space in a manner somewhat different from that of many modern physicists. He wrote:

> . . . since the atom is naturally co-extensive with the whole of the space in which it is situated—and since, on the other hand, we have just seen that a universal space is *the only space there is*—we are bound to admit that this immensity represents the sphere of action common to all atoms. The volume of each of them is the volume of the universe. The atom is no longer the microscopic, closed world we may have imagined to ourselves. It is the infinitesimal centre of the world itself.[16]

Logically, of course, there is little difference between Teilhard's conception of space and that of modern physics if we remember that physics severly limits the scope of investigation to certain entities such as the atom. Conceivably, if we had instruments sensitive enough to record all phases of atomic existence, we could show that the atom extends its influence to all parts of the universe. At least there is no good reason to limit the spatial influence of the atomic nucleus to the present capabilities recorded by our measuring devices.

Teilhard combined the idea of physical space with the requirements of an emerging consciousness, and his definition of space transcends physical existence to include the influence of consciousness. Even though consciousness is understood as radial energy, its influence extends to the rest of the universe through its awareness of things. Space includes awareness for Teilhard, and in this respect his radial energy is comparable to modern physics' contention that matter conforms space to itself. Space is thus, in a very complicated manner, both the distance between things and the geometric shape that things must take to manifest themselves. It is universal and unique to each center. This understanding enables us to combine the insights of modern physics and modern biology to reach a more comprehensive definition than is possible relying upon the discoveries and theories of either science alone.

Time presents a much more difficult concept to capture in Teilhard's philosophy. "Everything does not happen continuously at any one moment in the universe," he maintained. "Neither does everything happen everywhere in it." [17] His understanding of time appears to be similar to that of relativity in that both theories have not relied on universal events having simultaneity. Teilhard would appear to deny a cosmic and absolute time, but we are never certain whether this definition of time is consistently used in Teilhard's thinking. For example, if we have time as an internal phenomenon of growth within organisms, which his limitation on simultaneity would seem to advocate, each organism creates its own sense and tempo of time, and we have a multitude of times that can be measured individually in a theoretical sense. But as we move up the scale of life to increasingly larger units of existence, reaching the galactic level, we achieve at every step a sense of time internal to the system under consideration. There would seem to be no good reason to deny a cosmic time that expresses the total sense and experience of the universe itself.

Teilhard seemed to imply a universal time when he discussed the history of the planet. The evolutionary history of the world, according to Teilhard, would:

> ... thus appear no longer as an interlocking succession of structural types replacing one another, but as an ascension of inner sap spreading out in a forest of consolidated instincts. Right at its base, the living world is constituted by consciousness clothed in flesh and bone. From the biosphere to the species is nothing but an immense ramification of psychism seeking for itself through different forms.[18]

The tempo of this history would appear to be a constant factor in the universe in that a spreading sap, whether considered on a planetary basis or in terms of the entire universe, must certainly imply a continuous experience of time. That everything does not happen at once does not preclude a simultaneous sense of happenings in the universe, and in the interpretation of time Teilhard never seems to give a satisfactory answer to the possible questions that can be asked.

We can combine Teilhard's idea of time, liberally construed, with his treatment of causality, and suggest that the definitions quoted above place his thought within the definitional confines of modern physics. In this way we can maintain a consistency of interpretation for our basic concepts of the physical world—space, time, matter-energy, and causality—thus reconciling the thinking of Heisenberg and Teilhard. Teilhard found no causation inherent in the world prior to the emergence of nervous tissue in organisms. And then, he speculated, "The differentiation of nervous tissue stands out, as theory would lead us to expect, as a significant transformation. *It provides a direction; and therefore it proves that evolution has a direction.*" [19] With the emergence of a direction to evolutionary processes, the observer can introduce causality when attempting to make sense of phenomena; but apart from a sense of direction, there can be no way of determining the sequence of things, and causality remains an empty concept.

Teilhard attempted to bring the *kosmos* and the *oikumenē* together by making the evolution of biological forms lead directly into the history of the human species and thereafter suggesting that human history will produce a spiritual transformation leading to an Omega point at which the universe will become predominantly conscious and spiritual. At the point where Teilhard attached human history to the biological evolution of species, his religious bias began to dominate his thinking. As this influence became increasingly dominant, he moved beyond biology, physics, and history into the areas of metaphysics and theology. Such a sequence of development is a natural unification of the important elements in human existence and is a magnificent effort to reintegrate the separate fields of human knowledge and belief. But Teilhard's error lies in his assumption that the specific operating principles, which he derived from biology and paleontology, lead directly into the specific religious doctrines of Christianity. His understanding of evolution, therefore, often takes on an artificial stance, as if it were mustered in support of Christian beliefs instead of serving as a tool for interpreting the biological world.

Human history represented a new phase of the cosmogenetic process for Teilhard, but it begins with the emergence of the human species from the multitude of vertebrate organisms. "Thus *in the eyes of science,* which at long range can only see things in bulk," Teilhard explained, "the 'first man' is, and can only be, *a crowd,* and his family is made up of thousands and thousands of years." [20] The human species emerges simultaneously around the planet, but it concentrates its best efforts, according to Teilhard, in five basic areas: "Central America, with its Maya civilization; the South Seas, with Polynesian civilization; the basin of Yellow River, with Chinese civilization; the valleys of the Ganges and the Indus, with Indian civilization; and lastly the Nile Valley and Mesopotamia with Egyptian and Sumerian civilization." [21] From these five foci of human activity, Teilhard concentrated on the history of the Nile and Mesopotamian traditions and moved into a full-blown justification of Western civilization.

The final goal of the cosmogenetic process, according to Teilhard, is the Omega point in which autonomy, actuality, irreversibility, and transcendence characterize the universe. The purpose of the universal process, which at first seemed to emerge with consciousness, now becomes clear when we understand Teilhard's vision of the Omega condition:

> In Omega we have in the first place the principle we needed to explain both the persistent march of things towards greater consciousness, and the paradoxical solidity of what is most fragile. Contrary to the appearances still admitted by physics, the Great Stability is not at the bottom in the infra-elementary sphere, but at the top in the ultra-synthetic sphere. It is thus entirely by its tangential envelope that the world goes on dissipating itself in a chance way into matter. By its radical nucleus it finds its shape and its natural consistency in gravitating against the tide of probability towards a divine focus of mind which draws it onward.[22]

Logically, Teilhard's system folds back into its premises, making it ultimately a self-contained body of knowledge. As such, Teilhard's system must find its religious, cultural, and philosophical consistencies within.

The necessity of discovering religious truths within the system created immense difficulties for Teilhard. In the first place he had to rearrange the operative principles of evolution to include a major role for his religious doctrines. Second, by incorporating the beliefs of a particular religious tradition, Teilhard destroyed the universality of religious insight by restricting his interpretation of the meaning of the cosmogenetic process. Thus he wrote of the Western belief in Christ:

> . . . Christ, principle of universal vitality because sprung up as man among men, put himself in the position (maintained ever since) to subdue under himself, to purify, to direct and superanimate the general ascent of consciousness into which he inserted himself. By a perennial act of communion and sublimation, he aggregates to himself the total psychism of the earth. And when he has gathered everything together and transformed everything, he will close in upon himself and his conquests, thereby rejoining, in a final gesture, the divine focus he has never left.[23]

Developing a specific place within an evolutionary interpretation of reality for the major religious figure of Western culture does not guarantee either the validity of the system or the validity of the blend of theological and biological data. Aggregating psychism, as Teilhard visualized the Christ principle, would seem to be a function of unification rather than vitality if we remember the initial structure of Teilhard's system in which energy-matter is divided into two manifestations, working at least in part against each other. If we combine Teilhard's definition of the Christ and his definition of the Omega point, we discover that the tendency of the universe to dissipate itself through the expenditure of tangential energy and the propensity of the Christ principle to manifest itself through the generation of radical energy come into direct conflict. Teilhard seemed to follow the traditional Western tendency to pit spirit against matter, producing a universe in which the personal dimension of human existence is always threatened by alien entities and energies.

Magnificent as Teilhard's system is, and it brings many scientific understandings into one cohesive whole, its general failure is not its effort to incorporate the Christian religion into a biological interpretation of the structure and processes of the *kosmos*. Rather Teilhard does not directly confront the difficult problem of explaining exactly how species originate. Balancing radical and tangential energies would seem to produce a stability that could not transcend itself. Teilhard raises in our minds the question whether any evolutionary interpretation of the biological dimension of the *kosmos* can give an adequate understanding of reality. How do we interpret the similarities we see at all levels of organic and inorganic life if not in an evolutionary sense? Is there a reasonable alternative to the conception that life evolves from the simple to the complex, making physical and psychic changes over a prolonged period of time?

VI. Whither Evolutionists?

Teilhard's evolutionary philosophy provides a systematic analysis of the origin and development of the biological world. By attaching concepts of modern physics and human history to his basic biological outline, Teilhard attempted to reach a modern metaphysic that would embody three fundamental fields of knowledge. Incorporating Christian theology into his exposition of biological processes does not damage Teilhard's position because the question of ultimate meaning is a theological question that can only be resolved in theological terms. The question we must pose first, however, is whether in fact Teilhard's understanding of the *kosmos* is correct.

I have already suggested that the balancing of radial and tangential energies within the individual promotes the most complete development of that individual but does not enable the individual to mutate itself, thereby becoming a member of a new species. The alternative to evolution, if we are unable to discover the process by which organisms progress up the scale of complexity to produce new species, may theologically be the doctrine of special creation. But in scientific terms it will only mean that the explanations we have given to biological phenomena that incorporate a purpose in morphological and psychic change are invalid conclusions, that such changes are not changes in physical structure or psychic capability but simply the unique expressions of the unity of life which the universe contains.

If we adopt this second interpretation our task is to discover the manner in which all entities share certain basic ways of manifesting life. The change is more radical than we should wish to contemplate because our present evolutionary interpretation of biological phenomena is based on the premise that similarities in structure and behavior indicate the origins of species. This is not necessarily true. If we consider carefully the manner in which we have built up our knowledge of the biological world, we shall discover that our first efforts to understand life were simple classifications of similarities that species appeared to share. Evolutionary thinking has simply made these classifications mobile when considered over a long period of time. Animating our classifications does not guarantee an absolute knowledge of origins, however; it simply causes us to draw conclusions that have no basis in fact.

Let us return to Teilhard's analysis of the operative principles of evolution and see if the animation of classification categories can be justified as an adequate explanation of how organisms originate. If Teilhard's analysis holds together, we can conclude that his understanding of biological development is a proper interpretation of the similarities that the physical world contains. However, if he cannot solve the problem of how species originate, then we must reduce our expectations of how much understanding we can actually have concerning the nature of the biological world and its possible origin and development.

The basic agent of change, for Teilhard, was the individual, and we must be certain that all aspects of individual existence, which he felt important, are brought together in our discussion of his philosophy. We are told that the atom, and by extension every other entity including the universe, encompasses space and, in doing so, establishes a center.[1] This space is not symbolic in a theoretical sense. Neither is it simply a spiritual space in the old sense that spiritual indicates primarily a mental rather than a physical reality. Rather it is a space that we feel, that scientists are able to measure, given the proper instruments, and that is expressed, in a variety of ways, by every individual.

Identifying this space and establishing objective relationships to other spaces and other entities within their spaces are functions of the individual. Consciousness is responsible for establishing and maintaining sufficient space to create individual identity. By creative extension of tangential energy the center of the individual is transformed into what we have commonly called an "ego." In the Darwinian scheme of interpretation this ego recognizes the principle of the survival of the fittest, whether on a conscious or unconscious basis, and proceeds toward fulfilling that principle.

When we examine Teilhard's analysis of the role of the ego in the organism, we find, not a recognition of the value of ego development, but the assumption that the ego is more relevant to theological reality than to biological functioning. Thus where we would expect the development of ego to become the primary tool of survival for Teilhard, he informs us that the ego is a destructive step in the evolutionary scheme:

Egoism, whether personal or racial, is quite rightly excited by the idea of the element ascending through faithfulness to life, to the extremes of the incommunicable and the exclusive that it holds within it. It *feels* right. Its only mistake, but a fatal one, is to *confuse individuality with personality.* In trying to separate itself as much as possible from others, the element individualizes itself; but in doing so it becomes retrograde and seeks to drag the world backwards towards plurality and into matter. In fact it diminishes itself and loses itself.[2]

When one considers them in an evolutionary framework, it is difficult to see how individuality and personality can be separated this precisely. These two aspects of the organism would seem complementary and inseparable in the sense that each contributes a dimension that cannot be denied and without which life would not exist. Like space-time, personality and individuality cannot be separated into two isolated concepts that are pitted against each other.

If cosmogenesis is directed toward the development of personality and must produce increasingly complex expressions of itself in the lives of its individual constituents, individuality must accompany and probably always precede (at least logically if not actually) personality. That Teilhard confused theological doctrines with biological necessities (desiring unity and spirituality rather than plurality and physical reality), should not be allowed to intrude into an exposition of the requirements of the biological world. If we are to produce increasingly complex organisms from simpler ones, and we see increasing evidence that complex organisms become independent individuals with an efficient means of existing in space-time, plurality and individuality are the essential ingredients in the cosmogenetic process.

Teilhard understood the production of new species as a function of a process of transformation which, generated within the organism, produces a biological quantum leap of great significance. As he explained the process of emergence of new species, "The increase of the synthetic state of matter involves . . . a corresponding increase of consciousness for the *milieu* synthesized. To which we should now add: the *critical* change in the intimate arrangement of the elements induces *ipso facto* a change of *nature* in the state of consciousness of the particles of the universe."[3] We have here the contention that as consciousness increases it reaches a situation of immense tension within the organism or milieu. Suddenly the radial energy seems to transform itself into a new tangential expression, changing, as Teilhard understood it, the *nature* of the individual or milieu.

This proposition seems difficult to accept because it is the tangential energy alone that establishes relationships with the rest of the universe, controlling morphological growth and physical innovations. Radial energy is basically psychic energy, and how, in a practical sense, this energy can be transformed into physical growth remains a mystery. In practical terms Teilhard was saying that a fully developed organism with intense psychic energy can spontaneously mutate into an entirely new individual, initiating a new species with new genetic properties and a new body structure. The closest practical example we can suggest that illustrates this condition would be intense forms of genius or madness that can be observed in our own species and in animals. We find nowhere in nature any individual of any species generating within itself sufficient energy, either psychic or physical, to transform itself into an entirely new creature or producing sufficient physical changes to appear as a representative of a new species.

Teilhard's introduction of the Christ principle was an effort to ensure this type of change, since it coordinates and dominates the process of cosmogenesis. If we accept his thesis that egoism individualizes the world backward into plurality and matter, we cannot have the radical change in nature that the emergence of a new species would require. Teilhard's Christ principle ensures that radial energy will always dominate tangential expressions of energy, giving internal and psychic functions of an organism superior to physical functions, thus preventing morphological change of any kind. Changing the *nature* of an organism is thus impossible within a system in which the quality of change always dominates the quantity of change.

Other thinkers commenting on the possibility of spontaneous change as advocated by Teilhard do not find it possible to generate the change of nature Teilhard attributed to the rise of intense consciousness. Etienne Gilson, French neo-Thomist philosopher, writing in an essay entitled "Concerning Christian Philosophy," directs his criticism of the process of self-generated change to the point at which inorganic entities would have transformed themselves into organic expressions of life. He contends that "inorganic form is a principle of structure and of arrangement of energies, but not a source of energy which is calculable, or experimentally demonstrable, nor an inner spontaneity giving rise to observable quantitative variations." [4] Inorganic existence means possessing a structure but lacking both the energy and spontaneity to introduce radical change in the structure that would produce a new species or individual. The physical requirement that such a change would seem to suggest would be the actions of an external agent that produced both the new structure and the energy necessary to transform the inorganic substance or individual into an organic substance or individual.

Evolutionists would argue, of course, that completely new species do not originate spontaneously but that a series of small changes in both structure and psychic constitution produce, over a period of time, sometimes infinitely long, a new species. Laying aside small variations that occur in each generation of individuals in any species and which are not transmitted as new characteristics, we must ask if it is possible for individuals to pass along to their descendants any changes they might have experienced. Ernst Cassirer pointed out that "every perfection that an organism can gain in the course of its individual life is confined to its existence and does not influence the life of the species. Even man is no exception to this general biological rule." [5] The qualities, strengths, talents, experiences, the skill and knowledge of survival techniques, and any other basic skills the individual might acquire in the course of a lifetime cannot be genetically passed down to his or her descendants, producing a superior specimen of one species which in turn transmits even more skills and perfections to its descendants, eventually producing a new species.

The problem Teilhard faced and which all evolutionists confront concerns the unit of survival that operates in the evolutionary scheme. Gregory Bateson notes that most evolutionary theories are based upon "the breeding individual or the family line or the subspecies or some similar homogeneous set of conspecifics." He feels that this focus is inadequate because "the last hundred years have demonstrated empirically that if an organism or aggregate of organisms sets to work with a focus on its own survival and thinks that that is the way to select its adaptive moves, its 'progress' ends up with a destroyed environment." [6] And the destruction of the environment usually results in the destruction of the individual.

When we combine the arguments raised by Cassirer and Bateson against the principles of evolutionary change, we leave Teilhard with few concepts of any value. Self-generated change through the increase of individual energies appears to be impossible. Genetic transmission of learned behaviors to one's descendants is also highly unlikely, and while we may transmit behavioral patterns through cultural tradition, we hardly incorporate these responses genetically. It would appear that we must take the concept of progression away from Teilhard, leaving his philosophy with descriptions of similar structures inherent in the biological world but devoid of the inevitable march from the simple to the complex.

Evolutionists will not surrender this theory without further discussion, however, and we would do well to review the broadest basis upon which evolutionary doctrines can rest. Gregory Bateson writes that "all theories of biological evolution depend upon at least three sorts of change: (a) change of genotype, either by mutation or redistribution of genes; (b) somatic change under pressure of environment; and (c) changes in environmental conditions." [7] We will investigate the second and third sorts of change first in order to see exactly how environment relates to biological change. Then we will return to the question of changing genotypes since it is the original thesis of Teilhard and seems to hold some promise of redemption when placed in a different context.

When we speak of somatic change under pressure of the environment, we usually talk about organisms changing their body structure to correspond to environmental demands. Thus biologists sometimes explain respiration rate as a function of atmospheric pressure or human skin color as a function of exposure to sunlight. Robert Ardrey, a successful playwright who has in recent years turned to the study of the nature and origin of the human species, tells us regarding the variations in human skin color:

> The white skin, lethal baggage in the sun-smitten tropics, admitted larger doses of the northern latitudes' weak ultraviolet rays to produce our necessary Vitamin D. Through a remarkable adaptation, it retained a capacity to tan when occasion demanded. In tropical areas tan-to-black skins became permanent assets offering protection from the excesses of the tropical sun. [8]

Such an explanation borders on flights of fancy although many scientists accepting evolution would regard it as reasonable. White skin seems to be characteristic of the Aryan peoples who originated in the area north of the Indian peninsula, moving to the European area in historical times. The American Indians, inhabitants of a northern latitude for thousands of years, did not have the white skin which, following Ardrey's theory, they should have had. If we carry this explanation to its logical conclusion, we should expect to find Eskimos, Aleuts, and Lapps with a nearly albino skin because of their need to absorb Vitamin D. We conclude, reluctantly, that tropical peoples had no need for Vitamin D and thus maintained a dark skin to eliminate the intake of the vitamin. It is not difficult to see that we approach difficult, if not ridiculous, conclusions when we attempt to apply the principle that somatic change under pressure of environment accounts for variations in the biological world, eventually producing new species.

A more popular explanation of evolutionary change relies upon the changes in environment alone. Ian Barbour, usually a cautious and reliable thinker, gives an interpretation of evolutionary theory that relies chiefly upon environmental change:

> The history of evolution on earth has been influenced by long chains of contingent circumstances: mutations, genetic recombinations, competition between particular species, and environmental changes. The exact dates of successive ice ages, for instance, had a profound effect on the development of species. Again, nothing similar to dinosaurs has appeared before or since; the pattern does not repeat itself.[9]

We can hardly debate the proposition that patterns do not repeat themselves since everything we know indicates this to be true. But it is difficult to imagine that ice ages had a radical role in the emergence of new species or had much of a role in the extinction of old ones. Robert Ardrey warns in his last book, *The Hunting Hypothesis,* that a new ice age may be rapidly approaching. One indication that this may be so, cited with approval by Ardrey, is the activity of the armadillo, which is moving south from the heartlands of the continent to warmer climes. Ardrey remarked that such news as armadillo migrations was great fun for the press that reported it as a serious scientific discovery, but "for the student of the Ice Age ... or for an ethologist such as myself, any unscheduled migration of animals is disturbing." [10]

We are thus informed by evolutionists such as Ardrey that climatic changes are an important part of the evolutionary process, that they are responsible for the emergence of new species and the demise of old ones, and yet the migrations of animals at the slightest hint of climatic change is cited with approval as evidence that a major geological phenomenon, which we detect at present only with great difficulty, is upon us. The natural tendency of animals and other organisms when confronted with rapid environmental changes would be to begin a migration to a different region where climatic conditions would be compatible with their physiological capabilities. Climatic change would have to be nearly instantaneous to radically affect animals. In 1976 Ardrey suggested that we may have an ice age within six years, and this immediate threat has already been intuited by the armadillo. It is extremely unlikely that environmental changes could have any but the minimum effect on species, certainly not the radical effects that evolutionists credit to environmental change.

Even the latest expressions of evolutionary doctrines have a hollow ring. "It is a truism of modern biology that anatomical change comes about *as a consequence* of behavioral change," Robert Ardrey declares. And he emphasizes this idea in *The Hunting Hypothesis:* "And so I have chanted again and again and again the new refrain: 'Birds do not fly because they have wings; they have wings because they fly.' As it is with the wing, so it is with the brain. We do not think because our brain is big; our brain has grown big because we think." [11]

Such an explanation may seem reasonable when applied to the human brain, but it is hardly convincing or reassuring to hear that birds have wings because they fly. According to such doctrines, birds were already flying long before they developed any wings, and because they were already flying, they developed wings to make their peculiar activity more efficient. We must reject this "truism of modern biology" because it seems to mean that organisms are already performing feats and tasks prior to the development of those organs that specifically allow them to perform these feats and tasks. Accordingly, we should find fish developing fins and tails and gills because they were already living in the water, or we should find monkeys developing tails because they were already swinging from trees.

Whenever we draw specific examples from the biological world to illustrate evolutionary principles, we arrive at a dead end in our explanation, or we begin to make ridiculous statements, which the logic of evolutionary principles demands. Ardrey himself mentions monkey body-structure as an evolutionary puzzle: "New World monkeys have even developed that fifth arm, the prehensile tail, of such immense selective advantage for a life in the trees that one cannot understand why Old World monkeys did not develop one too." [12] We can only conclude that Old World monkeys did not swing from trees, or they would have developed anatomically to conform to their behavioral activities. Yet we know that both Old World and New World monkeys swing from trees.

Ardrey pushes the principle of morphological change following behavioral change to its ridiculous limit in an example of rapid evolutionary adaptations taken from American Indian life. "Adaptations of heritable sort could be rapid and sometimes wonderful," he writes in *The Hunting Hypothesis.* "In the woodlands of northern New York State and adjacent Canada are the Mohawk Indians, a canoe people. One must speculate that sufficient generations of canoeing placed a heavy selection against those with inadequate balance. Today, long after canoes, no iron-worker can match the Mohawk's skill on high, hazardous construction jobs . . ." [13]

The difficulty with this example is that the Iroquois, of which the Mohawks are a constituent tribe, only moved to the New York area within very recent times, perhaps as late as A.D. 1200, and their former homelands, the Ozark region, did not require them to use canoes to any great extent. Ardrey would have us believe that within the short period of six hundred years these Indians achieved a remarkable sense of balance when active at great heights by using canoes. Under such reasoning we would have to allow that the Indian tribes of the Pacific Northwest—the Makah, the Lummi, and the Quinault, peoples who have used canoes skillfully for thousands of years—would be much better at working the high steel construction jobs than the Mohawks. Such is not the case, and we can eliminate the canoe as an evolutionary factor in developing a remarkable sense of balance in the human being.

No current explanation of the emergence of species which follows evolutionary principles adequately explains observable life-phenomena in either a practical or scientific sense. But evolutionary doctrines create an additional problem: the extent of time required by the complete evolution of species. Changing either the physical or psychic structure of an organism involves an experimental situation in which various possibilities must be explored. All variations in structure, when considered as the product of a random process of innovation by individual organisms, have a theoretical possibility of realizing themselves prior to the organisms adopting that particular characteristic most useful in the game of individual and species survival.

The permutations and combinations that any particular organism would test before it emerged as the complex species we observe today must be incredible, and each innovation and experiment takes a certain amount of time to realize. When we expand this process of testing, discarding, and adopting new characteristics to include several billion species that must have once existed on the planet, we face the problem that the production of this number of species would require an almost infinite period of time. Werner Heisenberg reported a conversation with Niels Bohr (1885–1962), the Danish physicist, wherein the two scientists expressed suspicion that modern biology, in adopting progressive selection as an explanation of the origin of life, had moved beyond the mathematical possibilities that the present age of the universe allows.

As Heisenberg remembered the conversation, Niels Bohr commented that "physical and astrophysical studies tell us that no more than a few thousand million years have passed since the appearance of the most primitive living beings on earth. Now, whether or not accidental mutations and selection are sufficient to produce the most complicated and highly developed organisms during this interval will depend on the time needed to develop a new biological species. I suspect that we know much too little about this factor to give a reliable answer." [14] We must remember that Bohr was expressing doubt that, given a primitive living being already existing on the planet, we should have sufficient cosmic time to produce a new species. When we begin without a primitive being but simply a possibility of the most fortunate chemical reactions producing the necessary conditions for life, and seek to produce not simply one species but billions of species, if we accept biological theories of evolution, we necessarily come into direct and irreconcilable conflict with other fields of science, which project a relatively limited period for the existence of the universe.

We can return now to the first category of evolutionary change mentioned by Bateson: change of genotype, either by mutation or the redistribution of genes. This explanation of change lacks only the identification of a specific agent to appear reasonable. Teilhard's philosophy, although lacking in specific identification of the agent of change, is based in fact upon genotypic mutation or redistribution, for he wrote: "Either by arrangement of the parts or by the acquisition of another dimension, the degree of 'interiority' of a cosmic element can undoubtedly vary to the point at which it rises suddenly on to another level." [15] Teilhard, of course, viewed the new arrangement as a self-initiated process, but we have already seen that such a process fails to correspond to observed facts. If we take Teilhard's two alternatives, arrangement of the parts and the acquisition of another dimension, and consider them as initiated by an external agent of change, we would then have reason to accept his theory as a logical explanation of the origin of life.

Robert Ardrey suggests in *African Genesis* that radiation is an external agent of change that has quite possibly produced the biological world as we know it. "Radiation is the killer," Ardrey tells us, but "it is also the creator. Its impact on the gene is mutation, and on life, change. Drawn from hot, molten sources within our earth or from cold masses of our ancient granitic rocks; from sources beyond our planet, beyond our sun, beyond our galaxy; drawn from the the most turbulent natal sources of intergalactic space, radiation is the force that has brought us where we are." [16] If we have taken Gregory Bateson's categories seriously, then we can see that mutation or redistribution in the genetic sense is possible primarily through radiation or, as another possibility, intense and prolonged heat or sound. But radiation certainly emerges as the most easily understood of the possible agents of genetic change.

We have a problem when we discuss radiation as the agent of genetic mutation, however, because if we suggest that some species are formed from the mutations of other species, we must find an occasion when radiation was loosed upon old species, mutating its genes. Ardrey further speculates that the reversal of the earth's magnetic field, which has occurred at specific times in the geologic past, may provide an answer to this question. "Cores drilled from the sea bottom," he informs us, ". . . reveal that during the course of a reversal the earth lacks for about five thousand years any magnetic field at all. And it is that field which provides protection from incoming cosmic rays." [17] If we accept Ardrey's suggestion that reversal of our planet's magnetic field has produced the necessary exposure to radiation to mutate species, then we have provided the necessary agent of change and occasion for change to make evolutionary theories again comprehensible.

Such a theory would resolve many questions in both biology and geology. A perennial question of paleontology concerns the extinction of many species at the end of geologic eras and the emergence of many new species at the beginning of other geologic eras. This question is particularly important in relationship to the Pleistocene era, which featured giantism in many species and which saw, at its conclusion, the extinction of many animals that appeared to have made the proper adaptation to the lands in which they lived. The horse, for example, is a natural inhabitant of the North American continent, and in previous geologic eras a North American version of the horse did exist on our continent, but it perished at the end of the Pleistocene era. When the Spanish brought horses to North America in the 1500s and the horse was allowed to breed freely in the middle part of the continent, it took very few years, comparatively speaking, for the horse once more to dominate the grasslands.

So we can apparently save the theory of evolution by introducing genetic change through radiation exposure initiated by the lack of a magnetic field created by the reversal of the earth's poles. But does this solution really save evolution? Or does it hammer the last nail into evolution's coffin? We have formerly conceived the evolutionary process as one in which random variations, the natural selection of the best variations, and the survival of the fittest species and individuals combine to produce the species we observe today.

If we admit that no fundamental change occurs genetically without radiation exposure on a planetary scale, we have to introduce radiation exposure every time we wish to change species, and we have to allow intense radiation exposure at the beginning of life in order to initiate the process of existence. We then jump from one catastrophe to another each time we need a change of species, and if we work our way up the alleged biological ladder from the simplest organism to the most complex, we have simply created a planetary and possibly cosmic history that features a series of catastrophes instead of a smooth and uniform passage of time in which minute changes occur. We have in fact destroyed evolution in attempting to save it.

We have done much more than destroying evolution as an interpretive theory explaining the origin and development of biological groups and individuals. If our planet is subject to occasional and severe exposures to radiation, then how can we be sure of the age of either the planet or the universe? We have tended to date the ages of the universe and the planet respectively by assuming a constant rate of radioactive decay in certain elements. If we introduce the occasional overexposure of radiation into the picture, we have no guarantee that our figures for the age of the planet or the universe reflect a constant rate of decay. We might have had several severe catastrophes that radically changed our mineral elements in the same way that our genetic structures were changed. Our planet could be several times as old as we now conceive it, or it could be a mere several hundred thousand years old—in accordance with the most conservative estimates of fundamentalist Christians.

Obviously this problem needs serious attention and careful consideration. It raises once again the theological question of a special creation. It involves the supposition that many ancient legends and myths may not be symbolic representations of primitive superstitions but literal reports of cosmic disturbances. We finally have the problem of reconsidering the manner in which we conceive and classify the biological world; indeed, we must reconsider our interpretations of both animal and human behavior. We must find some common basis for understanding the manifestation of life, the similarity that organisms seem to share, without forcing into that understanding a process of gradual evolutionary change which may not, in fact, exist.

VII. The Structure of Life

We are no longer bound to interpret biological phenomena in an evolutionary framework because we have seen that the mechanism for genetic change remains an open and serious question. Lacking a satisfactory solution to this problem, we face the possibility that life-forms make genetic quantum jumps from species to species according to the manner in which they are subjected to mutations from radiation or severe heat or sound, any of which arise in a cosmic or plantery catastrophe or major disruption.

The original approach of Western peoples to the biological phenomena was to classify life-forms according to their similarities, with categories formed according to the identification of major morphological differences. Evolution simply introduced a process whereby organisms were thought to have transcended the categories of classification by making adaptations in response to changes in environment, to environmental pressures, or to genetic mutation or redistribution. When we stop conceiving the origin and development of life as an evolutionary process, we are still left with the similarities and differences that we have identified in the biological world. And we still have to account for and understand both.

Let us return to physics and recall some of the insights that field has given us. We recall from the explanations of Werner Heisenberg that reality comes in an organic unity in which space, time, energy, matter, and causation are functions of one another and not absolute qualities or entities of reality itself. We have no good reason to reject this picture of the world when we leave the field of physics and enter the field of biology. If the structure of existence at the atomic and the stellar level seem to incorporate space-time-energy-matter unity, we should expect to find that unity expressed in the biological world. If we keep the lessons of modern physics in mind as we review biological phenomena, we will come to realize that new tools of understanding are available.

Teilhard stated frankly in his evolutionary philosophy: "I am obliged to recognize that the assumption of a dimensional *milieu* in which space and time are organically combined is the only way we have found to explain the distribution around us of animate and inanimate substances." The very existence of the world, as we have learned from modern physics, is contained in the peculiar way that space-time manifests itself. "Indeed," Teilhard continued, "the further we advance our knowledge of the natural history of the world, the more clearly we realize that the distribution of objects and forms at any given moment can only be explained by a process whose duration in time varies directly with the spatial (or morphological) dispersion of the objects in question. Every distance in space, every morphological deviation, presupposes and expresses a duration." [1]

If space-time is a precondition of existence, then we should find it as a function of the biological world as well as of the world of physics. Frank A. Brown, Jr., a noted biologist, in his famous article, "The Rhythmic Nature of Animals and Plants," discusses a variety of new experiments that seem to indicate the presence of a sense of time in certain plants and animals. Reviewing some of the patterns of behavior that Bermuda shrimp, California grunion, and Australian reef-heron exhibit, Brown suggests that "living things behave as if they possessed both 'clocks' and 'calendars' by means of which many vital processes are appropriately timed even in the absence of such well-known daily, monthly, and annual changes as those of illumination and temperature." [2]

The experiments that Brown reviews featured efforts to isolate organisms, plants, and animals from any contact with the sun and moon in order to determine how organisms react when deprived of any contact with the larger rhythms represented by these bodies. Cross-checking the organisms' ability to measure time when subjected to a rise in temperature which, under ordinary circumstances would increase the rate of biological processes, Brown says:

> When we studied critically this problem with fiddler crabs about 10 years ago, we found to our amazement that, through a wide range of temperature, the period of the rhythm remained the same, precisely 24 hours. The animals had available some method of time-measuring that was independent of temperature, a phenomenon quite inexplicable in any currently known mechanisms of physiology, or, in view of the long-period-lengths, even of chemical reaction kinetics. [3]

Time appeared to be an organic phenomenon that remained constant even when environmental changes of great magnitude occurred. The results of these experiments would seem to indicate that space-time is more fundamental than adaptation to the immediate environment, making evolution a less satisfactory explanation of universal existence than space-time, as I suggested above.

Space-time is a more satisfactory explanation of universal existence because conditions were so varied in these experiments as to preclude evolutionary concepts as an interpretive device of organic behavior. "Living things might conceivably possess inherited, regular rhythms," Brown observed, "but it is quite inconceivable that they are born with an inherited plan of all the erratic temperature, barometric pressure, and background-radiation fluctuations which are to occur during their lifetime." [4] If environment were a significant factor in influencing organic behavior, the experiments described by Brown should have indicated as much. His conclusion supports the suggestion that space-time is an essential element in understanding the biological world:

> The demonstration that the physical environment of living things is organized *temporally* in terms of still unknown, subtle and highly pervasive forces, which the living organisms can resolve, encourages one to speculate that there may be some comparable subtle and pervasive *spatial* organization of the environment which is contributing at least in a small way towards accounting for geographical distribution or periodic migrations of organisms.[5]

It is not just time that determines organic existence; space may also perform a mysterious function. Claude Levi-Strauss, the noted anthropologist, supports this view with a casual remark concerning the growth of organs of certain crustaceans. He points out that in order to formulate laws that can describe the growth of crustacean claws "it is necessary to consider the relative dimensions of the component parts of the claws, and not the exterior forms of those organs." [6] Growth, and presumably innovations in organic development, would seem to be a function of spatial relationships among the respective organs of the crustaceans and not a function of either internal energies manifesting themselves in new ways, as Teilhard would understand it, or as adaptations to environmental changes, as other thinkers would explain. Levi-Strauss concludes that "here, relationships allow us to derive constants—termed parameters—from which it is possible to derive the laws which govern the development of these organisms. The object of a scientific zoology, in these terms, is thus not ultimately concerned with the forms of animals and their organs as they are usually perceived, but with the establishment of certain abstract and measurable relationships, which constitute the basic nature of the phenomena under study." [7] We may eventually discover that organic growth, is a function of geometry, spatial relationships, and ratios.

When we review Teilhard's analysis of mineral existence, which must certainly precede his discussion of the origin of life, we discover how evolutionary thinking precludes a careful understanding of the nature of the physical world. Discussing the process of crystallization of minerals, Teilhard stated: "We may say that it is characteristic of minerals . . . to have chosen a road which closed them prematurely in upon themselves. By their innate structure the molecules are unfitted for growth. To develop beyond a certain size they have in a way to get out of themselves, to have recourse to a trick of purely external association, whereby the atoms are linked together without true combination or union." [8]

Viewing the process of crystallization in a space-time sense means that minerals have not chosen a road that prematurely closed them in upon themselves at all. They have fulfilled the space-time dimensions that minerals possess. The "trick of purely external association," which Teilhard considered a futile and incomplete effort to continue some form of external growth, is another manifestation of the spatial dimension. It indicates that community, with its spatial relationships, is another example of the space-time nature of universal existence. We shall find this organic unity of space-time in the larger vertebrates in a recognizable form if we understand how it initially occurs with reference to mineral existence.

The spatial dimension to organic life, as we have previously noted, expresses itself in a geometric relationship among the various parts of the individual body and in most instances seems to control the body's growth as an integrated whole. This aspect is internal to the organism and, when we discuss vertebrates, is naturally assumed to be taking place. But vertebrates are, for the most part, mobile, highly complex organisms that have a definite duration of life in a temporal sense and live in a particular environment with specific behavioral patterns. Robert Ardrey, in a series of popular books— *African Genesis, The Territorial Imperative, The Social Contract,* and *The Hunting Hypothesis*— explores the mass of material that has been gathered in the fields of biology anthropology, paleontology, geology, and related sciences to present a concept of territorial instinct, which he feels both dominates and explains our behavior.

"Territoriality is a vertebrate instinct touching fish and amphibia, reptiles and mammals and birds," Robert Ardrey writes in *African Genesis.* "While it therefore must be several hundreds of millions of years old, still it came into being after the evolutionary separation of the ancestral insect line from our own." [9] Territoriality is defined as "the drive to gain, maintain, and defend the exclusive right to a piece of property," [10] and Ardrey finds it as ancient and powerful as the reproductive drive or any other instinct manifested by vertebrates. Indeed, when we begin to understand the manner in which territory dominates the activity of individuals, we discover that this desire for individual living space must certainly be the most fundamental drive, even more basic than the sexual instinct.

To illustrate his point about territory taking precedence over sexual instincts, Ardrey notes that the male bird seizes a piece of land or an area and marks it out with his song, warning all other birds that he has established himself there. "On this territory he will mate and breed," Ardrey explains, *"but the seizure and struggle take place before the coming of the female and without consciousness of sexual significance."*[11] Mating does not seem to be a casual thing conducted without first establishing a sense of personal identity within a particular environment. Seizing territory and establishing personal identity seem to be prior to any other vertebrate activity. Ardrey observes that "in the absence of females, on the territorial battleground, there is only conflict," [12] leading one to surmise that sexual competition is a fantasy of Western science and that underneath our crude observations about sexual drives exists a substratum of behavior in which territory forms the major consideration.

Ardrey says that all territorial animals respect the territorial rights of other individuals. Their behavior indicates, not a desire to invade and exploit, but to preserve social order and territorial existence. "The bird attacks an intruder not with the objective of destroying him or of seizing his territory in reprisal. Victory is accomplished by driving him away." [13] There are, of course, predatory activities that must be considered in any understanding of territory, for the different species have long since determined which of their fellows is a tasty meal, and the territorial imperative does little to inhibit the search for food. But each species and family recognizes that territory forms the basis of individual life, and protection of the territory surpasses any other motivation for conflict.

Territory is conceived by vertebrates in much the same manner that Teilhard suggested all entities begin to take on individual identity, by forming a center around which the milieu takes on a significance for the individual. "The fighting inclination may be stated with mathematical exactness," Ardrey maintains, because "it decreases in direct proportion to the distance from the nest." [14] Perhaps we have previously interpreted the individual's inclination to fight for the nest as a sexual drive, but Ardrey seems to indictate that the nest forms the center of the territory and that conflict revolves around a desire to preserve living space rather than around sexual jealousy.

Territory is not the only instinct to which vertebrates respond. Ardrey suggests that the instinct driving individuals toward dominance within their species is as powerful, although perhaps not as fundamental. "It is a force at least as old and as deep as territory," he informs us, and "like territory it benefits sex but stands independent of it; . . . among social animals it is universal, and among our primate family the source of society's most mysterious subtleties; . . . that among all animal sources of human behaviour . . . may in the end prove the most important." [15] Dominance is the drive for ranking and status that is competitively determined, and thus could be said to provide a mechanism, if that is how we can characterize it, by which the various territorial possessors organize into groups.

Unfortunately Ardrey places both territory and dominance in the evolutionary framework, suggesting that "self-awareness in the limited sense of consciousness of rank seems to have appeared at some very early moment in the evolution of things." [16] If we accept the evolutionary interpretation, we can be fairly certain that such an instinct arose after the separation of vertebrates from insects because insects rank their societies by inherited status and do not participate in social competition to determine rank and status. But unlike territory, dominance can easily become perverted through misunderstanding or overemphasis. "Whereas territory acts invariably as a factor promoting the interests of individual and species, and whereas society furnishes creatures in a state of nature with their most striking instrument of survival, still dominance over-developed can do damage of an absolute order, upsetting natural balances otherwise so carefully protected." [17]

Whether we view animal behavior or human behavior, this warning strikes a familiar chord. Whenever charisma and leadership burst the ordinary bounds of behavior in an individual, there is generally an unusual change in the manner in which a group of society behaves. Ardrey cites the example of the "extraordinary endowment of dominance in the personality of an individual male lion [which] may act as a magnet to effect coalition of prides into super-prides, and the creation of a hunting unit so efficient as to be self-defeating." [18] We can certainly see, looking back at the foibles of human history—our wars and conflicts as well as our demonstrations of genius—the negative impact of dominating personalities in many societies and the evil that theories of racial superiority have spawned when dominance has emerged as an ideological belief affecting behavior.

Following territory and dominance in the hierarchy of instincts is the need for social order. We see indications of social order in nearly every vertebrate, in the gathering together of individuals and their ranking within that gathering. Recognizing that an equal society of individuals would be an impossibility in the animal world, Ardrey suggests that the instinctual drive for social order aims for a just society. "The just society, as I see it," he writes, "is one in which sufficient order protects members, whatever their diverse endowments, and sufficient disorder provides every individual with full opportunity to develop his genetic endowment, whatever that may be. It is this balance of order and disorder, varying in rigor according to environmental hazard, that I think of as the social contract." [19] Basically the social contract is an uneasy truce between individual desires and group behavior. "We may therefore speculate that at some early moment in the evolvement of living things," Ardrey suggests, "natural selection found in duality of purpose a superior endowment for the creatures in its charge. The individual creature must survive; but so must his group, his population, his race, his species. And so the anarchistic instincts favour the demands of the individual creature, the instincts of order the demands of his kind." [20]

We cannot help but speculate that these instincts must manifest themselves on a totally unconscious level since it is a rare individual who consciously regards the efforts to establish a family and express oneself as an anarchistic tendency. But Ardrey finds the instinctual drives complementary in this respect, and since we can see indications of each tendency in our behavior and in the behavior of some animals, we have no reason to quarrel with his understanding. Perhaps any quarrel with the definition of three basic instincts would be premature because Ardrey combines the basic three with another instinctual drive: "deep-set, unaccountable, and perhaps unproveable: a mysterious need for order." [21] This need for order, coming after and transcending the need for social order, appears to be a manifestation of culture and institutional behavior, which we see primarily in primate societies but particularly, and perhaps exclusively, in human societies.

Robert Ardrey is an avowed and devoted evolutionist, and he takes the knowledge of vertebrate behavior as an indication of the source of human patterns of behavior, feeling that our species has evolved from the larger group of primates. If this proposition be true, and the majority of modern biologists, anthropologists, paleontologists, and archeologists would seem to accept it, then a mechanism must be found that would trigger the proper adaptive responses in our species to enable us to transcend the threshold of primate activity and become a separate species. Ardrey finds this threshold in several types of behavior, notably in our accidental adoption of the hunting, carnivorous life (due to a severe drought in the Pliocene era) and to the increasing sense of awareness our instincts brought us concerning the need to make survival choices.

"Man is a primate. All primates are social animals," Ardrey explains. "As social animals, all primates have developed to one degree or another such instinctual bundles as guarantee the survival of their societies. There is no reason to suppose that man in his African genesis inherited from primate ancestors a bundle less complex." [22] The major characteristic which primates share that distinguishes them from other vertebrates is the body-brain ratio, and within the crowd of primates the human species apparently made specialization of mental activities its major evolutionary invention. According to Robert Ardrey, this development occurred and continues to occur, "as an extension of the animal debate of the instincts. Our primate line developed such an increasingly complex instinctual pattern that thought as we know it became necessary." [23]

According to Ardrey's evolutionary explanation of the origin of our species, then, the primate faced an increasing sense of awareness that instinctual drives were in competition with one another, and primate behavior began to reflect deliberate choices of specific instinctual response rather than an immediate organic response. "Human thought," Ardrey writes, "is an extension of the animal debate of the instincts. It carries in itself no police power. It cannot act with final authority to impede this instinct, or advance that. But it can probe through experience and ingenuity the various means to a variety of ends." [24] But "our reasoning power," Audrey admits, "is scarcely unique to man; it is simply the peak of a trend that we share with all lemurs, all monkeys, all apes." [25]

Obviously an exposition of this type takes the classifications of vertebrate and primate species and sees in the different characteristics an evolutionary continuum in which a hierarchy is created. Through some incredible accident in nature, the higher organisms are seen to evolve from the lower ones. Ardrey insists on his explanations but in fairness mentions divergent observations that would tend to undermine his thesis. He connects the development of the primate brain with an accident of the Pliocene era in which an intense planetary drought forced our species to descend from the trees and enter the grasslands in search of food. When we arrived in the grassland plateaus of eastern Africa, we became hunters of other animals. *"If among all the members of our primate family the human being is unique, even in our noblest aspirations, it is because we alone through untold millions of years were continuously dependent on killing to survive."* [26]

The drought apparently caused the human species, of all the vertebrates, to adopt a new pattern of behavior. We picked up clubs, transformed our simian feet into instruments for the chase, and began a history as killers. "It is *because* we were hunters, *because* we killed for a living, *because* we matched our wits against the whole of the animal world, that we have the wit to survive even a world of our own creation," Ardrey maintains.[27] But we have little in the way of behavioral observations to suggest the validity of this thesis. The hunt required an organized group that would conduct its activities in concert and provide a focus around which food could be acquired. This is not primate behavior. It is the behavior of social predators—the large felines such as the lion, tiger, panther, and the large canines such as the wolf, coyote, fox.

The idea of roving bands of quasi apes invading the quiet grasslands in a severe planetary drought, with clubs in their hands and swiftly adapting feet that give them superior mobility in the face of other carnivores, may be appealing in a scientific sense, but it does not sound reasonable. Certainly the larger predators would have arrived at the African savannahs at approximately the same time as our ancestors did, and they would have delighted in catching us in the open, stumbling along on feet designed for trees, with primitive clubs in our hands, determined to adapt our bodies to the requirements of the open plains. But we have additional scientific evidence that the African scene pictured by Robert Ardrey could not have taken place.

In his attempt to relate observed simian behavior to the hypothetical circumstances in which our species emerged from the crowd of primates, Ardrey quite frequently cites studies of primate behavior. Although these studies indicated a propensity of some individual apes, chimpanzees, monkeys, and other simians to perform certain functions comparable to human behavior, on the whole it was determined that "natural selection in a normal environment could not account for chimpanzee capacities in an experimental setting." [28] "The chimp in the wild," Ardrey explains, "does not seem to have the 'idea' of the weapon. But in captivity, he has." [29] If, then, our first real accomplishment in arriving at the African grasslands was to bring weapons into play as an evolutionary innovation, extending our physical organs by artificial means, the uniqueness of this accomplishment must surpass human understanding because it has been shown that only in captivity does the chimpanzee reach the same conclusions, using the same powers of reason that we use.

Ardrey is the first to admit the difficulty with this view of human emergence as a separate species. Discussing the hunting motivation of the great transitional form of human primate, which he suggests inhabited the Pliocene era, he writes:

> They did not hunt for immediate gratification. They hunted for the nourishment of their females and their young. And while it is all very well to presume that they *knew* that they would have no inheritors if they did not bring the meat back home, still, such a concept would give any biologist the shudders, and I am a Darwinian. The sudden access of altruism smacks of divine intervention.[30]

And with a complete honesty rare in an advocate of a scientific theory, Ardrey forecloses the suggestion that our apelike ancestors had projected into the future some probable state of society, acting in response to the needs of their descendants, at least in part, in their adaptations to immediate environment. There is no "reason to believe that we, with our ape brain encountering the challenges of the hunting life, had any impressive advantages over our ancestors in terms of *knowing* what the next generation would demand. We show little enough such propensity today." [31]

The mechanisms whereby our species emerged from the variety of other primates to become something unique may still be the subject of great debate. It is important, however, that we do not reject some of the insights which Robert Ardrey's masterful journey into vertebrate behaviors can give us. Territorial-dominance, social-order, and need-for-order instincts seem to be so widespread among vertebrates that we cannot doubt our relationship with that group. But identifying a relationship does not necessarily imply a common point of origin. The alternative interpretation of such behavior would be the admission that for organic entities of approximately the same physical size as ourselves, the cosmic unity of space-time manifests itself in behavioral patterns as well as in morphological complexity.

In speaking of our human behavior, which he finds deeply rooted in the vertebrate past, Ardrey argues persuasively: "To conclude that human obsession with the acquisition of social status as material possessions is unrelated to the animal instincts for dominance and territory would be to press notions of special creation to the breaking point. To conclude that the loyalties or animosities of tribes or nations are other than the human expression of the profound territorial instinct would be to push reason over the cliff." [32] If, therefore, we cannot escape our common vertebrate-primate heritage, it is because such a heritage is a natural part of universal existence, and in territory, dominance, and social order we find, not an evolutionary tradition pushing backward to the beginnings of life, but the manifestation of space-time.

"The contemporary revolution in the natural sciences presents us with what seems to be a most unpromising portrait of man," Ardrey concludes in *African Genesis*. "He is a creature dominated by ineradicable animal instincts, with sapient powers devoted largely, thus far, to the task of hiding from himself all those truths which he deems disagreeable."[33] It is, perhaps, prophetic that Robert Ardrey mentions the disagreeable truths from which we hide, for in his last book, *The Hunting Hypothesis,* he makes the following statement:

> If we are to accept the human line of evolutionary origin—I suggested this in my first chapter—as independent of other small-brained hominids, we are right back to special creation, if not to divine intervention. And the question, Why is man man?, can be referred to the department of neometaphysics.[34]

The question of what makes the human being specifically what we believe ourselves to be, once we eliminate evolutionary speculations and fantasies, is metaphysical because it involves a determination of reality. At almost every decisive point in the evolutionary interpretation of the biological world, or of the origin of our species from the crowd of vertebrates and primates, evolutionists rely either upon fanciful projections of some phase of primate or vertebrate behavior or upon some incredibly fortunate accident. Rather than articulating a closely knit, scientifically sound theory that explains the development of organic life and the morphological inventions that various forms of that life have made in response to their environment, evolutionists give us vague, although highly imaginative, scenarios.

One major distinction must be recognized when dealing with the subject of territorial instincts and the correlating instincts of dominance, social order, and the still-emerging instinct for order which Ardrey intuits from the organic unity of the first three. Every indication is that individuals and species do in fact behave in certain easily identifiable, predetermined ways. The error in Ardrey's brilliant articulation of these similarities of behavior is his supposition that if we compile a sufficiently large and impressive list of behavioral similarities we can imply an evolutionary development of individuals and species across established categories of classification.

Let us return to some of the better insights that Robert Ardrey and other evolutionists have used to verify their evolutionary overtones. By removing doctrinal considerations from the interpretation of information, we can understand the relationship of species to one another, come to see the unique place our species occupies, and suggest further investigations of the new metaphysic that must emerge as we search for a method of interpreting the biological aspect of the *kosmos* and, within that conglomerate, the physical and external aspects of our species.

We are replacing an outmoded metaphysic with a more modern and comprehensive one. Although evolutionists such as Ardrey may deny the metaphysical basis of their interpretation of instinctual drives, in fact they have covered overscientific knowledge with a mysticism equally as bizarre as any vaguely defined theological doctrine. "Nature," Ardrey writes in a summary of the principle of the territorial imperative, "by instilling in the individual a demand for exclusive living space, insures two consequences: first, that a minimum number of individuals in any population will be enabled to breed in relative security and pass on in fair certainty the conformation of their kind. And second, that the surplus will be cast to the wolves . . ."[35] The first purpose of territory, a safe breeding ground, may be a valid reason for the territorial instinct. But the second reason, to ensure that a surplus of each species will "be cast to the wolves," is little more than evolutionary fantasy, and no respectable scientist would affirm this as inherent in the territorial concept. It is, without a doubt, the present ill-defined but tenaciously held metaphysic that supports the theory of evolution.

VIII. Transforming Instincts

We return to the question of our relationship with the other life-forms, ready to take up the task of interpreting our present knowledge of the biological world in a nonevolutionary sense. The many examples cited by Robert Ardrey to support an evolutionary interpretation of our behavior, grounded in our origin as a primate species, can be used to illustrate both the great similarities and the essential differences between ourselves and other vertebrates. We have suggested that the basic instinctual drives for territory, status, and social order are manifestations of the space-time structural unity expressed in modern physics. The analysis we used in physics included a process of transformation in which matter and energy became equivalent expressions of the ultimate constituent of the universe, each a function of the other and together forming a boundary beyond which we cannot conceive or observe.

Can we understand this process of transformation as an integral part of the universe by showing that the functioning of organisms contains the same process of energy-matter transformation? How does such a process manifest itself? Subatomic transformation involves the twin faces of matter and energy emerging as elements of finality. Teilhard based his philosophy of organism on the premise that life consists of a complicated interaction between two kinds of energy: radial and tangential. In radial energy we confront psychic, mental, and spiritual energy; tangential energy appears as mechanical force and physical exertions, indicating both growth and life. The ebb and flow of these energies produces the organic unity of life as we know it.

Since everything in the universe has form and substance, we can rest assured that these elemental transformation processes of physics continue to operate at the subatomic level. Karl Heim saw in the subatomic existence a picture comparable to our own lives. Remarking that the elemental particles of physics observed at the most minute scale execute purposeful movements like living individuals, Heim cautioned that "we are simply being naively presumptuous if we suppose that because these worlds in which the electrons and protons circle, infinitesimally small as they are according to human standards, have nothing in common in shape or size with a human body . . ."[1] He went on to suggest that, however slight the experience of these tiny beings, they have joys and sorrows, struggles and defeats like we do.

We always encounter the space-time unity and the transformation process whenever we begin to observe entities and individuals in the universe, although the manifestation of the structure and process appear in increasingly complicated layers of activity and behavior as we observe increasingly complex organisms. Lyall Watson, a biologist, writing about organic existence in *Supernature,* says that living systems, and by this expression he means organisms, "create order out of disorder, but it is a constant battle against the process of disruption. Order is maintained by bringing in energy from outside to keep the system going. So biochemical systems exchange matter with their surroundings all the time . . ."[2]

The transformation process involves an environment and an individual exchanging energy and matter rather than the stark transformation of matter and energy themselves. The more complicated the organism, the more complex this transformation process appears. At a certain degree of complexity, information is exchanged in addition to energy. This information is essential for the survival of the individual, and it "arrives in three forms—electromagnetic waves, such as light; mechanical pressures, such as sound; and chemical stimuli, such as those giving rise to taste and smell," according to Lyall Watson. And, he observes, "If the organism is an animal, all three kinds of signals are converted by sense receptors on the outside of the body into impulses of electrical energy that carry messages in to the central nervous system."[3]

Simple plants and animals convert the information they receive from their environment into life rhythms. We cannot detect the responses they make to their environment without very sophisticated measuring devices, but some scientists have been able to show electrical impulses that would indicate the presence of joy and pain within plants and simple animals. The current popular fad of playing music to assist plants in achieving better growth stems from this initial perception of the psychic nature of plants. The jump between simple plants and animals to more complicated species involves a radical change in our definitions because we come to understand that, in Gregory Bateson's words, "in so far as animals can signal at all about the external universe, they do so by means of actions which are parts of their response to that universe."[4] Actions by animals are comprehensible as responses to incidents and events when viewed by other animals, and we have entered the realm of communications, transcending the simple intake of information.

The change is as radical as it might appear. Gregory Bateson carefully distinguishes between the phenomena observed in the world of physics and chemistry and the phenomena experienced in the more complicated world of animals and complex organisms. "In the hard sciences," he writes, "effects are, in general, caused by rather concrete conditions or events—impacts, forces and so forth. But when you enter the world of communication, organization, etc., you leave behind that whole world in which effects are brought about by forces and impacts and energy exchange. You enter a world in which 'effects' . . . are brought about by differences."[5] Actions and responses are not predictable to any great degree but depend in large measure on the individual's relationship to the environment.

We observe in the human-sized animals easily detectable patterns of response comparable in many respects to our own emotional responses. Because of this similarity evolutionists are inclined to seek the origin of our species in the behavior and instinctual drives of other animals, particularly in the primates to whom we are closely comparable in body structure. But if we examine the similarities with the rigor, that scientific thinking requires, we conclude that while there are startling similarities, even close resemblance in types of response patterns, we cannot logically cite these parallels as evidence of a common biological ancestor. We have rather to conclude, with Gregory Bateson, that "mammals in general, and we among them, care extremely, not about episodes, but about the patterns of their relationships."[6] And that conclusion is the limit beyond which we cannot safely proceed.

Sharing, as we do, a total organic response to events and similarities in the external world, what makes us different from other animals? Robert Ardrey suggests that we incorporate a sense of purpose into our communications that is absent in other animals. "Specialized though the animal call may be," he writes in *African Genesis,* "—as specialized as the howler's 'infant dropped from tree!'—it is never purposeful. Never does the animal cry out with the motive of enlisting aid. The cry is simply an expression of mood, and the mood catches."[7] Thus while animals can *vocalize* emotions, they cannot *verbalize* emotions. Animals are incapable of transmitting a sense of meaning but merely summarize conditions. They report; they do not interpret.

Ardrey echoes an insight of Ernst Cassirer, who wrote that "we have no psychological evidence whatever for the fact that any animal ever crossed the borderline separating propositional from emotional language. The so-called 'animal language' always remains entirely subjective; it expresses various states of feeling but it does not designate or describe objects."[8] Bateson, writing in a more evolutionary context, says that our chief distinction from animals in the field of communications, and perhaps the first great step in emerging from the crowd of vertebrates, was "not the discovery of abstraction or generalization, but the discovery of how to be specific about something other than relationship."[9]

If we take these two ideas out of their evolutionary context and consider them in the space-time-transformation process that we have been using to illustrate a nonevolutionary understanding of the world, we would simply remark that our species has two major areas of communication, one of which distinguishes us from the other animals. We communicate both verbally and nonverbally. "The discourse of nonverbal communication," according to Gregory Bateson, "is precisely concerned with matters of relationship—love, hate, respect, fear, dependency, etc.—between self and vis-à-vis or between self and environment."[10] In this type of communication we are equal with other animals. We are also capable of verbalizing feelings, moods, and abstract propositions, and this ability separates us from animals and makes us, with respect to survival tactics, superior to animals.

Via our ability to use two forms of communication with respect to the external world, we enter a complex series of relationships with other individuals and with our environment. Edward T. Hall, a contemporary anthropologist, lists ten separate kinds of human activity which he feels demonstrate that complexities of human behavior derive from biological roots, having evolved in the course of human history. These different kinds of activities Hall calls "Primary Message Systems," indicating that human behavior, considered in a communications sense, involves a series of complicated responses, many of which are uniquely human and not exhibited by animals or other organisms. The list includes: *interaction, association, subsistence, bisexuality, territoriality, temporality, learning, play, defense,* and *exploitation* (use of materials).[11]

Obviously these Primary Message Systems are not all equally important. Territoriality and temporality might well be understood in the universal context as preconditions for life rather than as specifically human patterns of behavior, and Robert Ardrey's thinking would seem to indicate that there is no hard and fast way to categorize human responses as primarily our invention. Defense appears to be a function of the territorial imperative; learning and play would seem to be cultural factors rather than biological responses. But the listing is important because it indicates the possibility of cataloging nonverbal communications according to instinctual responses void of any transmission of meaning, which communications sometimes seem to imply. By eliminating the transmission of meaning from our initial discussion of communications we are able to see the whole phenomenon of communications as a manifestation of the basic process of transformation we discussed earlier. Such a cataloging enables us to consider what are the truly human inventions in communications.

If our chief distinction from other animals is our ability to be specific about something other than relationships, then it would seem to follow that we are specific because we are able to examine our situation as objective fact rather than simply respond emotionally to events of the external world. This ability to view ourselves and our condition objectively is what Teilhard called reflection.

It is, according to Teilhard, "the power acquired by a consciousness to turn in upon itself, to take possession of itself *as of an object* endowed with its own particular consistence and value; no longer merely to know, but to know oneself; *no longer merely to know, but to know that one knows.*[12] It is in knowing that one knows that we find the ability to be specific about something other than relationships.

Reflection, for Teilhard, was a phenomenon of consciousness that appears simultaneously with and is indistinguishable from the emergence of what we call the ego, the individual sense of identity. Like the space-time unity, the process of reflection and the emergence of the ego which reflects cannot be conceived or discussed as separate items but must always appear in tandem as an organic unity. This process provides an understanding of how the individual can be specific about something other than relationships. It occurs, according to Teilhard, when "the living element, which heretofore had been spread out and divided over a diffuse circle of perceptions and activities, was constituted for the first time as a *centre* in the form of a point at which all the impressions and experiences knit themselves together and fuse into a unity that is conscious of its own organization."[13] The individual does not simply know, but knows that he or she knows.

When we attempt to apply this insight to animals and to our own species, we run into obvious difficulties because the animals and our own species are both distinguished by separate and identifiable genders. As individuals of either gender fuse their experiences into a unity, different perceptions result. Ardrey notes that this phenomenon, sexual dimorphism, affects the manner in which humans and other animals approach the various basic instinctual drives such as territory, status, and social order. Such a discussion may not be popular in these days of women's liberation, but the order of nature seems to recognize two sexes in the animals and in our own species, and we would be remiss if we refused to discuss differences brought about by the genders in the perceptions individuals have concerning their world.

In *African Genesis* Ardrey illustrates the territorial imperative by referring to the male bird's tendency to establish his territory prior to any sexual activity, and he notes that the arrival of the female brings peace to an otherwise brutal struggle on the territorial battleground.[14] In *The Hunting Hypothesis* Ardrey becomes more specific about the territorial imperative, noting that the male conceives territory as an economic entity, but the female views it as a home and breeding ground. Ardrey finds that the survival of the species cannot rest on the response of either male or female; both must contribute their perceptions of territory in order for the species to continue.

> What we can guess, with fair authority, was that the male, viewing from a hilltop the Texas-like space of Africa, saw it one way; the female, viewing the antics of her children in a quite different geographical perspective, saw it another. Again and again I must reassert that had not both males and females, each in their own way,

relighted the fires of the ancient territorial imperative, the human being would not exist.[15]

Ardrey, of course, sees the combination of these two perpectives on territory in an evolutionary sense, but his knowledge of male and female behavior is without error. "It is a curious charateristic of the instincts of order," Ardrey writes in *African Genesis*, "that most are masculine. There are exceptions, but the species are few." [16] If we consider the instinctual drives for order to be masculine and to be concerned with establishing territory, ranking individuals within a society, and founding a social order, all of which can be considered as spatial dimensions of one sort or another, we would have to find in the feminine the temporal dimension in order to complete our comparison with the space-time unity.

Ardrey does not deal directly with the feminine instincts of temporal dimension other than referring to sexual periodicity, which, considered primarily in a physical sense, does not seem to adequately parallel the masculine propensity to seek order. However, Carl Jung, (1875–1961), the famous Swiss psychologist and psychiatrist, in discussing the femine aspects of psychological archetypes, found in the feminine the manifestation of a temporal sense:

> . . . every mother contains her daughter in herself and every daughter her mother, and . . . every woman extends backwards into her mother and forwards into her daughter. This participation and intermingling give rise to that peculiar uncertainty as regards *time:* a woman lives earlier as a mother, later as a daughter. The conscious experience of these ties produces the feeling that her life is spread out over generations—the first step towards the immediate experience and conviction of being outside time, which brings with it a feeling of *immortality.*[17]

Insofar as masculine and feminine complement each other as a unity and seem to manifest propensities toward spatial and temporal dimensions, we can outline the possibility of space-time as a human experience in sexual terminology.

Ardrey seems to prefer to view the feminine as fulfilling a generative role, and this function can be easily viewed as having a transforming aspect comparable to the transformation process we discovered and discussed earlier. "It is female responsiveness, as a rule," Ardrey writes in *African Genesis*, "that guides and excites masculine attention." [18] We could possibly rely upon that insight as indicative of the role of the sexes, that females attract and males compete, except that Ardrey rejects this interpretation of vertebrates' sexual instincts. "The concept of the female as a passive sexual attraction for which competing sexually aggressive males struggle has moulded our views for many centuries," he comments. "And we have imposed the human preconception on our observation of animal affairs, despite full knowledge that it is the male who through all of the natural world bears the brilliant plumage, the fancy mane, the handsome markings, whereas the female is invariably drab." [19] Ardrey concludes his observations with the comment that "the law of the sexes that females attract and males compete exists not in observations of nature but only in the nature of the observers." [20]

It is important to identify the duality of perceptions present in vertebrates, particuarly in animals, and specifically in the primates to which we appear to be related, because we must recognize that an adequate understanding of the *kosmos,* in the objective sense our metaphysical search would require, demands that we include both views of the world. Establishing an understanding of the world that reflected simply a masculine interpretation of phenomena would preclude coming to grips with the reality the universe presents. If we can speak of the instincts of order as being primarily masculine, we must also speak of the instincts of time and generation as being primarily feminine. The unity of these two gives us an understanding of the full dimension of human existence. Without either set of instincts we would find life impossible to realize or understand.

When we concentrate on the human species alone, and consideration of our species in an objective sense is the last remaining task in our effort to survey the *kosmos* to discover the outlines of a new metaphysics, we must discuss the manner in which the human species acts as a group of reflective individuals in a social unity. Traditionally, evolutionists have insisted that "cultural evolution has now replaced genetic change as the main method of transmitting the past and modifying the present." [21] If we were to accept the contentions of the evolutionists that we originated from a specific group of primates, we would expect our institutions to follow some of the major lines of primate instinctual propensity, with cultural evolution having changed our instincts into institutional behaviors.

A great deal can be said for this viewpoint. We have the natural confusion concerning the object of sexual attraction which "is a state of affairs far more likely to come about among domesticated or captive animals than among animals in the wild," [22] indicating that our institutions have radically changed our perception of biological reality. Robert Ardrey suggests that this condition has come about because of a feminine liberation movement in the remote past in which the male accepted the role of provider, not only for the young, but for females as well. He argues that the human infants, being helpless for so many years in comparison with the infants of other species, required the constant attention of the mothers, effectively eliminating the female as provider of food.[23] From the redefinition of the male role as provider must also have come the confusion concerning the nature and function of sexual activity and, ultimately, the object of sexual attraction.

But human infants must have been helpless from the very start of our species unless we consider that in evolving to a super-species of primate we produced an increasingly helpless offspring that hampered our mobility and reversed our sexual roles considerably. The same problem arises when we consider the feminine territory of the home. "The concept of the home as focus for a social group of mixed ages and mixed sexes as other than a nocturnal refuge," Ardrey comments, "finds no indication in the history of apes and monkeys," [24] leading us to suppose that the home is another reversal of primate instinctual drives of great significance. Or we could have possessed that conception of the home from the very start of our existence as a species.

The concept of the family involves us in more difficulty. "Natural selection," according to Ardrey, "has favoured among primates that institution of collective female sexual action which has come to be called polygamy." [25] We certainly can see in many non-Western societies, and in the ancestor societies of Western peoples, the acceptance of polygamy as a form of institutional marriage. "No successful primate, with the exception of the gibbon, maintains a society limited to the family unit," [26] Ardrey writes in *African Genesis*. Most societies tend to maintain a family based upon extended clan or kinship group rather than a nuclear unit, making any investigation of the family difficult at best when we attempt to distinguish our species from other primates.

We seem to reach a vague area in which it is exceedingly difficult to distinguish between primate activities and our own activities on any systematic basis. Ardrey, being a good evolutionist, develops the theme of cultural evolution by expanding on the idea of a social mind that develops through the cooperative interaction of the individuals of our species linked together in a group. We reached a point, according to him, when "brain-size could mean only so much. Smaller brains could be effectively far superior to larger if they combined their efforts. An there would be a consequence. Once selection pressure rested on the effectiveness of the social mind, any advance in communication would have its selective value." [27]

The shifting of concepts from brain to mind is perceptible and leaves us puzzled at the change from a physical reality that we can understand to mystical, nonphysical entity we cannot understand. Ardrey sees the process as one in which the brain gave way to the mind, which he defines as "variable, extra-anatomical, immeasurable aspect of the standardized human brain, and it can act not at all according to the animal laws of self-interest." [28] Introducing such an ill-conceived element into an exposition that built directly on our intimate relationship with animal laws of self-interest gives evidence of the threadbare state in which evolutionary thinking finds itself in attempting to jump the real boundaries that separate species. Ardrey's conclusion, that the mind, "unlike the anatomical brain, . . . is a fraction of that larger entity, the social mind," [29] leaves us totally baffled, wondering how the emergence of the social mind could transcend all the instinctual drives that Ardrey suggested composed the human individual.

But we must not belabor Robert Ardrey for his valiant effort to produce a consistent explanation of the human species conceived in evolutionary terms. His hesitancy to arrive at a final and satisfactory conclusion in *African Genesis* and *The Hunting Hypothesis,* regarding the nature of our species, is forgivable when we consider his conclusion of *The Social Contract.* "Social order," he writes, "with its rules and regulations, its alphas and omegas, its territories and its hierarchies, its competitions and xenophobias—has been the evolutionary way. And if I am correct, then it is the individual as we know him that has been the human invention." [30]

Ardrey is absolutely correct when he suggests that the individual is what makes the human species unique among the life-forms of the biological world. But we must insist that this individual be taken out of the evolutionary framework of interpretation so that we can declare in a straightforward manner that the individual is what makes us a unique species. We depart from the discussion of how instincts may have been or might be transformed in the course of our human experience. We must admit that the unity of space-time-transformation process becomes exceedingly muddled when we attempt to understand it on the human scale. That is because we have reached the end of our chain of evolutionary connections. We have now to investigate the functioning of the human mind, the concluding concept that Ardrey discovered in his evolutionary scheme.

We approach the investigation of the human mind with certain problems needing resolution. They are: (1) the role of instincts in the human psyche, (2) the possible existence of the social mind, (3) the manifestation of space-time as a mental phenomenon, (4) the role of the male and female viewpoints in mental processes, and (5) the manner in which transformation occurs as a function of the human mental processes. The next obvious step, from both a scientific and a metaphysical viewpoint, is to discover in psychoanalysis, the science of the mind, the answers to these questions.

IX. The Human Mind

We have seen in previous chapters that when we began to examine the physical world—atoms, minerals, plants, animals, and human beings—the human mind or psyche was the last objective entity to demand our attention. The questions we discovered in our criticism of the evolutionary interpretations of the biological world must be resolved in some form in our investigation of the human mind. If the space-time-transformation process unity, which we have suggested as an explanation of phenomena, can be demonstrated to exist in the human mind also, we will have sketched an alternative to evolution, completing our search for a new metaphysic, at least insofar as the *kosmos* is concerned.

The problem of instinctual drives, which Robert Ardrey so eloquently argues as evidence of our species' vertebrate and primate origins, remains a continuing problem, for we cannot deny that much of our behavior is instinctual. We must determine if these instincts are a precondition for existence or are derived from an evolutionary journey. And we must also determine whether masculine and feminine roles originated in an evolutionary adaptation or are manifestations of the universal organic structure, thereby orienting these aspects of the human situation with respect to the structure or the history of the universe.

How are we to choose from the many systems of psychology and psychoanalysis we have available today one particular system capable of answering so many diverse questions? The choice is not as difficult as one might suppose, for we are looking for a thinker who recognizes the existence of instincts but who also transcends instinctual problems to draw conclusions from the study of the human mind which have universal implications. Carl Gustav Jung would seem to qualify as the thinker who has actively inquired into the realms we wish to cover.

Robert Ardrey, in developing his interpretations of the biological world, continually remarks that science once viewed animal behavior as if it were inspired by the same motives that people believed moved humans. Discussing the object of sexual attraction, Ardrey insisted that our human beliefs made us look at the female as the passive partner. Appealing to actual observations of the animal world, Ardrey declared, "If that most all-powerful judge, natural selection, saw the female as the attracting force, then the decisions handed down from the natural bench for the last half billion years have for the most part been in singular error." [1] The problem with previous scientific efforts to interpret the sexual instinct in animals, according to Ardrey, was that "the science of Freud's day acknowledged no human instincts other than sex and individual survival, and no social inheritance larger or more complex than the family group." [2] With such a viewpoint it was a natural mistake to project human understandings upon the nonhuman species of the biological world, attributing to them instincts and institutions we detected in ourselves.

Jung recognized this error of science early in his career, and he distinguished his system of interpretation from others by maintaining that:

> Medical psychology, growing as it did out of professional practice, insists on the *personal* nature of the psyche. By this I mean the views of Freud and Adler. It is a *psychology of the person,* and its aetiological or causal factors are regarded almost wholly as personal in nature. Nonetheless, even this psychology is based on certain general biological factors, for instance on the sexual instinct or on the urge for self-assertion, which are by no means merely personal peculiarities. [3]

Manifestations of psychic difficulties, according to Jung, transcend personal origins and find their roots in deeply embedded instinctual drives hardly unique to the individual.

The psyche was Jung's basic structure of personality, and he did not consider it primarily mental or personal in distinction to both Freud and Adler. "Nowadays we have to start with the hypothesis that, so far as predisposition is concerned, there is no essential difference between man and all other creatures. Like every animal," Jung continued, "he possesses a preformed psyche which breeds true to his species and which, on closer examination, reveals distinct features traceable to family antecedents." [4] The psyche is all-encompassing although much of its structure obviously descends to the individual according to the physical-mental structure of the species. But, Jung maintained, "We have not the slightest reason to suppose that there are certain human activities or functions that could be exempted from this rule." [5]

It would seem, therefore, that Jung's conception of the psyche is compatible with Ardrey's idea that we inherited a bundle of primate instincts from our simian ancestors, our task being to make these instinctual drives a concrete and objective form of behavior. And Jung is certainly close to Teilhard's contention that "the consciousness of each of us is evolution looking at itself and reflecting upon itself." [6] But this comparison of Jung with Ardrey and Teilhard serves only to orient us with respect to the wider relationships that the human species may have with other entities in the biological world. Jung's analysis of the phenomenon begins at precisely the point where Ardrey surrenders and suggests the presence of a "social mind" [7] and where Teilhard lamely suggested that we are evolution's most profound product.

In order to understand Jung's point of departure, we must understand the careful distinction between consciousness and the unconscious. These distinctions are not radically different from Teilhard's considerations, but they appear more precise because of the limitations Jung places on himself. He restricts his inquiry to the human mind, whereas Teilhard describes the process of evolution, arriving at the human being as our contemporary end product. It we consider Jung's analysis of the psyche in its "ultimate nature," we find a convergence of thinking between him and Teilhard. "The deeper 'layers' of the psyche lose their individual uniqueness as they retreat farther and farther into darkness," Jung said. " 'Lower down,' that is to say as they approach the autonomous functional systems, they become increasingly collective until they are universalized and extinguished in the body's materiality, i.e., in chemical substances. The body's carbon is simply carbon. Hence at 'bottom' the psyche is simply 'world.' " [8]

Teilhard would view Jung's explanation of the substance of the psyche as compatible with his own thought because he began and concluded his philosophy on an organic note. *"In the world,"* Teilhard wrote, *"nothing could ever burst forth as final across the different thresholds successively traversed by evolution (however critical they be) which has not already existed in an obscure and primordial way. If the organic had not existed on earth from the first moment at which it was possible, it would never have begun later."* [9] Taking Jung and Teilhard together, we can see that the contents and processes of the psyche are objectively real in the same sense that the activities of the atom or the organism or the mineral are real. We are not discussing an opposition between "spiritual" and "physical." But we are also not bound to an evolutionary interpretation, for we could as easily conclude that the substance of the psyche, being ultimately a universal element, simply roots the psyche in the structure of the universe.

For the purpose of discussion, Jung divided the psyche, which he conceived as the major organ of emotional or, in Teilhard's terms, radial energy into the conscious and the unconscious. He noted that although the identification of the unconscious was certainly not original with him, it is not simply the residence of forgotten and suppressed memories and experiences as Freud and Adler believed. Jung saw the unconscious as having a Janus face, a duality of experience and structure. "On one side its contents point back to a preconscious, prehistoric world of instinct, while on the other side it potentially anticipates the future—precisely because of the instinctive readiness for action of the factors that determine man's fate." [10]

Evolutionists, of course, would see in this statement verification of their theory. But Jung's understanding of the psyche and its conscious-unconscious structure seems to indicate more precisely the space-time unity of which we have been speaking. "I have often encountered motifs which made me think that the unconscious must be the world of the infinitesimally small," Jung mused. And he suggested that such an intuition "could be derived rationalistically from the obscure feeling that in all these visions we are dealing with something endopsychic, the inference being that a thing must be exceedingly small in order to fit inside the head." But Jung saw no alliance between himself and the rationalists on this matter. "It seems to me more probable," he remarked, "that this liking for diminutives on the one hand and for superlatives—giants, etc.— on the other *is connected with the queer uncertainty of spatial and temporal relations in the unconscious.*" [11]

The space-time structure of the unconscious would appear to be conceptually different from the space-time structure in which we spend our waking hours, paralleling perhaps Heisenberg's conception of space-time as fundamentally different from Newtonian concepts. Since the motifs of which Jung spoke are involved in the process he called "individuation" [12] or the growth of personality, the difference between motifs as they appear in the dreams of his patients would seem to indicate that the process of personality growth has a structure and duration distinct from anything we have previously considered. We find a perfect analogy between this intimate relationship of space-time in the motifs of the psyche and the analysis which we have previously made suggesting that space and time appear in different forms as we examine different complexities of organization and individual expression.

Jung did not deal with the deepest levels of the unconscious because, as we have seen, they constitute in an objective sense the *kosmos*. But he found in the unconscious a level of reality that he called the "collective unconscious," and this element is in large measure the substance of the unconscious insofar as we can experience it. It is, we can guess, the concept toward which Ardrey was struggling when he spoke of the "social mind." Jung called the collective unconscious by that name "because this part of the unconscious is not individual but universal; in contrast to the personal psyche, it has contents and modes of behaviour that are more or less the same everywhere and in all individuals. It is, in other words, identical in all men and thus constitutes a common psychic substrate of a suprapersonal nature which is present in every one of us." [13]

Jung chose to call the contents of the collective unconscious *archetypes*. These archetypes are not personal; according to Jung they "have never been in consciousness, and therefore have never been individually acquired, but owe their existence exclusively to heredity." [14] In this sense they are parallel in many respects to Ardrey's bundle of instincts, but not strictly identical with them. Deriving from human heredity instead of the general instinctual experience and heritage of mammals, archetypes are clothed in human form and appear in dreams in the forms of personages that express certain familiar human growth patterns. Archetypes are thus specifically human. They are *designed to both initiate* and *record* the stages of *growth in the human personality*. Whether they are an evolutionary product indicating a direction in which consciousness is proceeding is doubtful since they seem to originate in the human past rather than appearing as indications of a new pattern of development.

Jung specifically denied that archetypes could be rationally subsumed under a principle of knowledge. He found that the archetype can best be understood if one conceives it as a psychic organ:

> The archetype . . . is a psychic organ present in all of us. A bad explanation means a correspondingly bad attitude to this organ, which may thus be injured. But the ultimate sufferer is the bad interpreter himself. Hence the "explanation" should always be such that the functional significance of the archetype remains unimpaired, so that an adequate and meaningful connection between the conscious mind and the archetypes is assured. For the archetype is an element of our psychic structure and thus a vital and necessary component in our psychic economy.[15]

But the archetypes, even though incapable of reduction to rational categories of interpretation (which would reduce them to mental constructs), are a representative group of figures that denote stages of growth and expression specifically characteristic of human beings. Jung said that among the archetypes that can be arranged as a cast of characters are major figures, which represent typical human conditions. "The chief of them being," according to Jung, "the *shadow,* the *wise old man,* the *child,* . . . the *mother* . . . as a supraordinate personality . . . and her counterpart the *maiden,* and lastly the *anima* in man and the *animus* in woman."[16]

These figures compose Jung's cast of psychic characters for the most part, although they are certainly not the only figures that have content and therefore archetypal significance. One of the more important archetypes Jung discussed does not appear in this list: the trickster. He is described by Jung as "a primitive 'cosmic' being of *divine-animal* nature, on the one hand superior to man because of his superhuman qualities, and on the other hand inferior to him because of his unreason and unconsciousness."[17] The trickster was a difficult figure for Jung to describe. Although the trickster is a prominent figure in North America, fulfilling an important role in American Indian mythology, he does not appear historically in Western European myths until quite late when he becomes an anti-Christian figure serving to alleviate the seriousness of medieval ceremonial life. Whether Jung should have included a figure so intimately tied to specific cultural traditions is a serious question. There is little doubt that Jung was never able to integrate this figure into his general system of archetypes.

In this archetype we can perhaps see one of the categories that Edward T. Hall understood as characteristic of human societies: play. If this correspondence holds, then perhaps learning and the complexities of logical process it entails indicate that the human species is indeed the next step in the Teilhardian process of evolution, which is qualitatively distinct from the previous stages of growth. But we have insufficient evidence to prove one way or the other the actual function of the trickster. Jung seems to suggest at some points that the trickster prefigures the symbol of Christ, but in the cultural context of the American Indian, the trickster is by no means a salvation figure.

In addition to personalized archetypes such as the wise old man, the mother, and the anima and the animus, Jung described another class that he called "archetypes of transformation." They are not understood as personalities but as places, situations, and incidents that seem to symbolize the type of transformation and growth which the individual personality is undergoing. "Like the personalities, these archetypes are true and genuine symbols that cannot be exhaustively interpreted, either as signs or as allegories. They are genuine symbols precisely because they are ambiguous, full of half-glimpsed meanings, and in the last resort inexhaustible." [18]

Our previous investigations of the *kosmos* suggested that a process of transformation always appeared with the space-time unity and was in fact inseparable from it except for purposes of discussion. Jung's archetypes of transformation fit precisely into this pattern of interpretation and thus would indicate that our metaphysical search for a more encompassing interpretation of phenomena can be consistently applied at every step of our investigation. The archetypes of transformation are often motifs of a particular pattern of events in which the personality archetypes play an internal role as characters in a drama or myth. The interplay of personal archetypes and archetypes of transformation, considered as an organic unity and revealed in the dreams of an individual, indicate the condition of the unconscious of the individual at that particular moment in life.

The reliance of Jungian psychoanalysis on the dream is built on the recognition that the unconscious is a process of nature in which conscious and unconscious energies seek to balance themselves. "Dreams are the natural products of unconscious psychic activity," Jung claimed. "We have known for a long time that there is a biological relationship between the unconscious processes and the activity of the conscious mind. This relationship can best be described as a compensation, which means that any deficiency in consciousness—such as exaggeration, one-sidedness, or lack of a function—is suitably supplemented by an unconscious process." [19]

The supplemental functioning between conscious and unconscious led Jung to interpret dreams as indications of an unbalanced situation. "The psychological rule says that when an inner situation is not made conscious, it happens outside, as fate." [20] Other psychoanalysts have suggested that dreams indicate a semirational experiment with alternative realities rather than an unbalance in the interplay between conscious and unconscious. One cannot reject Jung's insistence on the objective resolution of psychic problems because of a failure to resolve internal difficulties in view of the many instances in human history of what we call fate actively pursuing an individual. The idea that the energies present in both conscious and unconscious act to transform behaviors or result in objective mistakes in confronting problems certainly indicates the indeterminate nature of the psychic transformation process in which archetypes appear to be involved.

Jungian psychoanalytic theory treats the instincts that Ardrey describes in much the same way that Ardrey does. They are not personal in the sense that archetypes illustrate personal problems and stages of growth. They are universally distributed, are probably predetermined by hereditary factors, and have a dynamic or motivating aspect that triggers individual actions on an unconscious level. Jung seemed to feel that followers of Freud and Adler more often confronted instinctual problems than problems of personality growth. He cautioned against treating instinctual problems lightly, however, insisting that "the instincts are not vague and indefinite by nature, but are specifically formed motive forces which, long before there is any consciousness, and in spite of any degree of consciousness later on, pursue their inherent goals." [21]

There appears to be no conflict between Jung and Ardrey on the subject of instincts insofar as we can describe and understand their role in human behavior. But Jung tended to brush aside the instinctual problems as simply the preamble to human personality growth, annoying adolescent problems that must be resolved before we can embark on the great adventure of becoming fully human. It often seems as if Ardrey is being deliberately reductionist in insisting that instincts describe and motivate the major human concerns, our present beliefs and institutions being already existent in the universe as vertebrate instincts that cement us firmly into the evolutionary process. Jung's archetypes qualitatively distinguish human psychic energies and problems from those of any other species.

All the above entities—the archetypes of personality, the archetypes of transformation, and the instincts—are residents of the unconscious for Jung. They form a collective structure that impinges upon the conscious mind to force and direct its objective growth. The major constituent of that mind, and here we encounter difficulties in conceptualization, is the "ego." Jung understood the ego as "the complex factor to which all conscious contents are related. It forms, as it were, the centre of the field of consciousness; and, in so far as this comprises the empirical personality, the ego is the subject of all personal acts of consciousness." [22]

Jung's conception of the ego appears comparable to Teilhard's characterization of it, but it is not. There is a universal dimension of Teilhard's conception of the ego, because of his reliance upon the cosmic evolutionary process, and so Teilhard's understanding encompasses much more than the field of consciousness. Jung's concept of the self, the totality of psychic action when the conscious and unconscious are considered in an organic unity, is probably comparable to Teilhard's conception of the self. I shall use Jung's concept of the self as if it and Teilhard's concept of the ego were identical.

Using these specific structural elements—the archetypes, the instincts, and the self—as operative in psychic life, Jung explored the human mind and the manifestations of psychic problems in individual and social life. A more careful examination of the respective archetypes of personality will indicate how Jung applied these elements to an understanding of the individuation process, the formation of the mature person.

The Shadow. According to Jung, the shadow coincides with the "personal unconscious" [23] and is therefore the side of personality that has been derived from experiences of the individual. The shadow includes not simply the individual's experiences but the values and concepts that structure his or her society, how that society views the world, and the extraneous information and beliefs the individual has been taught. It is thus a composite of information and beliefs that can easily be reprogrammed into new groupings to produce a different understanding of the world.

For the person in the Western world the shadow would include all those beliefs and superstitions which that cultural tradition accepts about the nature of the world and the place of the human species in it. One can easily see that the shadow for the Christian and the Buddhist differ considerably. Males and females necessarily have different ways of organizing their shadows. And the racial or ethnic group from which one comes plays a considerable role in fashioning the manner in which information and beliefs are organized.

Dealing with the shadow is a major problem, according to Jung, because it involves confronting moral issues and beliefs. It "challenges the whole ego-personality, for no one can become conscious of the shadow without considerable moral effort. To become conscious of it involves recognizing the dark aspects of the personality as present and real." [24] In a fundamental sense the shadow stands in the way of every individual creating a new metaphysic, for such a creation inevitably involves destroying or rearranging one's shadow as a deliberate process guided by the conscious mind. The shadow, while manifested on an individual basis, tells us a great deal about the cultural influence an individual feels, and this archetype is Jung's major effort to account for this part of human experience.

The Anima. The anima seems to appear in the experiences of males as a young woman, and she represents life. She is spontaneous, promiscuous, flighty, irrational, and apparently immune to human tragedy. Yet Jung said that for the person who takes her seriously, behind the anima "lies something like a hidden purpose which seems to reflect a superior knowledge of life's laws." [25] The picture Jung drew of the anima as an archetype is not radically different from the role Ardrey sees the female performing in the animal world—the initiator of all action.

The Animus. This archetype appears in the unconscious of the female as a counterpart to the anima of the male. "The animus corresponds to the paternal Logos just as the anima corresponds to the maternal Eros," [26] Jung wrote. When this archetype appears in the dreams and experiences of women, it calls forth a drive for order, direction, purpose, knowledge, and the creation of structures and organization of data fulfilling a masculine role in the life of women much as the energetic and irrational sensitivity of the female appears to call forth enthusiasm and spontaneity in the male. The two archetypes, anima and animus, provide a sense of balance in what would otherwise become wholly unisexual functions of the psychic life of men and women.

The Wise Old Man. This archetype seems to have been Carl Jung's favorite. We no doubt see in it the objective manifestation of his own life, for it represents "the superior master and teacher, the archetype of the spirit who symbolizes the pre-existent meaning hidden in the chaos of life." [27] The wise old man would seem to personify the direction in which Teilhard saw the evolutionary process pointing, for it gives, according to Jung, "knowledge, reflection, insight, wisdom, cleverness, and intuition on the one hand, and on the other, moral qualities such as goodwill and readiness to help, which make his 'spiritual' character sufficiently plain." [28]

The wise old man's appearance in dreams is often at the end of the therapeutic process when the patient seems to need an affirmation of the universal wisdom. It is important, for our purpose, to note that a substantial number of human societies have chosen, deliberately or intuitively, to represent deity in some form of this image, either as the old gentleman we see walking in the Garden of Eden in the cool of the evening or in the somber Grandfathers of the American Indians, or the adepts and masters whom the esoteric religions picture as the ultimate repository of wisdom. The figure may contain more than the effort by males in a society to dominate the females, and we will return to this important figure in later chapters in another context.

The Mother. Jung, recognizing the duality of the feminine, understood the mother archetype as having two aspects: the primordial mother and the earth mother. He found a positive aspect to the mother archetype in that the maternal instinct is "identical with that well-known image of the mother which has been glorified in all ages and all tongues." [29] The other aspect, essentially a negative connotation, is the "secret, hidden, dark; the abyss, the world of the dead, anything that devours, seduces, and poisons, that is terrifying and inescapable like fate." [30] In this duality we see both the immediate human experience of the family and home of childhood and the universal experience of familarity and danger, which the physical world presents with some ambivalence. In general we could say that Western peoples have emphasized the human mother and non-Western peoples have concentrated on the universal, generative, and dangerous aspect of the mother. Depending on the specific dream, of course, the mother archetype fulfills the function of presenting the context in which the individual problem can be understood.

The Child. The child is another dual-natured archetype. "One of the essential features of the child motif," Jung wrote, "is its futurity. The child is potential future. Hence the occurrence of a child motif in the psychology of the individual signifies as a rule an anticipation of future developments, even though at first sight it may seem like a retrospective configuration." [31] But it is much more than the future if we take Jung at his most profound sense, for he also said that the child archetype "is an incarnation of *the inability to do otherwise,* equipped with all the powers of nature and instinct, whereas the conscious mind is always getting caught up in its supposed ability to do otherwise." [32]

Like the figure of the wise old man, the child has been a popular and frequently used religious image. Particularly in the Christian tradition the Child has been conceived as that individual so pure in relationship to the world and to other humans that *he or she cannot do otherwise than follow the natural tendency to do good.* Being "childlike" implies a type of faith without guile, the perfect attitude that people are taught to emulate. But there is another aspect of the child image that has found its way into the popular religious vocabulary: the idea that non-Western peoples have a "childish" understanding of religious reality. This implies a superstitious and ignorant nature that rejects or cannot comprehend the higher wisdom of religion. Unfortunately, this latter meaning represents an egotistical cultural attitude that precludes understanding and forecloses the future, degrading the positive image of the child by association.

It is difficult to determine exactly which interpretation of this archetype represents Jung's true feelings. Both he and Teilhard considered a reflective consciousness as the ultimate product of their respective processes of nature, and the wise old man would seem to represent this conclusion much better than the child. Insofar as the child represents the beginning of a therapeutic process, we can restrict its appearance to the stirrings of the self in initiating individuation, or maturity. But we cannot place too much emphasis on this archetype as indicating an open-ended future when it appears within the Jungian system of psychoanalysis.

The primary psychological tasks during the initial stages of personality growth are to confront and bring under control the instinctual drives that dominate spontaneous behavior. These instincts are, for all practical purposes, identical with the instincts described by Robert Ardrey. Instincts are always with us, drive us unwittingly to respond to basic tendencies which all organisms seem to possess, and channel our physical response to the environment and to others of our species into restricted patterns of behavior.

But human personality is designed to proceed through a series of growth stages that are represented by the wise old man and the Great Mother for males and females respectively. The anima and animus trigger in males and females respectively the unbalance needed to initiate a process of synthesis between unconscious drives and conscious activities. As personality growth proceeds, dreams begin to inform us of the proportion of unbalanced psychic energy in the conscious and the unconscious. As the proportion between the two aspects of the self becomes critical, dreams warn of the existing lack of compensation. The dream situational motif describes a condition, a place, or an incident that symbolizes the nature of the problem and often suggests a pattern of growth capable of solving the problem. The story line or situation represents what Jung called the archetype of transformation.

Within the story line, situation, place, condition, or incident of the dream appear a cast of characters, sometimes the major archetypes which we have discussed, sometimes animals, reptiles, and other organisms, symbolizing specific fears, beliefs, or tendencies. Sometimes recognizable plots appear in which universal characters move in and out of the sequence of action describing a nebulous condition. As growth takes place in normal personalities, these dreams and the appearance of the major archetypes record the progress of growth. In individuals with specific problems the sequence shifts about until the process of growth compensates for inadequacies, bringing the personality back into a statistically normal growth pattern.

The end product of both the psychic growth process and of the human individual physically is described as either the Wise Old Man or the Great Mother in their best and most complete manifestations. The male personality achieves a sense of wisdom tempered with a well-developed body of knowledge. The female personality achieves a sense of propriety together with a concern for the gathering of other humans into a social unity, most commonly the family. The combination of youth and age often acts across sexual lines with the younger male and the older female and the older male and the younger female bringing out the most complete development in each other. In the female we find manifestations of a sense of time, and in the orderliness of the male we find the manifestation of a sense of space. Inherent in the growth process is the transformation of personalities from young man and young woman to Wise Old Man and Great Mother.

The Jungian system contains many more useful analogies and insights, but we must end our discussion of Jung's thinking at this point. We have investigated the basic structure of the human personality, using his ideas, but we cannot push Jung's thinking beyond the point of objective investigation. To do so would be to violate our initial point of investigation, which involved a survey of the *kosmos*. We will now analyze some aspects of the other half of the Greek division of the world, the *oikumenē*, the world of human affairs. There we shall find several analyses of how human institutions and beliefs have channeled our behavior as a function of our conscious and deliberate intention to follow those beliefs.

The *oikumenē* is, from this viewpoint, wholly artificial in that it is not a natural process of development that can be traced in all entities and elements we can observe in the universe. The *oikumenē* stands apart from the *kosmos* because it is a world that we have deliberately created. And where we can make no certain statement concerning the origin of the physical world, we can determine how our technology arose, how we conceive laws and institutions, how religions arose and affect our behavior, and how we conceive our historical experience. To borrow a phrase from Pierre Teilhard de Chardin, we become, in an investigation of the *oikumenē* evolution looking at itself, because we can chart and follow the social behavior of our species in a reflective sense. If we cannot affirm evolution as a physical process, we can raise it again as a means of interpreting our history and behavior.

X. The Quickening Pace

Unlike the *kosmos* which consists of the physical entities and natural processes that we observe, the *oikumenē* is composed of those parts of our experience that are generated by purposeful human activity. A number of distinctions must be made in looking at the *oikumenē*. We deal with data that traditionally falls into the area of social science rather than physical science. Our concern centers on the effects and influences of institutions on our behavior, not on the composition and operation of elements of the natural world. Nearly everything we will examine in the *oikumenē* is encompassed by a historical dimension. In this manner the *oikumenē* contrasts with the physical world of experimentation and observation, the methods by which we get information and knowledge concerning the attributes of the thing under consideration.

Our first subject of investigation in the *oikumenē* is the most visible product of our minds and activities—technology. How does it influence our behavior? Where does it originate? What principles does it incorporate? How do we presently understand technology? What changes can we expect it to make in our lives? Many other questions could be devised that would enable us to draw some conclusions regarding technology, but it will be sufficient to concentrate on a general review of the abstract principles that seem to appear in conjunction with technology and describe their probable influence. A historical survey of technology might be interesting, but it would have little immediate relationship to the metaphysical search.

Technology, even the most primitive, is regarded by many thinkers as the distinguishing mark that separates us from the other animals. Louis Leakey

(1903–1972), the distinguished British anthropologist who revolutionized our conceptions about human evolution, showed Robert Ardrey a photograph of an ancient bone pile with a worn lump of lava which he thought represented the first human weapon. This discovery impressed Ardrey and convinced him that with the discovery and use of weapons our species crossed the threshold that forever separated us from the other animals. Many animals use tools, Ardrey admitted, and he illustrated that contention by describing a chimp using a twig to dig termites from a rotting log. "But when we took a stone and chipped it into a pattern that would suit our needs," Ardrey argues, "then we created something that does not exist in nature. We were fashioning something to a design existing only in our own minds." [1]

Our use of instruments, tools, and weapons represents a very complex form of adjustment to the natural world and is the first indication that we have transcended ordinary requirements for physical existence by projecting abstract ideas to create additional capability which nature did not give us. If, in the field of communication we are the only species to exhibit a sense of purpose in our outcries, in using tools, weapons, and instruments, we begin to bring an artificial order to our relationship with nature and initiate the *oikumenē*. We thus introduce into the general animal propensity to use tools a process of manufacturing that depends upon the purpose which we abstractly conceive for the tool. This abstraction which enables us to better confront our environment can be seen as a deliberate effort to create a new space for ourselves.

Ardrey sees a major innovation in the creation of the bow and arrow and the spear. Prior to the invention of these weapons our species had to engage in virtual hand-to-hand combat with larger predatory and game animals in order to eat. Using clubs and rocks our ancestors invaded the grazing and hunting territories and either stampeded larger animals into places where they would destroy themselves by running over cliffs, or surrounded a game animal and cooperatively killed it in a brutal manner. "But when the bow and arrow and the far-thrown spear made death at a distance a new fact in the life of the animal," Ardrey explains, "men for the first time stood apart." [2] He goes on to describe the fear of humans that animals learned when men became efficient hunters with death-at-a-distance weapons.

These weapons were more an innovation than Ardrey is willing to claim. The bow and arrow, sling, and far-thrown spear were revolutionary inventions because they enabled us to transcend space in a very short time, substituting the time it would have taken us to physically assault our prey and the distance we would have had to travel to come into contact with our target, for a new type of technology that eclipsed both space and time. If weapons were regarded by anthropologists and evolutionary thinkers as appendages of artificial nature to extend the capabilities of our physical bodies, they were also efforts to bring physical space and time under our control.

The same can be said for both transportation and communications. Domesticating the horse and dog and inventing the horse-drawn litter and the wheel enabled us to transcend space and time by substituting these innovations for our physical capability. As late as the Greek city states, communications were dependent upon the human runner, as evidenced by the famous run after the battle of Marathon, but with the improvement of transportation facilities, communications became more and more a means of telescoping time and reducing it to a manageable quantity.

Once the basic principles of tools and transportation became common knowledge, it was a simple matter for generations of people to improve upon them. The lessons learned in modifying these basic inventions encouraged people to seek relief from the drudgery of human existence by building machines that could perform more and more arduous functions. Werner Heisenberg suggested that inventions were modeled after functions we were already performing. "Starting in the eighteenth and the beginning of the nineteenth centuries, there was developed a technology which rested on the exploitation of mechanical processes," he explained. "Often machines did nothing but imitate the action of our hands in spinning, weaving, lifting loads or forging large pieces of iron. Thus, this form of technology was at first merely the development and extension of old handicrafts, and outside-observers could understand it just as they had understood the old handicrafts themselves . . ." [3]

Our species had transcended the simple requirements of conquering space and time by artificially extending our limbs. We now patterned machines after the actions of our hands, a process whereby the physical capabilities of our bodies were represented mechanically in our machines. Coinciding with the development of tools and machinery was the discovery that time could be measured as a function of the distance traveled. This recognition resulted in the imposition of precisely measured uniform units on our experience of time and space. Marshall McLuhan suggests that "great cultural changes occurred in the West when it was found possible to fix time as something that happened between two points. From this application of visual, abstract, and uniform units came our Western feeling for time as duration. From our division of time into uniform, visualizable units comes our sense of duration and our impatience when we cannot endure the delay between events." [4] This sense of dread at the thought of unfilled time is precisely the experience from which Christianity freed us according to Paul Tillich. He failed to recognize that the anxiety was created by our attachment to a particular interpretation of time that was almost exclusively a creation of our minds.

The sense of impatience which measured time generated became an influential force in its own right, and triggered the incessant desire for activity that has characterized Western peoples. The movie *Around the World in Eighty Days* seems to symbolize this attitude wherein speed in transportation dominates all other considerations. Although the story was fiction, it represented the optimistic belief of an era when it seemed that science would bring all of nature under our control. That we were imposing a wholly artificial interpretation on the natural world and denying its most precious insights was overlooked. Our view of the world prior to 1850 was one in which people believed that with certain minor adjustments our species had come to know the natural world completely and had reduced it to our harmless possession.

But, according to Werner Heisenberg, "a decisive change in the nature of technology did come about with the development of electro-technics in the second half of the last century. There was no longer a direct connection with the old handicrafts, since natural forces hardly known to man from his immediate experience of nature were being exploited." [5] Electricity increased the speed with which machines could operate from a rate compatible with and conceivable by the ordinary person to an instantaneous rate in which the simple flick of a switch produced the desired results immediately.

Marshall McLuhan has a piercing insight when he maintains that "with the arrival of electric technology, man extended, or set outside himself, a live model of the central nervous system itself." [6] The importance of this change cannot be underestimated because we had already created a mechanical universe in our technology that mirrored our bodies but which, until electricity, was powered by an energy source of time expenditure comparable to our own bodies. Electricity coupled to our existing machinery made our created universe a complete model of our total selves because our technology could operate as fast as our spontaneous reactions. We have observed, of course, the many differences that electricity has created in our lives by providing a dependable and almost inexhaustible source of energy. "But the final, qualitative difference between this and all previous lifetimes," Alvin Toffler writes in *Future Shock,* "is the one most easily overlooked. For we have not merely extended the scope and scale of change, we have radically altered its pace." [7]

Altering the pace of life is a change of qualitative difference without precedent in the history of our species. McLuhan indicates how the introduction of electricity changed our lives. "In the mechanical age now receding," he writes, "many actions could be taken without too much concern. Slow movement insured that the reactions were delayed for considerable periods of time. Today the action and the reaction occur almost at the same time. We actually live mythically and integrally, as it were, but we continue to think in the old, fragmented space and time patterns of the pre-electric age." [8]

Our exploration of the *oikumenē* therefore, must take into account this basic fact of contemporary existence. Nearly all our cultural traditions originated in the period of history in which we were restricted to a ponderous mechanical form of expression. Space and time were absolute elements of our experience that were overcome with great difficulty and played an important part in our lives. The best example of the inhibiting nature of space and time in the old mechanical world is the Battle of New Orleans, fought weeks after the conclusion of the War of 1812 by generals who had not yet received word of the war's conclusion. We live today in exactly the opposite situation: A war could start and nearly conclude instantaneously through the ability of electricity to make our decisions not simply instantaneous, but irreversible.

Marshall McLuhan describes our present situation as the creation of the global village. "Many analysts have been misled by the electric media," McLuhan explains, "because of the seeming ability of these media to extend man's spatial powers of organization. Electric media, however, abolish the spatial dimension, rather than enlarge it. By electricity, we everywhere resume person-to-person relations as if on the smallest village scale."[9] But it is a village that has no history because, according to Alvin Toffler, "not only do *contemporary* events radiate instantaneously—now we can be said to be feeling the impact of all *past* events in a new way. For the past is doubling back on us. We are caught in what might be called a 'time skip.'"[10] We are in a time skip because we can instantly retrieve data from any source whatsoever, but also because as we link together the various human societies, the events of the past that plague some societies become important factors in the new linkages created by electric media. McLuhan describes this condition as being the greatest of all reversals: electricity has ended the idea of sequence by making things instant.

Making things instant and reversing the idea of sequences, which formed the basis of the old perception and understanding of time, has certain perilous consequences. " 'Rational,' " according to McLuhan, ". . . has for the West long meant 'uniform and continuous and sequential.' " And he maintains that Western people "confused reason with literacy, and rationalism with a single technology."[11] Toffler agrees with McLuhan's analysis, arguing that "rational behavior, in particular, depends upon a ceaseless flow of data from the environment. It depends upon the power of the individual to predict, with at least fair success, the outcome of his own actions. To do this, he must be able to predict how the environment will respond to his acts. Sanity, itself, thus hinges on man's ability to predict his immediate, personal future on the basis of information fed him by the environment."[12] But the difficulty is that because of electricity "speeding up change in the outer world, we compel the individual to relearn his environment at every moment."[13] Rationality, in the former sense of the word, in which we are able to file information into learned categories of explanation and interpretation, is the victim of our electric world.

When we discuss the environment of the electric world, we discover that it no longer exists. "Our electric extensions of ourselves simply by-pass space and time," McLuhan writes, "and create problems of human involvement and organization for which there is no precedent."[14] The precedent does not exist, we learn, in the Western tradition, but it does exist in the tribal tradition. For, according to McLuhan, "Literate man, civilized man, tends to restrict and enclose space and to separate functions, whereas tribal man had freely extended the form of his body to include the universe."[15] We have already seen that technology in the pre-electric age was an extension of our own bodies. We can therefore conclude that energizing those mechanical extensions of our bodies provides an organic universe in which we have the space-time-transformation process as our own creation rather than as a natural process. The pattern of existence we discovered in modern physics and biology we now confront as the result of coupling technological progress in building machines with the energy of electricity.

If McLuhan is correct that tribal man adapted to the environment by extending his body to include the universe, we should expect descriptions of tribal or primitive peoples' viewpoints to reflect this understanding of the world. The psychologist Heinz Werner (1890–1964), described the primitive concept of reality as "a world of behaviour, a world in which everything is seen as gesture as it were—physiognomically—and where everything either personal or thing-like exists in action. It is not a world of knowledge, but one of deed; it is not static but dynamic, not theoretical but pragmatic."[16] This view of reality is precisely the view that our electric universe now forces upon us. "Concern with *effect* rather than *meaning* is a basic change of our electric time," McLuhan writes, "for effect involves the total situation, and not a single level of information movement."[17] The pragmatic and practical and not the theoretical and informative are the marks of our new situation.

We are not simply advancing to a state in which tribal responses to phenomena become the proper patterns of behavior, but we are seeing the emergence of new understandings of life, which had been covered up by the inexorable logic of pre-electric Western science. McLuhan insists "that media as extensions of our senses institute new ratios, not only among our private senses, but among themselves, when they interact among themselves."[18] The new ratios of which McLuhan speaks are the organic unification of sciences, technologies, and human values. "The entire world, past and present, now reveals itself to us like a growing plant in an enormously accelerated movie. Electric speed is synonymous with light and with the understanding of causes. So, with the use of electricity in previously mechanized situations, men easily discover causal connections and patterns that were quite unobservable at the slower rates of mechanical change."[19]

We view a universe of our own creation that has transcended its cultural and intellectual roots in Western society and now seeks to bind all societies together instantaneously. The best comparison McLuhan can make between our world and any other is to the world of tribal people. The manner in which primitive, tribal people understood the world and the way we must now understand the world are identical. We stand at the dawn of a new creation, for we can no longer process our experiences into predetermined categories of explanation; we require a generalized approach to life which can give us a meaning that transcends the immediate intake of data.

McLuhan finds the solution to our immediate problem as one of emphasizing and perhaps emulating the artist and the liberally educated person. Survival has become a matter of perceiving a pattern of reality over and above the overwhelming amount of data we receive from our electric media. "Paradoxically," McLuhan writes, "automation makes liberal education mandatory. The electric age of servomechanisms suddenly releases men from the mechanical and specialist servitude of the preceding machine age."[20]

"The new society offers few roots in the sense of truly enduring relationships," Toffler warns. "But it does offer more varied life niches, more freedom to move in and out of these niches, and more opportunity to create one's own niche, than all earlier societies put together."[21] But this new freedom entails a sacrifice of major proportions because "across the board the average interpersonal relationship in our life is shorter and shorter in duration."[22] These new temporary relationships produce a type of human behavior that Toffler characterizes as searching activity. It is "a relentless process of social discovery in which one seeks out new friends to replace those who are either no longer present or who no longer share the same interests."[23]

Communities are no longer based upon locality, racial background, or tradition. Instead they reflect a similarity of interests and relationships devised to resolve personal problems. We might characterize such a process of establishing relationships as a retribalizing effort as McLuhan does except that we know the permanency of the tribe does not reside in modern social forms. Philip Slater describes the present method of deriving personal relationships as following a network pattern rather than a traditional community pattern. Writing in *Earthwalk,* Slater finds that "urban and suburban Americans do not live in communities, they live in networks. A network is an address book—a list of people who may have little in common besides oneself. Each network has only one reference point that defines it. No two people have the same precise network. This means that everyone controls her own social milieu, and if she likes can subsist entirely on interpersonal candy bars. The persons in her network do not know each other, so she is never forced to integrate the disparate sides of herself but can compartmentalize them in disconnected relationships."[24]

In this type of individual existence there really are no criteria to guide people. "The entire knowledge system in society is undergoing violent upheaval," we are warned by Alvin Toffler. "The very concepts and codes in terms of which we think are turning over at a furious and accelerating pace."[25] Two solutions are offered to this terrifying problem of devising a new sense of reality. Toffler seems to see in the creation of new institutions a way out of our dilemma. "No man's model of reality is a purely personal product," he writes. "While some of his images are based on first-hand observation, an increasing proportion of them today are based on messages beamed to us by the mass media and the people around us. . . . And as experience and scientific research pump more refined and accurate knowledge into society, new concepts, new ways of thinking, supersede, contradict, and render obsolete older ideas and world views."[26]

With a great expansion of refined and accurate knowledge Toffler feels that it would be possible for us to devise communities based on working models of human existence from which people might choose their alternatives. "While Utopia A might stress materialist, success-oriented values, Utopia B might base itself on sensual, hedonistic values, C on the primacy of aesthetic values, D on individualism, E on collectivism, and so forth." The accumulated experiences and productions of these various utopias, Toffler feels, might bring forth a new flowering of arts, science, books, plays, films, and television, "thereby educating large numbers of people about the costs and benefits of the various proposed utopias."[27] Such a scheme assumes that individuals would conduct themselves with good will in experimenting with the various utopias, searching out that combination of experiences which they feel would contribute best to the welfare of society and the individuals within it.

We have no such indications upon which to rely. For the most part, our society tends increasingly toward instant gratification because the mass of information and experiences flooding our emotional lives deal with gratification and sensuality. We are now trained to be entertained in much the same way that masses in every society have been trained when the society reaches the point at which it cannot provide a meaningful vocational life for its people. To attempt to channel individuals into the various utopias that Toffler suggests would be to drop all pretense of civilized life and simply return our societies to a presocial state. Toffler sees this alternative clearly, remarking that "unless we are literally prepared to plunge backward into pretechnological primitivism, and accept all the consequences—a shorter, more brutal life, more disease, pain, starvation, fear, superstition, xenophobia, bigotry, and so on—we shall move forward to more and more differentiated societies."[28]

Differentiation into smaller societies—cults, groupings by interests, and other forms of organization—appears to Toffler to be the path to take to avoid the future shock of instantaneous existence. We cannot quarrel with his suggestion because it was one of the important movements, the breaking into cults and subgroups, that Revel identified as indicating America's potential for leadership in the coming world revolution. But there is much to recommend the alternative solution suggested by Marshall McLuhan, and that is basing our hope for the future on the individual.

McLuhan draws his comparison of our times and tribal or primitive times by insisting that the electric media is in the process of retribalizing our societies and ourselves. He continues this comparison with an analysis of work, showing that the effect of our electric media is to reconstitute work in a primitive sense. "The primitive hunter or fisherman did no work," McLuhan notes, "any more than does the poet, painter, or thinker of today. Where the whole man is involved there is no work. . . . In the computer age we are once more totally involved in our roles. In the electric age the 'job of work' yields to dedication and commitment, as in the tribe."[29] Ultimately, for McLuhan, we go not to the tribe, but to the dawn of creation. "The very toil of man now becomes a kind of enlightenment," McLuhan tells us. "As unfallen Adam in the Garden of Eden was appointed the task of the contemplation and naming of creatures, so with automation. We have now only to name and program a process or a product in order for it to be accomplished."[30]

The electric media, we might say, bring the individual back together, creating a perceiving person who views everything in an organic sense, eliminating the fractionation of individuality which the mechanical universe had created. "Man the food-gatherer reappears incongruously as information-gatherer. In this role, electronic man is no less a nomad than his paleolithic ancestors."[31] And "our quarry now in this new nomadic and 'workless' world, is knowledge and insight into the creative processes of life and society."[32]

McLuhan does not, however, describe the old manner of looking at the individual. "Toynbee urges again and again the cultural strategy of the imitation of the example of great men," McLuhan remarks. But he rejects this avenue as fruitless because it "is to locate cultural safety in the power of the *will,* rather than in the power of adequate *perception* of situations."[33] So we are never advocating the increase of education as a solution to the acceleration of experiences created by electricity, but we are now speaking of the accumulation of wisdom in the ancient tribal sense. Gathering information, which is arriving at an incredible rate of speed, is a difficult task at best, and the only way this activity can make sense is by perceiving situations, not by attempting to absorb the data intellectually.

We can make a number of observations about the influence and change which the electric media has had on our lives, and it is important, before we move to other human inventions in the *oikumenē* to list the types of changes that we must consider when attempting to formulate our metaphysic. The first consideration is that we have made machines do our work and have made them perform functions that our bodies could already do, thus extending our bodies spatially and organically by our own inventions. With the introduction of electricity to power these machines and the invention of automation to guide the operation of machines, we have extended our own nervous system to the world of machines, in effect creating a wholly artificial universe of machinery patterned after ourselves. Our technology and industry is a complete model of our minds and bodies. We have created a world in our own image.

The second consideration is that in harnessing electricity to our machines, and particularly in inventing new forms of communication, we have created a situation in which the world comes to us as an organic unity, and it comes instantaneously, binding the various human societies into a tribal, or village, situation. The result of this instantaneous media-connected world is the destruction of our old patterns of interpreting data. We can no longer categorize, separate, and intellectualize about our experiences. We can simply perceive the larger picture that confronts us and attempt to come to grips with it. Thus we are speaking of perception as a means of gathering knowledge about the world. We can no longer derive concepts that will explain the world to us, for the world moves too fast. We must perceive situations in a total experience in order to make sense of our lives.

The third consideration we must make is that we seem to have two options.

We can begin to differentiate our larger mass society through the creation of smaller societies and cultic activities in which we explore the variety of human experiences. Or we can begin a process of liberal education in which information-gathering becomes our chief focus, relying upon individuals to absorb the world through perceptions, as a serious artist would, transcending the immediate situation by accumulating a type of wisdom that tribal societies have tended to produce. Either alternative can be effective without negating the other, and, in fact, the two solutions would appear to complement each other.

Insofar as our first venture into the *oikumenē* finds a structure comparable to what we discovered in the *kosmos,* we are well within the space-time transformation process that we suggested occupied the central position in the universe. We can now investigate the two alternative avenues of future development, the nature of human society and the nature of individual growth, conceived as a learning process, in order to see if there are any developments presently taking place that would support our analysis of the influence and effect of technology on our lives.

XI. Our Social Groupings

Carrying our investigation of the *oikumenē* into the area of human societies is a difficult task. Both Teilhard and Ardrey found our social organizations to be at least partially an expression of ancient vertebrate instincts shared, with some modifications, by most organisms in the universe. Even minerals, if we give Teilhard's description of them an alternative reading, quickly form associations comparable to our most rigid and conservative institutions. The territorial imperative articulated by Robert Ardrey can be understood as the basis of nationalism, private property, and the accumulation of wealth, reducing our most cherished values to a sophisticated form of vertebrate response to planetary existence.

Although instinctual behavior is an important aspect of social existence, it does not determine our social existence, and we can eliminate from discussion those social institutions that seem to derive from instinctual behavior. If they are indeed instinctual, while they may parade in social forms, they are not essential to the creation and maintenance of social institutions. They may be present in one form or another in the behavior of every living thing and thus form a body of information that remains relatively constant throughout any investigation of human behavior. We are looking for those types of social behavior that can be clearly identified as our creation—intuitions, apprehensions, and purposeful activities that we introduce into the world.

It may be impossible to consider our species apart from a complex social organization. In 6500 B.C., according to Robert Ardrey, the people of Jericho began constructing a new set of walls, surrounded by a ditch twenty-eight feet wide, eight feet deep, and carved out of solid limestone. The Jericho fortifications rival anything built in the Middle Ages, and construction on a scale this large would tax the economic resources of most small towns even today. The fortifications indicate two things: people were already highly organized to perform complex and specialized tasks, and they had already experienced concentrated and organized attacks against their community.

Two other facts emphasize the importance of these walls. These were the *third set* of walls built by the good citizens of Jericho. In 6500 B.C. the great world agricultural revolution was well under way. Agriculture is usually conceived to be the motivating factor in establishing permanent centers of human society. Yet these people had already established permanent homes a considerable time prior to this date. The Jericho discoveries cast a doubt on the role of agriculture in domesticating our species and require that we look for a different motivating factor when explaining the origin of social organizations among members of our species.[1]

Two contradictory processes seem to affect human societies. Erich Neumann (1905-1960), the Jungian psychoanalyst, stated that "primitive culture is characterized by a rigid isolation of separate groups, sometimes carried to such grotesque length that different tribes inhabiting the same island do not know one another and remain in a state of xenophobia that is prehistoric."[2] We are not certain what factors create this type of social behavior. In religious terms a great many societies have viewed themselves as the true representatives of humanity, or as the chosen people, thereby isolating themselves, at least in their beliefs, from other peoples. In nearly every society of which we have knowledge, the tendency toward isolationism can be found, and while it is generally associated with a conservative view of the world, it does not necessarily represent a reactionary attitude toward all of life.

Quite distinct from the orientation toward separateness is the process of differentiation. "In any domain," Teilhard wrote in *The Phenomenon of Man*, "whether it be the cells of a body, the members of a society or the elements of a spiritual synthesis—*union differentiates*. In every organised whole, the parts perfect themselves and fulfill themselves."[3] Unification of a group and the recognition that unity has been achieved (the product we must assume of the reflective process) seem to produce an erosion into newer forms of smaller structure but higher energy intensity. The individual members of a group appear to relish their identity and differentiate the larger whole into a series of smaller and different unities. Joachim Wach, speaking of the organization and reorganization of religious institutions, commented that as the population grows "what may be spontaneous in the smaller unit must be organized in the larger; instead of intimacy there may be impersonal relations, and individual initiative may be replaced by representative action."[4]

The dehumanizing aspect of larger organization may be sufficient to stifle individual expression and may serve to create disruptive tendencies that prove more attractive to individuals. It would almost seem that achieving relative homogeneity is a signal for differentiation to start. The phenomenon is not restricted to primitive societies or to societies in the process of adopting new technologies. Whenever human societies discover a way to create a unity, the elements creating that unity seem to emerge as centers for additional growth and unification under a new focus.

A case in point is our modern age. The electric media, as we have seen, have accelerated time and imploded space to present us with a global village homogenized by communications and bound together by an increasingly more efficient transportation system. As a result of this homogenization, Alvin Toffler detects "a new, more finely fragmented social order—a super-industrial order . . . emerging. It is based on many more diverse and short-lived components than any previous social system—and we have not yet learned how to link them together, how to integrate the whole."[5] The integration of the whole, in our modern world, is the coming planetary transformation of which Revel speaks, and the search for a unified understanding of human social existence, unless it takes into account the process of differentiation, will be transitory at best. Revel's initial fascination with American social change, in which he sees the creation of alternative life-styles as indicative of potential for growth and leadership, indicates a recognition of these growth and differentiation factors.

Not all social groups are participating in the present transformation in the same way that Western societies are. Marshall McLuhan comments that "backward countries that have experienced little permeation with our mechanical and specialist culture are much better able to confront and to understand electric technology. Not only have backward and nonindustrial cultures no specialist habits to overcome in their encounter with electromagnetism, but they have still much of their traditional oral culture that has the total, unified 'field' character of our new electromagnetism. Our old industrialized areas, having eroded their oral traditions automatically, are in the position of having to rediscover them in order to cope with the electric age."[6]

The oral tradition, having a unified field character, presents primitive societies with a total perception of the world, and this manner of confronting experience seems to be demanded of us in the future. If our future requires gathering knowledge in a total perception and if this characteristic is a feature of the ancient, primitive, and tribal societies, then our investigation of societies must concentrate on identifying how civilized groups, particularly Western countries, differentiated their view of the world from an original perception of totality into compartmentalized and specialized understandings that served to structure Western civilization as we know it today. In the process of discovering how Western countries transformed their understanding of the world, we fulfill, in a sense, Revel's suggestion that we make a critique of culture and civilization-as-sanction.

Societies are composed of generations of people. The activities of any selected group of individuals do not constitute a society unless they extend in space and time long enough to establish an identity. Thus history is the most important category for identifying a society because it provides sufficient evidence to understand the nature of the society. Arnold Toynbee (1889-1975), the world-renowned historian, made an important point in the understanding of history when he attached civilization to history. "It goes without saying that some civilizations go back to 'the dawn of history' because what we call history is the history of man in a 'civilized' society, but if by history we meant the whole period of man's life on Earth we should find that the period producing civilizations, far from being coeval with human history, covers only two per cent of it . . ."[7]

History, at least from a Western point of view, is the story of Western societies and their antecedents, an understanding that Toynbee suggests is similar to producing a book entitled *World Geography* that contained only maps of the Mediterranean Basin and Europe.[8] Johan Huizinga presented an understanding of history more to the point in distinguishing primitive from civilized societies. "The character of the civilization determines what history shall mean to it, and of what kind it shall be. If a civilization coincides with a people, a state, a tribe, its history will be correspondingly simple. If a general civilization is differentiated into distinct nations, and these again into groups, classes, parties, the corresponding differentiation in the historical form follows of itself."[9]

The simplest history is the oral tradition, for it incorporates only the experiences of a single people. As classes and parties emerge within the single history and as divergent points of view arise, we get the complicated histories that are familiar to Western peoples. And we get a corresponding change from remembrance of events past to a variety of interpretations of remembrances of things past. We therefore look for the manner in which societies interpret their experiences in the world, and this area of interest is generally a combination of religious understandings and orientations, historical interpretations, and philosophical systems of explanation.

Gregory Bateson, seeking a basis for understanding human efforts to understand the world, writes that "anthropologically, it would seem from what we know of the early material, that man in society took clues from the natural world around him and applied those clues in a sort of metaphoric way to the society in which he lived. That is, he identified with or empathized with the natural world around him and took that empathy as a guide for his own social organization and his own theories of his own psychology."[10] Our initial effort to understand the world and our society is structuring that society along lines suggested by the observation of natural events and entities. Considering the instinctual drives for territory and dominance as natural tendencies, we can see that it was a relatively simple procedure for early societies to extend the analogies with nature to include and explain human organizations.

We could rest content with this explanation were it not for the fact that societies, particularly in the Western tradition, easily transcend simple analogies with natural process and derive extended and complicated structures of organization. Claude Levi-Strauss may explain behavior when he writes that "men's conception of the relations between nature and culture is a function of modifications of their own social relations."[11] We apparently derive a model for social organization from nature, process and reflect on that model as an explanation of our social experiences, and then explain our relationship with the rest of nature as a function of, and perhaps as an analogy with, our own social system. Our models are derived from nature, given an interpretation that seems to introduce a sense of purpose, and then used to explain nature.

This process of transformation is not unique to primitive societies but may be considered a function of humans in their social condition. Alvin Toffler contends that "we all learn from our environment, scanning it constantly—though perhaps unconsciously—for models to emulate. These models are not only other people. They are, increasingly, machines. By their presence, we are subtly conditioned to think along certain lines. It has been observed for example, that the clock came along before the Newtonian image of the world as a great clock-like mechanism, a philosophical notion that has had the utmost impact on man's intellectual development."[12] We invented the clock in an effort to bring order into our experiences, and the clock gave us an empirical indication of the uniform passage of time. Time became a uniform process for us in a conceptual sense, and history became a reality. Time was not experience of uniformity on a personal level but on a social level; we regulated ourselves in a uniform manner, creating history. Then we used the analogy of a clock to prove the presence of an absolute time within the universe, which was conceived to operate in the absolute manner we had been taught to expect.

Either in the original perception of natural processes or in the differentiation of social groups we must discover the procedure by which Western civilized societies became complicated through the separation of functions into specialties. Joachim Wach, writing in *The Comparative Study of Religions,* described a process of differentiation in religious experiences that may give us a clue. "Where the family or the tribe or the people functions as a cult-group, the natural and the religious orders are identical," he writes. "If the pattern of religious organization is altogether independent of the natural, the organization can be kept at a minimum or developed maximally. In this case the structure of the religious group will at no point coincide with other orders such as the social, economic, or political."[13]

Conceiving the original order as one modeled after the processes of nature, we discover that the society maintains a total-field view of reality insofar as all orders remain identical. When any phase of our existence starts to separate, the logic of distinctions provides material for the differentiation, and the world view of the society shatters, creating specialists, separate disciplines, and the other accoutrements of civilized life. We can trace the differentiation process in religious terms fairly easily if we follow the theological explanations given of primitive conceptions of religion. Perhaps tracing the religious differentiation will provide a sufficient pattern of interpretation to enable us to see how other orders of society become separated from the original wholistic view shared by members of a social group.

Gerardus van der Leeuw (1890–1950), a German Protestant theologian who taught religion, theology, and Egyptian philology, said that "primitive men do not have the ability to think at one time about God and at another time about the world. The most insignificant 'secular' occasion has a religious meaning; and religious activities are exceedingly practical in nature." Societies begin with a unified perception of reality in which religious understandings seem to best characterize their point of view. There is no distinction between sacred and secular; everything is permeated by a central vision of meaning, and life is not divided into categories. But, van der Leeuw explained, "Later thought, in the form of theology and philosophy, tries to eliminate intuitive apprehension and to replace it by conceptual ideas, and so to replace dependence on the emotions by thought as dispassionate and unprejudiced as possible."[14]

Squeezing emotion and intuition out of perceptions of reality is to reduce reality to a particular structure and make it a mechanical process with an aura of inevitability. It may be a proper intellectual analysis of what was experienced, but it suffers in translation because intuition and emotion are properly part of the experience, and without them we discuss structure, not content. Looking at history as an example of what happens to the original experience or intuition of natural processes, we find that history itself arises with the elimination of the human elements of experience. Leon Brunschvicg says that "in the guise in which history first appears to the philosopher there is nothing properly historical about itself: *Primitive people, like children, retain in their memory what has taken place before their eyes far less than what has been transmitted to their ears.*"[15] The oral tradition, therefore, contains a more precise rendering of experience than the reconsidered and reprocessed theologies, philosophies, and histories from which the emotions and intuitions have been eliminated.

Reflective processing of data alone does not distort the original perception by eliminating the human emotional elements. Sometimes the functioning of social orders creates the necessary transforming mechanism. Ernst Cassirer suggested that the division of labor was as important in religious development as any theological speculations or formulations. "Long before the appearance of the personal gods we meet with those gods that have been called functional gods. They are not as yet the personal gods of Greek religion, the Olympian gods of Homer. On the other hand they no longer have the vagueness of the primitive mythical conceptions. They are concrete beings; but they are concrete in their actions, not in their personal appearance or existence."[16]

We can verify the consistency of our analyses by referring to the previous chapter and Marshall McLuhan's contention that in the attitude of primitive man labor was not experienced as "work." The integration of vocational activities into a total expression of the individual will return us to the same condition as primitive peoples faced in understanding their experiences. Thus if the differentiation of life into functional labor specialities is an indication of the separation of the world view of a society from its original apprehension, restoration of the labor of individuals to a totality indicates the corresponding need to once again glimpse reality as a unity. Between these two poles of expression we must discover the structure of societies and the meaning they give to their members.

Instead of the social isolation that we find in primitive societies, the phenomenon of the more complex and civilized society is to produce individual isolation. Erich Neumann describes the growing sense of isolation that individuals feel in the more abstract social organizations that derive their structure from the reprocessed understanding of the original model. "Now, while the clan, tribe or village is as a rule a homogeneous group descended from a common origin, the city, office, or factory is a mass unit. The growth of these mass units at the cost of the group unit only intensifies the process of alienation from the unconscious. All emotional participations are broken down and personalized; . . . As has long been observed, in the place of a group or a people there now appears a mass unit like the State, a purely nominal structure which, *in the manner of a concept,* comprises a variety of different things, but does not represent an idea that springs as a central image from a homogeneous group."[17]

Our analysis seems to hold together. In place of the tribe or smaller primitive group we have the state, but the state is a wholly artificial means of organizing human beings. It is, in Neumann's words, "in the manner of a concept," that is, it is the structure of reality as perceived by human beings with the original intuition and emotions eliminated by objective thought "as dispassionate and unprejudiced as possible." Replacing a society that corresponds to natural processes with a society that corresponds to an objective knowledge of the manner in which natural processes mechanically operate produces the civilized state that we see in Western countries and produces the phenomenon of individual trauma characteristic of these countries.

Carl Jung felt that this substitution transforms the normal apprehension of human sensitivities. "Instead of the concrete individual, you have the names of organizations and, at the highest point, the abstract idea of the State as the principle of political reality. The moral responsibility of the individual is then inevitably replaced by the policy of the State (*raison d'état*). Instead of moral and mental differentiation of the individual, you have public welfare and the raising of the living standard. The goal and meaning of individual life (which is the only *real* life) no longer lie in individual development but in the policy of the state."[18] We can now postulate why differentiation becomes so important a process in the life of a society. The abstract patterns of behavior, which a society uses to control its members, become destructive of individuals, for they channel experiences into preconceived categories of interpretation. The purpose of social organization, being the fulfillment of the individual and not the replacement of him or her, is reversed to accommodate the inverted pattern of understanding.

Emotion and intuition are replaced by objective observation and reason. The moral sensitivities of the individual are reduced to codes of behavior, and when experience and knowledge fail to coincide, the process of differentiation begins.

The rationale for separating the various social orders is generally explained as an effort to understand the functioning of the world, and our motivation in attempting to understand this process is the creation of a proper society in which all individuals find adequate expression of themselves. Thus, fairly early in the history of civilized states, philosophers and theologians described the utopian society designed to accommodate all good human experiences and to eliminate all evils. Hans Meyerhoff (1914–1965), social philosopher who taught at U.C.L.A., in an essay entitled "Freud and the Ambiguity of Culture" in *Psychoanalysis and History,* traces the disintegration of utopian ideas:

> All human and cultural reality is under the governance of time. Utopias, being "timeless" constructions, cannot incorporate this temporal dimension into their own systems. Worse: they cannot establish a meaningful connection between their own system beyond time and the social reality in time. They cannot and do not answer the fatal question: What difference will the passage of time make to the realization of the utopian ideal?[19]

Abstracting the structure of human experience from its context of emotion and intuition and articulating a religion, philosophy, or history that purports to explain the nature of things is in reality the removal of spatial structures from a space-time organic unity. These utopian descriptions of reality and society eliminate the temporal dimension and advocate a timeless society in which the functioning of individual members is conceived as a mechanical process. Efforts to structure political, religious, and educational systems on the basis of ideal organizations simply reproduce the nonhuman elements that can be derived from an analysis of experience. These systems suffer the corrosive effects of human and temporal demands for freedom.

More often in human history, utopias have been partially reproduced in societies by powerful forces seeking to create for their people a heaven on earth. We see this inclination in the Communist governments of today and, in somewhat different forms, in the expanding social programs that Western democracies have developed. The impact is hardly what theoreticians expected, however, because utopian ideals give way to practical, political considerations. In these social welfare schemes, according to Carl Jung, "the individual is increasingly deprived of the moral decision as to how he should live his own life, and instead is ruled, fed, clothed, and educated as a social unit, accommodated in the appropriate housing unit, and amused in accordance with the standards that give pleasure and satisfaction to the masses."[20]

These results describe perfectly the conditions of Western democracies today. But Jung felt that the effect of social welfare programs organized by the state have even more serious effects. "The rulers, in their turn, are just as much social units as the ruled, and are distinguished only by the fact that they are specialized mouthpieces of the State doctrine. They do not need to be personalities capable of judgment, but thoroughgoing specialists who are unusable outside their line of business. State policy decides what shall be taught and studied."[21] The ultimate result, therefore, of abstracting the world view of a society and reproducing the principles discerned as an objective knowledge about the world is the creation of a social machine that eventually runs amok, destroying the individual members of a society and the society itself.

Gregory Bateson warned that when an organism attempts to adjust the environment to suit itself it eventually destroys the environment and itself. The alternative to homogenization of societies and their operation according to abstract principles would appear to be a return to the old tradition that smaller groups once treasured. We already see some effort to reclaim ethnic and racial heritage in the social movements within Western societies. Jean-François Revel, recognizing this process already operating in many countries, says:

> I have no intention of denying the right of a people to cultural originality, or their right to a diversity of cultures and life styles. But I must say that the practice of denouncing the uniformity of technical civilization in the name of traditional cultures, or of life styles inherited from ancient systems of production and social organization, seems to me to be erroneous. Uniformity will not be conjured away by evoking the past, but by the growth of individual creativity which has become possible with the advent of technical civilization and of liberal societies—regardless of the opinions of the detractors of the latter.[22]

Revel's solution, individual creativity, restores our conception of society to the original thesis of Teilhard, that a society must both differentiate itself and fulfill and perfect the members. But Carl Jung seems to have spoken more directly to the specific need of all societies on the planet. "Modern man has lost all the metaphysical certainties of his medieval brother," Jung wrote in his famous essay "The Spiritual Problem of Modern Man," "and set up in their place the ideals of material security, general welfare, and humanitarianism."[23] If this humanitarianism seems not to be working, our alternative to continued confusion would seem to be the re-creation of metaphysical certainties, thereby providing for our time a sense of identity and personal fulfillment that replaces and transcends utopian ideologies and practices.

XII. Our Transforming Institutions

We have seen how the acceleration of modern life, caused in part by electricity and in part by automation, has made the planet a global village and presented us with future shock on a scale unimaginable to previous generations. Our analysis of the nature of societies appeared pessimistic because it understood the generation of theology, philosophy, political science, and other fields of thought as a process of abstracting from our experiences all patterns and structures, eliminating the emotional and intuitional dimensions, which make human life possible and comprehensible.

The temptation of many people, upon hearing such things, is to pretend that such insights are applicable to a select few within Western societies, or that such discussions take a deliberately destructive view of culture and civilization. The traditional response to such discussions is the redoubling of efforts to make institutions work and the determination to reinforce beliefs that are already outmoded. Many people in Western societies truly believe that we can avoid the worst impact of future shock and preserve the free institutions and individual freedoms for the next generation by more intensive participation in such institutions and by advocating more human goals for societies.

Too few people understand that radical transformations have been occurring in the American politico-economic system with such magnitude that any shift in emphasis is now impossible without widespread economic disaster and political upheaval of unsuspected dimensions. The conditions that Carl Jung and Erich Neumann describe, wherein modern societies replace the moral dimension of individual life with the policy of the state, have already become entrenched in our society. Even if we exclude the impact of the electric media from consideration, we must still examine the social institutions that control and direct mass society. It may be that even without the electric media we have already passed beyond the point of no return in an institutional sense and are ready for total social collapse.

If we can restrict our investigation to the social and political institutions of the United States as representing part of the *oikumenē* that is highly developed and therefore in an advanced stage of growth and maturity, we may find the type of radical change that Revel would require. We may also use this investigation to check the assertions of Jung and Neumann that large and complex societies, motivated by humanitarian concerns and directed toward social welfare, result in the moral destruction of individuals and eventually the destruction of society itself.

Charles Reich is famous for his bestselling book *The Greening of America (1970)*, in which he comforted the weary youth of the antiwar movement with the thought that they could have the best of both worlds—the revolutionary thrills of rapid change and the economic security of corporate life. The thesis of this book was that American society was undergoing a quiet, nonviolent, evolutionary, and inevitable revolution and transformation because it was incorporating thousands of idealistic and enthusiastic young people into its institutions. These young people were supposed to have such a radical and humanizing viewpoint that in virtually no time they would reconstitute the corporate monsters into benign institutions, and benevolent social goodness would pour down upon our society like the waters of righteousness.

Reich was hardly a counterrevolutionary thinker in *The Greening of America*. He appeared to seek only a resolution of the bitter feelings the war had bred between generations. His book was not his best analysis of American society but an effort to provide a context in which healing could take place. It is enlightening, therefore, to realize that his other writings have emphasized the radical changes in American society, particularly in the field of law, that seem to be revolutionary and immediately frightening.

In 1964 Charles Reich published an article in the *Yale Law Journal* entitled "The New Property," which examined the proposition that the source of wealth in American society had imperceptibly shifted from private property to government largess. This transformation, Reich declared, was profoundly influencing the manner in which the average citizen was conducting his life. To Reich it looked suspiciously as if the old feudal system against which the farmers at Lexington had rebelled, was reasserting its influence.

From the earliest days of the republic, it had been readily apparent, to anyone who considered the matter carefully, that the government was partially responsible for generating wealth and income. The purchaser of land from the Indians, the federal government, had then turned to its citizens and offered them lands at minimum prices, eventually offering 160 acres free if a family would merely establish a home on it and declare an intention to farm it. Railroad companies, while constructing roadbeds, had been the beneficiaries of enormous grants of land from the federal and state governments, and the sale of these lands provided a substantial income for the transportation corporations for decades after the construction of the railroad tracks. Few industries had not sought the protection of government in developing a capability to compete in world markets through a variety of tariffs that restricted trade in favor of their products. Thus to assert, as Reich did in 1964, that government activity was changing American society irreversibly did not seem revolutionary or even noteworthy at the time.

"The valuables dispensed by government take many forms," Reich wrote, "but they all share one characteristic. They are steadily taking the place of traditional forms of wealth—forms which are held as private property."[1] Reich went on to list the many forms of government activity that tended to produce income and generate private wealth. The most obvious were Social Security, Aid to Dependent Children, unemployment insurance, veterans' benefits, pensions, and other forms of welfare. The employment of large numbers of people by state and federal agencies was also cited by Reich as a major source of income and wealth-generation.

Reich maintained that occupational licenses are one major source of government largess because of the unique manner in which they are regulated. One cannot be a doctor, lawyer, pharmacist, electrician, or practice any of hundreds of occupations and professions without a license obtained from a state agency. Qualifications for these professions and occupations are often not a matter of competence but rather a set of qualifications according to certain preconceived standards of behavior. Yet, Reich points out, with a certified profession or occupation, immense economic status is generated and bestowed, along with state recognition. "A profession or a job is frequently far more valuable than a house or bank account," Reich commented, "for a new house can be bought, and a new bank account created, once a profession or a job is secure."[2] Reich might have added that the official declaration of bankruptcy is an excellent recommendation for credit. It is interpreted by lenders as eligibility for loans. A person can declare bankruptcy only once in a stated period of time. Loans made following the completion of an individual's bankruptcy can be secured against any default for a stated period. A bankruptcy thus generates income in the form of credit where a person might not be able to secure loans for dubious purposes.

On the corporate and company level of economic activity, the franchise, the contract, and the subsidy replace individual forms of government largess. An exclusive franchise, such as a license to operate a radio or television station, is extremely valuable because it guarantees a field of economic enterprise virtually devoid of competition, thus enabling a company to dominate the price and profit structure completely. The telephone company is the best example.

Similarly, contracts to perform certain services for government agencies are lucrative: Massive government funding is obtained through contracts dominating defense-related industries. Corporations engaged to perform defense work under government contract generally have special conditions by which they receive the cost of performing the services plus a percentage of the contract price as profit. Since the beginning of the Second World War, private industries have become almost totally dependent on some form of defense or government-related contract work to remain in business. This continuing relationship has expanded the role of government in the free enterprise system beyond all reasonable expectations.

In the human services field, nonprofit organizations and educational institutions have evolved their own form of contracts in the fields of educational services, research, and social services. They are usually paid, or receive, the cost of the program plus an institutional or organizational overhead fee, which in some cases can run as high as 40 percent of the total contract price. These contracts, accumulated from many federal agencies by universities in the course of a year, can amount to substantial sums. In 1974 the top ten universities, figured on the basis of moneys received, looked like this:

(1)	University of Washington	$81.89 million
(2)	U.C.L.A.	73.68 million
(3)	University of Wisconsin	73.6 million
(4)	Harvard	72.5 million
(5)	Univ. of Calif. (San Diego)	71.1 million
(6)	M.I.T.	69.5 million
(7)	University of Minnesota	68.06 million
(8)	Howard University	67.02 million
(9)	Stanford University	66.78 million
(10)	University of Michigan	63.87 million[3]

Educational institutions today are viewing the federal government as the source of supplemental income, and programs are beginning to reflect this concern. Professors are often hired on the basis of their ability to bring government research funds to the university, not their ability to teach. Of all our social institutions, schools and colleges have been most radically changed by the availability of government funds.

For example, during the Second World War the federal government built a number of military posts in previously isolated rural areas in several states. The distribution of population in the United States was radically altered by relocating war industries and federal activities for various strategic reasons. People moved to the centers of federal activity to seek jobs, and overnight small towns became cities.

In 1941 Congress, aware of the inconvenience that war industries were causing local governments, passed the Lanham Act, which was designed to provide federal assistance to those areas experiencing a tremendous influx of federally related workers. Local governments and school districts suffering a disproportionate pattern of growth were eligible for federal assistance in meeting their educational budgets. Some school districts became almost wholly dependent on federal funds.

In 1950, the 81st Congress, struggling with continued federal aid to local communities because of the Cold War's need to maintain a strong defense posture, passed two major pieces of legislation designed to assist school districts that were affected by federal activities. P.L. 81–815 provided funds for school construction, and P.L. 81–874 provided federal assistance to maintain and operate schools suffering from the impact of federally created population increases in their districts. In subsequent years these laws were amended several times, and with each amendment eligibility requirements were expanded to include, not simply war-related federal activities, but other normal activities.

By the time the Elementary and Secondary Education Act was passed in 1970, the justification for providing services and funds to school districts had changed from that of subsidizing local areas because of increased federal activity in their vicinities to a new policy that recognized "the special educational needs of children of low-income families and the impact that concentrations of low-income families have on the ability of local educational agencies to support adequate educational programs."[4] In a twenty-year process of expanding the subsidies granted to local educational agencies, nearly every school district in the country had figured out a way to obtain funds from the federal government. A school district without any federal funds was in danger of collapse.

Subsidies are another massive form of wealth that the government manages to infuse into the private sector. States offer tax incentive programs to corporations that will bring industries to depressed areas. Local governments often build plants and business parks to attract industries, and major-league sports cities are now providing massive subsidies to professional teams by constructing stadiums and arenas. The federal government subsidizes almost everything from farm products to shipbuilding, airlines, railroads, the post office, and the development, by private corporations and consortiums of corporations, of new technologies for the production of energy and other things regarded as essential to our nation's welfare. During the fierce debate over the funding of the SST, arguments about the economic effects of the program aired as vigorously as arguments regarding the need and desirability of the airplane. Many supporters regarded the SST as an economic cureall for the employment problems of the state of Washington rather than as an opportunity to maintain aeronautical leadership.

When the government intrudes into an economic area that has previously been isolated from governmental relationships, the separate parts of that area must all seek some form of subsidy in order to adjust to the change in conditions created by the government intervention. Reich describes a worker who is made unemployable by a new technology developed by government funding. Since his skills are no longer needed by industry, he must turn to the government, which supported the developments that made his skills obsolete. Through political pressure or other means the worker seeks a retraining program that will give him the necessary new skills to once again be gainfully employed. Training programs require additional educational experiences. Additional taxes are levied to pay for these services, and the company developing the new technology for the government needs an additional subsidy to pay its local taxes, which support at least partially the training program. And so it goes in a vicious cycle.

We thus never talk simply about government assistance to any particular industry or educational institution. The entrance of new income into an area, an industry, or a field of human activity calls for all groups affected to adjust to conditions none of them anticipated. Normal patterns of economic relationships that have evolved over a long period of time are almost instantly changed by the introduction of new wealth from government sources. Wealth not internally produced is disruptive and continues to be disruptive until all parts of a system establish some relationship with its source.

Receiving government largess has a peculiar effect on institutions that transcends the economic impact. "To some extent, at least, the holder of government largess is expected to act as the agent of 'the public interest' rather than solely in the service of his own self-interest,"[5] Reich argues. That is, the government establishes a formal relationship with institutions and corporations in giving funds that require the surrender of a great portion of the private identity of the recipient. Those institutions or corporations receiving government funds are perceived, at least in the eyes of the government employees who are responsible for approving the contract or subsidy and who monitor the expenditure of funds, as representing the government in their behavior and demeanor.

A recipient of government largess therefore immediately assumes an organic relationship with the state that involves certain new responsibilities. It is responsible for assisting in transmitting and promoting the government's image of itself, and it supports and expands the government's image of American society. The rationale lies deep in the nature of public financing. Awarding government funds is not simply a matter of law; it becomes a matter of determining from a large number of actual or potential applicants those who will receive the benefits. Thus even in the conception of eligibility, a natural winnowing process eliminates a certain class of potential recipients.

Legislatures, both state and federal, are notoriously lax in establishing guidelines for carrying out the provisions of the laws they pass. Most laws contain procedures that are largely discretionary with the agency designed to enforce them. No criteria exist in many areas for determining which entities in the private area shall receive the benefits. Who shall become eligible for a program thus becomes a matter of bureaucratic definition and, ultimately, in long-established bureaus, a matter of personal administrative whim. Large segments of the private sector can be included or excluded by simply manipulating definitions.

"One of the most significant regulatory by-products of government largess,"

Reich points out, "is power over the recipients' 'moral character.' "[6] He illustrates this point with examples: Some people have been deprived of Social Security benefits because of a past, distant connection with the Communist party; a lawyer unfortunately incorporated a phrase from the Declaration of Independence in his essay for the bar exam, thereby revealing an independent spirit that appeared subversive to the bar examiners; and people on welfare suffer continual harassment from social workers who suspect them of violating some vaguely defined moral standard established by the caseworker.

Reich quotes a judge deciding a welfare case in which the recipient was accused of living in unsanitary conditions: "One would admire his independence if he were not so dependent, but he has no right to defy the standards and conventions of civilized society while being supported at public expense."[7] The difference between this attitude toward a recipient of direct welfare subsidy and the attitude toward the holder of property is noteworthy. A holder of property has his property protected by law; the person receiving welfare payments is not considered to have a right protected by law but is the recipient of a privilege bestowed by the government, a gift, as it were, that he must demonstrate moral worth to receive. The moral dimension of government largess falls directly upon the recipient and in a larger sense becomes more the standard of eligibility than written criteria. Thus economics is increasingly severed from a property base in tangible physical assets and transferred to a vaguely defined pattern of behavior that demonstrates personal or corporate loyalty to the standards and conventions of "civilized society." Those standards and conventions are generally the ones shared and supported by government employees who administer the programs.

This general feeling that loyalty to the state must be the final criterion for qualification for government largess extends to the employment sector. Reich sees in the federal loyalty-security program the roots of changes in political and legal thinking that are at the base of this transformation of wealth from physical property to government largess. In the federal loyalty-security program "the 'gift' of a public job has been the justification for a process by which countless individuals have been 'tried' for 'offenses' which vary from conduct approaching treason to the most trivial departure from orthodoxy. These security trials, and the character investigations which are made for innumerable licenses and permits, attempt to search out every crevice and recess of an individual's life. The agencies try not an offense but the whole of a man, his strengths and weaknesses, his moments of honor and of temptation."[8]

Qualifications for federal employment reflect a view of the world that is less flexible than the criteria for becoming a member of a church. Surveillance over the personal beliefs and behaviors of an individual, and attempts to discern the person's probable understanding of reality and its social components, are efforts to ensure that a particular view of the world be perpetuated as a government function. The government in this sense resembles an organism that seeks to ensure its health by hunting down and eliminating or neutralizing possible cancers within itself. It no longer behaves as an impartial objective structure designed to express the wishes of the constituency but takes on the ominous task of determing personal values and reshaping beliefs.

Reich, it should be added, does not see this development as organic but, in political terms, as a restoration, albeit unconsciously, of the old forms of feudal society. He reviews some of the more difficult cases decided by the Supreme Court in the 1960s to illustrate this principle:

> The philosophy of *Flemming* v. *Nestor,* of *Barsky, In Re Anastaplo,* and *Cohen* v. *Hurley,* resembles the philosophy of feudal tenure. Wealth is not "owned" or "vested" in the holders. Instead, it is held conditionally, the conditions being ones which seek to ensure the fulfillment of obligations imposed by the state. Just as the feudal system linked lord and vassal through a system of mutual dependence, obligation, and loyalty, so government largess binds man to the state. And, it may be added, loyalty or fealty to the state is often one of the essential conditions of modern tenure. In many decisions taking away government largess for refusal to sign loyalty oaths, belonging to "subversive" organizations, or other similar grounds, there is more than a suggestion of the condition of fealty demanded in older times.[9]

The fundamental nature of this shift in emphasis can be understood best in relation to the initial political philosophy of our society. In reaction to the prevailing European, late eighteenth-century form of feudalism, most especially the arbitrary exercise of power by the king over individual freedoms, the founding fathers saw a need to limit the powers of government over the individual. In the Bill of Rights they established certain rights for citizens, including the freedoms of religion, speech, press, and assembly. More important than the Bill of Rights, however, was the vesting of private property in the individual through the requirement that government could not extinguish the individual's claim to property without just compensation. Any government confiscation of property was restricted to certain procedures described as the "due process of law," which meant the elimination of arbitrary or capricious actions. The government had to show a public interest in any confiscation of private property. Under the Constitution, it could not take property arbitrarily.

Property, according to Reich, drew a magic circle around the individual, and within this circle he was allowed almost unlimited discretion in using its assets and benefits. The property owner had economic independence insofar as he could bring within the protection of law certain forms of wealth-production, and the legal protection of these assets gave him economic independence from government restrictions. An economically independent individual could not be destroyed financially for taking a politically unpopular stance. In a very real way, then, private property guaranteed the individual freedoms of the Bill of Rights.

The first breach in this protective circle came with the acceptance of the legal status of the corporation as an individual. Corporations were theoretically formed from the contributions of individuals seeking through joint efforts to accomplish what each could not do alone. This legal fiction, the corporate individual, introduced one dimension of abstraction between an individual and his property. Instead of maintaining a direct relationship with individual wealth, a corporate stockholder surrendered control to a corporate manager. The individual thereafter could not always control or influence the manner in which his property was used. Individual preferences had to be modified to conform to larger goals, and the stockholders surrendered a portion of their personal freedom, accepting in return a part of the corporate morality as their own.

As long as corporate competition flourished in the private sector, property expressed a degree of independence from outside control. The business world was in effect individual competition written large. But when, through mergers, agreements, consortiums, and other ventures, corporations choked or eliminated competition, the private area became a cooperative organism exploiting society. The freedom to act economically became transformed into a power that could be exercised over the lives of people who were not a part of the cooperative venture. The individual citizen was trapped between the opposing forces of government and corporations, neither of which was particularly friendly. When these giant institutions, the corporate structure and the government, made peace with each other, embracing a mutually beneficial stance, both society at large and the workers employed by corporations suffered exploitation. Ultimately reforms were demanded, and the era of trustbusting, initiated by Theodore Roosevelt, made some superficial changes in the regulation of corporations.

Almost from the beginning of corporate existence in America in the early 1800s and escalating after passage of the Sherman Anti-Trust Act in 1890, the power structure of society—corporations, educational institutions, churches, and the government itself—launched a vigorous defense of the sanctity of private property. But, Reich comments, "The defense of private property was almost entirely a defense of its abuses—an attempt to defend not individual property but arbitrary private power over other human beings."[10] With the success of various reform movements, limitations were placed on the arbitrary exercise of powers. The scheme of regulatory agencies—licensing, granting of selected franchises, along with restrictions on the exercise of economic powers—came into being.

By the time of the Great Depression, conditions had deteriorated beyond the point of simple adjustment. The reforms of that era were designed, therefore, to place a minimum floor beneath human economic existence. Citizens received certain guarantees from the government that they would not be totally abandoned to their fate. The Social Security program characterized the political theory of the times. The role of the government was perceived differently by citizens. It was now seen as a last but always present resort for redress of economic misfortunes. Social programs came to express this governmental concern for the neglected areas of American society. This formally expressed concern, the human quality in government, created what Reich calls "the public interest" society.

With the change in atmosphere, the idea was born that if the government expressed by its actions a concern for its citizens, it might correspondingly expect loyalty in return. Thus emerged the philosophy that citizens receiving largess from the government had to be worthy of the gifts. Since loyalty had become the condition of the relationship, rather than economic or political rights, the gifts were understood as "privileges" rather than rights. Rights could be enforced in court; privileges could not.

Defining major areas of income as privileges and demanding loyalty as the condition for receiving income meant a fundamental reversal of the relationship between the citizen and the state. The state, in granting privileges in return for loyalty, was in fact purchasing individual freedoms because dissent from government policies, for whatever reasons, was regarded not as the exercise of the freedom of speech but disloyalty. The irony of this situation was that many programs were not voluntary. Citizens were forced to participate in them but received the benefits only by a demonstration of loyalty to the government. American democracy had substituted government largess for private property and in the process had severely restricted the exercise of individual freedoms that made citizenship important.

"There can be no retreat from the public interest state," Reich warned. "It is the inevitable outgrowth of an interdependent world. An effort to return to an earlier economic order would merely transfer power to giant private governments which would rule not in the public interest, but in their own interest."[11] The prophetic nature of Reich's warning, written in 1964, becomes clear: As President, Richard Nixon attempted just what Reich warned against, with the exact results predicted. Following the Watergate investigations, we learned how various corporations had traded financial support for political privileges, transforming the effort to restore independence to the private sector into a farce.

"As we move toward a welfare state, largess will be an ever more important form of wealth," Reich predicted. "And largess is a vital link in the relationship between the government and private sides of society. It is necessary, then, that largess begin to do the work of property."[12] Reich suggested that the distinction between property and largess be largely erased, a task easily accomplished by recognizing largess as a right and not a privilege. Such a transformation would involve acknowledging that the rights of a citizen extend beyond political participation or economic independence, that these rights also include food, shelter, health care, and education.

"Finally," Reich concluded, "it must be recognized that we are becoming a society based upon relationship and status—status deriving primarily from source of livelihood. Status is so closely linked to personality that destruction of one may well destroy the other. Status must therefore be surrounded with the kind of safeguards once reserved for personality."[13] If we conceive status and personality in nonlegal terms, viewing them instead as McLuhan and Toffler might see them, as extensions of ourselves in space and time, we would conclude that Reich advocates the recognition of status as a means of uniting the separated parts of the individual in a consistent theoretical framework.

What conclusions can we draw from Charles Reich's analysis of the changing nature of our institutions? We can identify the role of private property in protecting individual rights and trace how the transformation of income-producing sources destroys the basis of individual freedoms and expressions. The recognition of individual rights to economic security without the surrender of rights that guarantee the sanctity of personal philosophical expression would seem to be an immediate goal of our society. The transformation of privileges into rights, vesting the individual with basic physical necessities as a matter of law, would become a major transformation but one advocated and described by many utopian thinkers.

It is interesting to note the characteristics of the new society such changes would produce. The new society would have respect for the individual, irrespective of age or sex, because all citizens would be entitled to full economic participation. The new society would have an amazing degree of social and political integration because ownership of physical private property would no longer distinguish one class from another in the basic areas of human concern. The new society would advocate and support a concept of personal security that transcends all governmental forms and all group interests and conflicts because neither the status nor the personal expression of the individual's beliefs would be subject to loyalty tests.

Such a society sounds utopian indeed. By a curious coincidence, these three major characteristics are not the outstanding positive features of modern civilizations, but Paul Radin's estimation of the major strengths of aboriginal civilizations. There is a substantial lesson here. McLuhan and Toffler find the electric media retribalizing our society. Reich's proposals to make the privileges of economic security vested legal rights of citizens produce a type of society best exemplified in tribal or aboriginal societies. Our metaphysical search for an understanding of reality is beginning to focus on the tribal way of life. Our technology and our social institutions are themselves guiding us in this direction.

XIII. Expanding the Legal Universe

Aboriginal peoples modeled their societies after the natural processes of the universe. In their oral traditions they carried forward faithfully the original perceptions of reality by repeating exactly the incidents and experiences that had impressed them. Western societies developed a tendency to reprocess the original perceptions of the oral tradition and seek more abstract understandings. People believed that by eliminating the intuitive apprehensions and human emotions of the original experience they could discern the structure of ultimate reality from the parade of transitory incidents. Emotion and intuition came to be regarded as untrustworthy.

As Western societies became more committed to intellectual pursuits, various fields of knowledge emerged. Theology, philosophy, history, and other subjects became specialized ways of understanding the universe and its processes. The field of law became a unique subject in this transition from perceptions to conceptual knowledge because it dealt with two major topics. Law regulated the relationships that peoples and nations shared, but it also incorporated in rules and regulations the world view of societies. Insofar as natural objects were thought to have any ultimate value for our species, they were protected by law. But more often the systematic articulation of a society's law represented its view of reality apart from nature, its relationship to the *oikumenē*, not the *kosmos*.

The most prominent feature of the natural world that finds a place in human systems of law is property, and the most common form of property is land. Our relationship to land has been the subject of a variety of legal concepts, generally revolving around the rights of the owner to exploit the resources thereof. Since land forms the natural context within which communities exist, our attitude toward land forms an integral part of the *oikumenē,* and we should consider how we have viewed land legally.

Until corporate stocks and bonds became influential, land was the dominant form of private property in the United States, a chiefly agricultural country. This meant that political and legal concepts had a landed population as a reference point. Jeffersonian democracy assumed the existence of a self-reliant constituency that solved its practical problems through community consensus. Income from land or its uses dominates much of our present economic existence. Massive suburban developments, the creation of super-airports, and the use of giant tracts of land for recreational purposes are some evidences of the current use and value of land.

Developments of real estate have been notoriously ad hoc. Individual owners, protected by constitutional provisions, have generally been able to use their lands in whatever manner produced income, regardless of the eventual costs to society. We have as yet no consistent theory of law as to the proper stance toward the natural world. With the increasing demand for energy and our ability to strip-mine large areas, leaving thousands of acres in desolation, we will soon have to develop a consistent legal theory that channels our use of land into beneficial and intelligent patterns.

Placing a value on land has always been a major problem for the United States. The motivating force in Western development was human greed. Gold rushes followed by silver rushes followed by oil field developments created a crazy-quilt pattern of land-use laws. In mining camps, oil fields, and later in the development of desert lands for agricultural purposes local conceptions of land use and customs of the early settlers produced a unique body of law regarding the use of land and water. These legal concepts became doctrines over the course of years, and for the most part they have not been amended since their inception.

The most destructive theory of water law is called the Colorado doctrine. It grants the first user of water on a particular stream or river an absolute right to its use. At first glance this doctrine appears reasonable, and part of its appeal for western people was that it rewarded the early settler who had helped tame the wilderness rather than the latecomer who arrived on the scene when it was relatively safe. Theoretically those who took the greatest risk were granted the greatest reward. The water rights on any particular stream in states accepting the Colorado doctrine are thus an incredible hodgepodge of priorities established chronologically. The first priority right may be located far downstream and reflect an early ranching operation, while the second priority right may be at the headwaters, originating from early mining operations.

Since water can be used only in the sequence in which the rights are established, irrational situations can occur in the Colorado system. A farmer located upstream may watch his crops wither in the fields while the water flows past his farm on its way to a user with higher priority downstream. Or water can be transferred from one watercourse to another because the original use allowed a transfer of water to the place of use. The place of use, at the beginning, depended upon the nature of the activities in operation, and miners were not adverse to changing the course of a stream to provide water for a mining camp.

With this concept of water rights as property prevailing in the western states, primarily in the Rocky Mountain area, it was not long before subsidiary theories of water-use began to develop. Controversies arose over the nature of irrigation works. Sometimes the seepage of water from the earthen ditches of an irrigation system meant that more water was lost in its transmission to places of use than was actually used at the location to which it was being sent. The most notorious irrigation system in the west, the first construction project, incidentally, of the federal government, the Orr Ditch in Nevada, actually loses two thirds of its water in transmission from the foothills of the Sierra Nevadas to the desert area near Fallon, Nevada.

One of the most important subsidiary doctrines in water law allowed a water user who "recaptured" surplus, or wasted, water to claim its use. Depending on the circumstances involved, the person who saved water was generally awarded a new type of use-right that recognized his initiative in making constructive use of water that would otherwise have been lost to everyone. While there are different interpretations of the idea of recapturing water in each state that deals with water rights on a large scale, this method has generally been admitted as valid.

In 1966 an Arizona case dealt with the recapture of water. *Salt River Water Users' Association* v. *Kovacovich*[1] dealt with a number of fundamental questions. Could an owner of land use water-saving devices and, in effect, "create" new water through technical efficiency? Could he then apply the new water to additional land which he wished to place under irriagation? Could he do all of this without the permission of the State Water Code, which held ultimate responsibility for recognition and allocation of water rights? The state court ruled against the water user without commenting on the basic question of the right to introduce new technologies to create water that otherwise would have been lost to the irrigation system.

Viewed in the ordinary legal context, the *Salt River Water Users'* case involved a technical point of procedure, but its inherent theories illustrate a fundamental point with respect to the place of the natural world in a legal context. The point of departure for such an analysis sidesteps the legal question of human rights to ask about the legal status of the water itself.

Water is a life-giving element of the physical universe. We cannot live for an extended period of time without it. Neither can the plants, animals, birds, and other life-forms that always cluster around watercourses. Water, even in a desert area, supports more life than our species, and appropriating water from a stream or river assumes that humans will use a certain proportion of the flow of the water but that they will leave the stream relatively intact for use by the rest of the creatures.

The Colorado water doctrine, particularly the subsidiary idea of saving water by adopting more efficient methods of use, understands water only as a representation of property in the legal sense. It completely eliminates the intuitive sense of life and emotional content that makes water important as an element of universal life and reduces it to a quantifiable income-producing entity. If we carry the theory advocated in the *Salt River Water Users'* case to its logical conclusion as a legal right that can be enforced, in the future a large corporation could arrive in a desert valley and completely replace the river system by an interlocking network of pipes that would deliver water to each user having a water right, reserving all of the "created" or "recaptured" or "waste" water for its own use.

Theoretically at least, our present view of the natural world has no place for natural features and entities themselves. Physical entities that support life, such as air, water, and land, are conceived in a legal sense as if they had no existence apart from the human legal rights that have been attached to them. We could easily and legally destroy all vestiges of natural life without ever violating the constitutional provisions regarding the protection of property. Our present conception of property revolves around our use of it, not around its existence as an element of the universe in its own right. Nature has no rights of its own in our legal system. If our legal system reflects our view of reality, then we believe that we exist over and apart from the physical world.

That our courts have not yet reached that abstract but very logical conclusion is partially due to the conservation movement. Early in this century various public figures recognized that unless the government made an effort to preserve parts of our natural heritage it would soon be destroyed by uncontrolled exploitation of resources. Proponents of conservation have introduced into American social thinking the idea that natural resources have more than a commerical use. They have argued, for example, that natural resources can be appreciated for their recreational value; that recreation can be as valuable a resource as the profits derived from destructive economic exploitation.

This point of view has been verified in recent decades. As affluence has worked its way down the American social and economic structure, and particularly since the end of the Second World War, more and more Americans have spent their summer vacations in national parks and recreation areas. The number of visitors to the Grand Canyon, the Tetons, Yosemite, the Black Hills, and other prominent natural attractions has increased dramatically every year. The interest in recreational activities in a natural surrounding was not a profound philosophical or religious movement that recognized a value in natural entities themselves, but it did indicate that the aesthetic values of American society could be expressed as a function of nature as well as an appreciation of paintings, music, and other forms of art.

Spokespersons for groups interested in conservation of natural resources were unable to frame their arguments in terms that would expand the consciousness of American society to include the inherent dignity of nature. At best the conservation movement saw nature as a means of providing an emotional outlet for human frustrations. Yet in 1966 an important conservation figure, Aldo Leopold, wrote in *A Sand County Almanac,* "There is as yet no ethic dealing with man's relation to land and to the animals and plants which grow upon it," indicating that he was aware of the deeper issues represented in our relationship with nature. He added that land was still property in the minds of most Americans, and that entailed people taking privileges from the land but acknowledging no corresponding responsibility or obligation. "The extension of ethics to this third element in the human environment is, if I read the evidence correctly, an evolutionary possibility and an ecological necessity."[2] The contemporary interest in ecology seems to partially fulfill Leopold's prediction.

As the pressure for additional recreational areas increased, with longer vacations and the greater mobility of a large part of our population, abetted by the interstate highway program, Disney Enterprises proposed to build a gigantic complex in the Mineral King Valley of California. The project was estimated to cost $35 million and included motels, restaurants, and recreational facilities. The Sierra Club, one of the most aggressive conservation organizations, discovered the plans for development and brought suit for an injunction to prevent construction. The case was decided favorably in the federal district court in California, but it was overturned by the United States Court of Appeals for the Ninth Circuit in San Francisco on the grounds that the Sierra Club did not have sufficient "standing" to raise the question in a court of law.

Standing is a technical concept that has many legal and philosophical implications. Basically, it means that a thing—be it a corporation, a ship, or a person—can institute legal actions in a court of law on its own account. Standing appears to be a procedural definition in legal theory that recognizes the legal existence of an entity. The usual requirement for standing is not simply that an entity have legal rights, but that in an action for damages or for injunctive relief, it be in direct conflict with the entity or action which it must claim affects it and infringes upon its rights. Standing thus depends on the old logical sequence of cause and effect, and the relationship between the two entities is often described in spatial terms. A subject is said to have "remote" damages when the cause and effect chain is evident but not considered sufficiently important by the court.

The loss at the appeals court level meant that the Sierra Club had to take its case to the Supreme Court, and everyone knew that *Sierra Club* v. *Morton*[3] (Rogers C. B. Morton was the Secretary of the Interior who had to approve construction plans of the project) would become a landmark case in conservation law. Christopher Stone, a young law professor at the University of Southern California, saw the case as a perfect vehicle for advocating a new theory of standing for environmental issues, and he decided to write a law review article expounding his theory, hoping to influence the decision. His article "Should Trees Have Standing?" was published in the *Southern California Law Review*[4] prior to the announcement of the Supreme Court decision. Stone mustered all the legal theories and analogies in Anglo-Saxon law that could be brought to the defense of natural objects, and the article is now considered a classic articulation of the standing issue.

"The world of lawyers is peopled with inanimate right-holders," Stone wrote, citing the various forms of business entities that had received legal standing in previous decades of American legal history.[5] The corporation, the trust, and the joint venture were some examples Stone mentioned as fictional entities that enjoyed legal status. He proposed now to add to that list of fictional characters with legal existence nature itself, in the sense that a guardian could initiate a law suit on behalf of a natural object, in its own name. (Had Stone's thesis already been an accepted legal principle, the case would have been titled *Mineral King Valley* v. *Morton,* instead of *Sierra Club* v. *Morton.*)

Stone pointed out that many entities were once considered outside the law, including members of minority groups and women. These groups were either considered to be subhuman or to have such different temperaments and tendencies as to preclude them from exercising legal rights equal to those of white men. "Every era is inclined to suppose the rightlessness of its rightless 'things' to be a decree of nature, not a legal convention—an open social choice—acting in support of some status quo," Stone argued. "It is thus that we avoid coming face to face with all the moral, social, and economic dimensions of what we are doing."[6] Thus it was, Stone argued, that the metaphysical world view of a society determined which entities would have legal rights and which would not. Such a determination was considered an unalterable part of reality, not simply an ethnocentric understanding advocated and supported by one culture.

It is difficult for most people to recognize that their view of reality is a cultural belief and does not exist in nature itself. Philip Slater, in his brilliant work *Earthwalk,* illustrated the type of thinking that reduces things and people to a reality derived solely from social conventions:

> Thirty years ago, when middle-class blacks were almost invisible to the dominant culture, most whites experienced the sight of a black man in a suit and tie as something incongruous. They felt that blacks didn't belong in this kind of costume . . . By the time they overcame this racist reaction many blacks themselves began to feel that such constricting garb should be relegated to whites—that free black bodies belonged in free, expressive clothing. The third state in the process was that many whites—especially young ones—began to experience the armored pomposity of suits and ties as unfit for *any* lively human body. The liberal phase, in other words, may be a necessary transition, since the application of the principle of consistency to pockets of variation serves to highlight absurdities in the dominant culture which are normally invisible because we are so used to them. *We become sensitized to the discomfort of a familiar cultural pattern by applying it to those for whom it seems unfamiliar.*[7]

Stone's use of analogies was the more sophisticated in a legal sense because lawyers and judges had already recognized corporations and other artificial entities as having legal existence. The analogy was neither farfetched nor unexpected. But to average citizens who equated their society with natural law and reality, the example seemed subversive at best. They did not know that the fourteenth Amendment, which freed the slaves, had also been one of the major planks in corporate existence.

When the Supreme Court's decision was announced, the Sierra Club had lost the case but won a moral victory. Three justices viewed Stone's theory favorably, and the majority hinted broadly that they would like to see the case amended and brought back to them. Stone's article was published in the *Congressional Record* by Senator Philip Hart of Michigan, and ecologists around the country took heart at the ease with which the justices had received the new theory within the conceptual boundaries of the federal court system and the precepts of Anglo-Saxon law.

Yet, as Stone himself had previously pointed out, there was a glimmer of hope within the federal court system prior to the *Sierra Club* decision. Several years before in the *Scenic Hudson*[8] case, the Federal Power Commission had issued a license to Consolidated Edison to construct a hydroelectric plant on the Hudson River at Storm King Mountain, and a consortium of conservation groups, under the name of Scenic Hudson Preservation Conference, had opposed the project.

When the case was heard, the federal court made a curious and favorable ruling on Section 313(b) of the Federal Power Act. That section gave a right of review to any party "aggrieved by an order issued by the Commission." Traditionally the courts had interpreted the word *aggrieved* as a technical term meaning "economically damaged," but the federal court did not restrict its interpretation to that narrow view. Instead the court found that "aggrieved by" did not necessarily mean economic damages but could include "those who by their activities and conduct have exhibited a special interest" in the aesthetic, conservational, and recreational aspects of the project.[9]

Stone felt that one benefit of including the cost of damages to the environment itself in a lawsuit, which would have been the practical result of a natural entity bringing a suit in its own name, was that "every well-working legal-economic system should be so arranged as to confront each of us with the full costs that our activities are imposing on society."[10] The personification of nature, then, would give to the legal universe a tangent point with the world in which we live, providing, in the metaphysical sense, an organic unity that other theories of ecological concern lacked.

But Stone recognized that there were still many problems to be resolved before lawyers would seriously consider his guardianship proposal. If a natural entity could sue in its own right via a guardian, what would be the effect of winning a lawsuit? Traditionally, damages had been allocated among the parties in interest, and some lawsuits had been settled out of court by the parties themselves. But what would be the effect, even in an out-of-court settlement, of a natural entity, perhaps in cooperation with human plaintiffs, winning an award? Stone proposed that a trust fund be established by the court on behalf of the natural object. The guardian would administer the fund under the direction of the court with the funds used to replenish or repair the damages or possibly used to underwrite some holding activity until the proper technology could be developed to make the natural entity whole again.

Rights in themselves, Stone warned, were not absolute. "One's life, one's right to vote, one's property, can all be taken away. But those who would infringe on them must go through certain procedures before they can do so. These procedures, in turn, are a measure of what we value as a society."[11] Procedural problems, then, determined how entities would be considered. And in this sense the natural entity would be placed in the same position as a human receiving government largess who must remain in a state of suspension while administrative and judicial agencies decide whether he has rights or privileges. In a sense, vesting rights makes a final judgment on "what we value as a society," but it is the procedural apparatus that informs us how these rights in an absolute legal universe are actually viewed.

In addition to the procedural problems, granting standing to a natural object would involve recasting traditional legal concepts into broader perspectives. The burden of proving the nature of the damages and the extent of the injury would have to be determined. Would a natural object be expected to prove that it would be harmed by a certain type of construction, or would the corporation proposing to construct a dam or recreation complex be required to prove that its project would *not* injure the natural object? How would the type of injury be determined? Is the natural object a part of the public when courts are required to consider the "public interest," or is it still conceived as being in opposition to the public? These and many other questions arise when we begin to translate Stone's concept of standing into legal language.

The determination of evidence, which a court or administrative agency charged with issuing construction permits would consider, would depend almost wholly on the scientific knowledge of the people making the decision and how they conceived the world. Evidence regarding the life-support systems necessary to protect a river valley might be scientifically valid in the eyes of a sophisticated scholar but might be viewed as mental fantasy to a hard-headed judge who was unfamiliar with contemporary insights into ecosystems. Many people would consider it ridiculous to balance the interests of a school of tiny fish against the development of a housing facility designed to provide homes for thousands of people. Yet preserving that school of fish might ensure a healthy aquatic environment for a region in which thousands of people were already living. The problems in conception and articulation are immense but important.

Stone fully understood these problems and the necessity of making the proper distinctions. Thus he felt establishing rights for natural objects was a better course to follow than trying to extend the sympathetic doctrine of *Scenic*

Hudson, which gave standing to those groups traditionally associated with conservation causes. A shift in a judge's attitude toward conservation groups could easily change the interpretation of aggrievement from continuous interest and involvement to the traditional meaning of economic injury. Part of the reason that Stone wanted natural objects to have rights is that rights are recognized by the ordinary citizen if they are recognized in court. Their meaning is "vague, but forceful—in the ordinary language outside the courthouse walls, and the force of these meanings, crossing the boundary between ordinary and legal thought, becomes part of the context against which the legal language is interpreted."[12] Stone's concern, therefore, was not that lawyers understand the niceties of standing or rights, but that from the courthouse use of "rights," applied to natural objects, ordinary people might begin to accept the idea that nature has a right to existence in and of itself.

Remarking on the trend of recent federal legislation that gives a measure of protection to natural objects by requiring the filing of impact statements prior to authorization of construction, Stone says he "looks forward to the time when such behavior need not be 'established by law' because it has become deeply enough rooted in decency and custom."[13] Such behavior could only emerge in a society totally compatible with the natural world or having the wisdom to recognize that our species is a part of that world in an organic sense. Thus Stone believes that "a radical new conception of man's relationship to the rest of the nature would not only be a step towards solving the material planetary problems,"[14] it would make us better people.

The traditional separation of our species from the rest of the universe has been a figment of our imaginations and has evolved from our propensity to derive abstract knowledge from our experiences, eliminating our intuitive apprehensions and emotional growth as factors deserving consideration. That we can construct a legal system which views nature apart from its physical reality as elements of "property" testifies to the degree of alienation we have achieved. Our understanding of reality is incorporated in our legal concepts, and, as we have seen, these are already in the process of transformation, escaping from the sterility of the past to a more comprehensive understanding in the future.

Stone's thesis—broadening our legal concept of the world by giving rights to nature itself—issues in the conclusion that this new vision of the world would make us better people. In almost every aspect of the *oikumenē* we have investigated, we have reached the conclusion that the changes in motion today are pressing toward a new understanding and way of life for individuals. Our understanding of societies, of technology, of institutions, and of the place of nature in our legal system points to a radically new conception of individual life and seems to indicate that all transformation of larger social organizations and concepts will eventually focus on ourselves as individuals. Our final task, then, in discussing the *oikumenē* is to examine our traditional understanding of the individual.

XIV. The Charismatic Model

Many disciplines purport to explain human behavior and the unique aspects of human personality. Sciences that have arisen in the last century view human beings as another object for study, and the knowledge we might gain from them must properly be consigned to the *kosmos*. Theology and philosophy have been the major subject areas to deal with human individuals in the Western tradition, and of the two, theology must certainly take precedence in time and in capability, for philosophy originates from the secularization of religious insights.

Paul Tillich wrote that all types of religion give an answer to "the question of the intrinsic aim of existence—in Greek, the *telos* of all existing things." Therefore, he suggested, "it is *here* that one should start every interreligious discussion, and not with a comparison of the contrasting concepts of God or man or history or salvation."[1] Beginning an examination of the various religious traditions with a discussion of the answer they propose to this question would take more time and energy than we can allot. So we will attempt to devise a means by which we can narrow our discussion to those religious traditions that have most affected the manner in which Western people have understood the world of human affairs, leaving until the end of our inquiry any comparisons between religious traditions that might provide an alternative understanding of our topic.

Our search through the doctrines of religion will also be restricted. We will discuss primarily the doctrines, conceptions, and theories concerning the meaning of human life and the models that the respective religions offer as evidence of their validity. In this respect Joachim Wach dealt extensively with the history of religions in his book, *Types of Religious Experience*. He provides a point of departure, for he said that we "find a *concept* of man in religions whose origins are lost in a dim past, like the Egyptian, the Greek, the Hebrew, the Ancient Persian and Indian religions, and a *doctrine* of man in the religions of revelation like the Christian, Judaic, Mohammedan, Zoroastrian, Manichaen, Hindu and Buddhist."[2]

There is a substantial difference between a *concept* of man and a *doctrine* of man. If we can recall the analysis of Gerardus van der Leeuw regarding the origin of theology and philosophy, we will remember that theology and philosophy attempt to replace intuitive apprehension with conceptual ideas and to replace human emotions with dispassionate and unprejudiced thought. Wach's analysis of religion omits a third category—those religions that preserve the original perception of our place in the universe and carry it forward in oral traditions as part of their tribal or cultural heritage. Therefore, we can identify three basic types of religious attitudes toward the human individual: (1) a preservation of the original perception, (2) a development of the original perception into a concept of man, and (3) the further development of the concept of man into theological doctrines concerning the relationship of man to the deity and to the rest of the universe.

The first category can be put aside temporarily, for it represents the unprocessed apprehensions of reality that have been passed down in the non-Western oral traditions. We can easily determine their understanding of the human individual in the original context by reference to their myths and customs. The second category represents religions no longer functioning. Whether or not these religions had an impact on our present understanding of the human individual, and certainly in the case of the ancient Hebrew and Greek we can identify strong influences, the insights of these religions have long since been merged with still-living religious traditions, and we need not spend time on them.

We will be concerned with the third category, the living or so-called higher religions. Arnold Toynbee identifies seven: "There are three Buddhaic religions: the Hīnayāna Buddhism of Ceylon and South-East Asia; the Mahāyāna Buddhism of Eastern Asia, Tibet, and Mongolia; and the post-Buddhaic Hinduism of India. There are three Judaic religions: Judaism, Christianity, and Islam. And there is the Zoroastrianism of the Parsee diasporà in South-East Persia and Western India . . ."[3] These living religions can also be roughly grouped into two categories: the Indian and the Judaic. The laymen conceives the difference between these divisions to be immense, but Toynbee didn't see a radical dissimilarity. In fact, he wrote, "The difference between the Indian and the Judaic vision of Reality proves, on examination, to be, not a difference in view, but one of emphasis. In both visions, Reality reveals itself in two aspects, as a personal God and as a unitive state of spiritual Being . . ."[4]

In dividing the living religions into two traditions, we further simplify our task of discovering the religious understanding of the human individual. Since Christianity and Buddhism are the major religions in each division, we can choose these two traditions as representative of the doctrinal approach to our species and seek a means of comparing and contrasting the difference in emphasis that Toynbee felt represented each division. Paul Tillich gave an excellent comparison of the nature of Christianity and Buddhism when he wrote that "in the dialogue between Christianity and Buddhism two telos-formulas can be used: in Christianity the telos of every*one* and everything united in the Kingdom of God; in Buddhism the telos of every*thing* and everyone fulfilled in the Nirvana."[5]

If we place this comparison within the context of the *kosmos* and *oikumenē*, which we have been using as a tool of analysis, we could suggest that Christianity places primary emphasis on the *oikumenē* and is secondarily concerned with the *kosmos*. Buddhism would be concerned foremost with the *kosmos* and secondarily with the *oikumenē*. Such an interpretation is not out of line with claims made by both scholars and followers of the two religions. Ian Barbour, for example, writes that "in the biblical understanding, God acts primarily though not exclusively in the sphere of the personal; he can reveal himself more adequately through the lives of individuals and communities, and through the life of Christ, than through the order of nature."[6] And Joachim Wach, writing of Mahayana Buddhism, commented that "philosophically speaking, salvation is achieved by and in the realization ('transcendental wisdom') of the impermanence of the phenomenal world (voidness, *śūnyatā*) . . ."[7]

These two emphases represent, in rough manner, the two possible approaches to human religious experience, if we divide that experience into its logical components. But in making this division we discover that already the integrity of the experience is shattered and that the point of view, whichever alternative is chosen, shifts dramatically. The *telos* of each religion, Paul Tillich explained, is "based on a negative valuation of existence: the Kingdom of God stands against the kingdoms of this world, namely, the demonic power-structures which rule in history and personal life; Nirvana stands against the world of seeming reality as the true reality from which the individual things come and to which they are destined to return."[8]

An important lesson can be demonstrated in Tillich's estimation of the teachings of Christianity and Buddhism. When we choose to emphasize either the world of human affairs or the world of physical happenings as the point of view from which a religious tradition develops its understanding of reality, the subject content becomes conceived as a negative entity, and the religion attempts to resolve this difficulty by advocating a technique or procedure for overcoming the portion of the world it has chosen to confront. A much deeper problem arises in conjunction with the single emphasis, however: The neglected portion of experience is defined as a function of the other part that attracted attention.

Christianity discovers itself at odds with the physical world and attempts to resolve that difficulty by conceiving the end of the world as an event that creates a new heaven and earth immune from all the corruptibility they purport to discover in the present world. Although Buddhism regards the emergence and continuance of human self-consciousness as tragic, it develops a long tradition of political theory in an effort to come to grips with the world of human affairs.

Although Christianity and Buddhism took alternative emphases in understanding the world, one choosing human affairs and the other choosing nature, they shared amazing developmental parallels, indicating, perhaps, that once the religious experience is divided, even for purposes of understanding, into two complementary divisions, a certain logic of development takes control and the tradition moves according to certain patterns. "For example," Arnold Toynbee wrote, "Christianity and Buddhism were, each, expelled from its homeland by a rival younger religion which had derived its inspiration from the older religion that it was opposing and evicting. Christianity was expelled from South-West Asia by Islam; Buddhism was expelled from India by a post-Buddhaic Hinduism whose philosophy bears indelible marks of its Buddhist origins."[9] One might add that both Christianity and Buddhism originate from even older religions that seemed to possess broader understandings of the relationship between the world of human affairs and the physical world—Judaism and Hinduism respectively.

Both Christianity and Buddhism were founded by individuals who either conceived of themselves as God or were so conceived by their adherents shortly after their death. The divinity of Jesus is well-known and is an acceptable article of faith in Western societies deriving from the Christian tradition. Whether Jesus was so conceived by his immediate followers is a question for New Testament interpretation, but standing outside the Christian faith and viewing the matter in an objective sense, one is tempted to conclude that Jesus' divinity was a doctrine that evolved rather slowly during the first several centuries of Christian existence. As for the Buddha, according to Nathan Söderblum, he "claimed to be superior to the gods, who, like men, needed salvation from suffering."[10] But "gods" in the Asian sense were not comparable to the Western conception of deity in its absolute sense. In discussing how the Buddha came to be regarded by his followers, Söderblum comments:

> Who is more worthy of divine worship than he who sacrificed his own bliss for the salvation of the beings, men and gods and all living things? The divine worship of Mahayana was not limited to Sakyamuni, but has been gradually extended to innumerable Buddhas and candidates for the Buddha dignity.[11]

If we add to the Christian side of the ledger the worship of the saints who were, in a religious sense, imitations of Jesus, we find the phenomena close enough for both comparison and insight into the nature of religious development.

We have insufficient knowledge of the lives of both founders, but it appears that their original teachings were substantially changed in the centuries following their deaths. Disputes concerning the status of both Jesus and Sakyamuni the Buddha continued until a system of doctrines evolved describing the cosmic role each had played. Some five hundred years passed before doctrinal systems satisfactorily explaining the Christ and the Buddha could be erected. Such a period of development appears not to be unusual in the case of revealed and founded religions. Joachim Wach, writing in regard to the original religious experience of different founders of religions, said:

> When Mohammed received his initial revelation, when the Buddha awoke to the realization of the impermanence of the phenomenal world, when Laotse became aware of the nature of the unalterable Tao, this original intuition (*'Ur-intuition'*) in each case implied an apprehension of ultimate reality, of the relation of the visible to the invisible, of the nature of the universe and of man's nature and destiny which invited further conceptual articulation.[12]

In the founded religions, therefore, we have an original intuition implying or directly describing an apprehension of reality, which, after reprocessing by the followers of the religion, forms the basis for theological speculations and disputes. "The theological and philosophical concepts in the religions of revelation," Wach noted, "are interpretive; they develop the theological, cosmological and anthropological implications of the founder's message by applying methods and categories evolved in earlier thought."[13]

If we return to Gerardus van der Leeuw's comment that "later thought, in the form of theology and philosophy, tries to eliminate intuitive apprehension and to replace it by conceptual ideas, and so to replace dependence on the emotions by thought as dispassionate and unprejudiced as possible,"[14] as an accurate description of the relationship of theological concepts and doctrines to the original intuitive apprehension of the founder of the revealed religion, we can conclude that the world religions have done their best to eliminate the religious experience of their founder from consideration or from realization by followers of the religion.

Two examples, one from the Buddhist tradition and the other from the Christian tradition, will indicate that elimination of the founder's perception of religious reality is probably the rule rather than the exception. Nathan Söderblum quotes Stcherbatsky in *The Living God* concerning the transformation of the Buddha's teaching by his disciples:

> The picture of the universe which suggested itself to the mental eye of the Buddha, represented thus an infinite number of separate evanescent entities in a state of beginningless commotion, but gradually steering to Quiescence and to an absolute annihilation of all life, when all its elements have been, one after another, brought to a standstill. This ideal received a multitude of designations among whom the name of Nirvana was the most appropriate to express annihilation. . . . In the Buddhist community itself it provoked opposition which grew ever stronger and resulted, 500

years after the death of the Master, in what may be called a quite new religion, reposing on a quite different philosophic foundation.[15]

The Christian transformation involved determining the trinitarian formula, which was a subject of controversy during the early centuries of the religion. Hermann Bauke (1886–1928), German Protestant theologican and pastor, in an essay entitled "The History of Christological Doctrine" in *Twentieth Century Theology in the Making,* wrote that "it seems probable that in the year 318 *Arius* was denounced in Alexandria for heretical pronouncements about Christ, by the Bishop Alexander, who subsequently excommunicated him in 320/321. The doctrine of Arius which was objected to was that God alone existed, uncreated and unbegotten, in perfect unity, whereas the Logos did not form part of his true being, but was the first creation of God in time; this was naturally even more true of the man Jesus Christ, who later in the course of history became united with the Logos."[16]

The trinitarian-formula controversy, therefore, did not concern itself with the teachings of Jesus but with the speculations made by theologians concerning the logical explanation of the relationship of the persons of the godhead. The controversy raged for several decades, with the different parties of the Christian religion winning and losing theological skirmishes, until the peace of the Roman Empire was totally disrupted and the emperor became distressed that the controversy would split the empire. Then, according to Hermann Bauke, the emperor:

> . . . tried to deal with the matter by sending one of his court bishops, Hosius of Cordova, to Alexandria (324). But when this was not successful, the matter was brought before the first General Council at *Nicea* in 325. Under the pressure of the Emperor, who was present himself, and probably above all as a result of the political skill of Hosius, who belonged to the West, and here succeeded in carrying through a dogmatic decision of the West for the first time, the Council established the view of Alexander as dogmatically correct, and condemned Arius, although this result by no means accorded with the view of the majority of Eastern bishops at the Council.[17]

Rather than a divine revelation of the nature of reality, the trinitarian formula came about as a political ploy of an emperor distressed that the bickering of theologians would destroy his fragile empire. The trinitarian formula hardly qualified under Gerardus van der Leeuw's characterization of theology as the replacement of intuitive apprehension by "thought as dispassionate and unprejudiced as possible."[18]

Regardless of the manner in which the doctrines of the two religions came to final formulation, both religions share a common insight into the nature of human existence. "The Prophetic Vision that has made its epiphany in the higher religions—pre-eminently, perhaps, in Christianity and in the Mahayana—consists, if we are right," Arnold Toynbee wrote, "of two intuitions. The first of these is that Suffering is something to be accepted as the price of acting on the promptings of Love, and indeed to be embraced as an opportunity for thus following Love's lead. The second intuition is that this attitude towards Sufferings is practicable."[19]

This twofold conclusion is not remarkable when we consider Paul Tillich's contention that both religions originally conceived the world, whether the world of human affairs or the world of nature, as a negative entity to be overcome. Defining the part of human experience one wishes to understand as negative, realizing that it totally overwhelms the individual on every level, and concluding that through Suffering one can pay the price of acting, and that Suffering is practicable, is not a major achievement. It is the logical conclusion that one would expect to reach, the alternative being self-destruction. The insights and intuitions with which we credit both Christianity and Buddhism are, therefore, not innovative nor do they make for a compatible life in a physical world in which the human species dominates other life-forms. The conclusion that Suffering is redemptive can only come from an originally pessimistic view of reality.

These two religions make the mistake of which Gregory Bateson accuses the evolutionists: "The unit which was believed to be crucial and around which the theory was set up was not with either the breeding individual or the family line or the subspecies or some similar homogeneous set of conspecifics."[20] In other words, the intitial point of analysis is wrong. Christianity and Buddhism focus on the individual primarily and secondarily on either the society, in the case of Christianity, or the natural world, in the case of Buddhism, and attempt to explain the reality of existence using only those reference points. The two religions attempt to resolve only one basic question—the ultimate identity of the individual in a cosmic sense—without recognizing that the solitary individual is an abstraction and that a group of solitary individuals—even millions of them— is not necessarily a society.

We can summarize the emphases of the two religions using a contrasting set of aphorisms. For the Christian, one is born again, never to die. For the Buddhist, one dies once, never to be reborn. In either case we appear to have solved the question of meaning for the individual, but in fact we have presented the individual with an understanding of the world that requires its rejection upon acceptance of the teachings. We negate the individual and foreclose an understanding of the world and the place of the human species in it.

It now becomes possible to understand why the followers of each man conceived and experienced him as a divinity. Both Jesus and Sakyamuni began explorations of the world as religious quests, and they chose complementary paths. Each followed the logic of his choice to its ultimate conclusion, thereby incarnating, insofar as possible, the logical elements of the world—*had the world been primarily as each conceived it.* The Buddha, realizing the ultimate nature of reality, if reality is conceived as he conceived it, demonstrated a compassionate inconsistency in refusing to enter Nirvana before he proclaimed the saving truth to all creatures. Jesus, realizing the ultimate nature of reality, if reality is to be conceived as he did, after a ministry of preaching and teaching, as Albert Schweitzer described it:

> . . . lays hold of the wheel of the world to set it moving on that last revolution which is to bring all ordinary history to a close. It refuses to turn, and He throws Himself upon it. Then it does turn; and crushes Him. Instead of bringing in the eschatological conditions, He has destroyed them. The wheel rolls onward, and the mangled body of the one immeasurably great Man, who was strong enough to think of Himself as the spiritual ruler of mankind and to bend history to His purpose, is hanging upon it still.[21]

The two founders therefore become not simply divinities but the classic examples and models for their societies and for those who subscribe to the presuppositions that Christianity and Buddhism separately advocate concerning the nature of the world. Neither man is a complete human being in the sense of achieving a balanced understanding of human experience, and neither set of doctrines is capable of adequately explaining the variety of human experiences or the ultimate meaning of human existence. Yet the life of consistency capped by a magnificent act of compassion illustrates for us both divinity and humanity, and one cannot blame the adherents of each religion for conceiving the nature of the human individual after these men.

Thus with reference to our understanding of the human individual we have the testimony of the followers of each religion. Ian Barbour writes that "for the Christian there is one supreme model for God: the person of Christ."[22] Generations of Christians have been admonished to "imitate Christ" in their personal lives. The essence of Buddhism, of course, is following the path of the Buddha, and the long line of Boshisattvas testifies to the importance of the original Buddha as a model. "It is not enough," Söderblum writes of the imitation of the Buddha, "to give men psychological advice how to get to Nirvana. They are referred to the vow of Buddha not to enter into Nirvana before the saving truth had been proclaimed to all creatures."[23]

Models, no matter how profound, cannot stand alone, just as the teachings of religions and the models of the Christ and the Buddha do not stand alone. No sooner does the model become apparent than a system of teachings clusters about it. "In higher religions," Joachim Wach commented in *The Comparative Study of Religions,* "the principle of *imitatio* is of special importance. This would correspond to the stages of the path of mystical search and spiritual perfection. The ideal of service is typified in the attitude and conduct of a man of God, a prophet, a saint, a mediator whom to emulate is the royal path to perfection or salvation."[24] But, Wach suggested, "While it is possible to conceive of serving God in terms of a paradigmatic figure (the ideal Jew, Mohammedan, Hindu, Buddhist, or Christian), a more abstract canon of virtue may be established. This has been formulated in the ethical systems of all major religions. Both in Buddhism and Christianity, love (charity) is central . . ."[25] The parallel that we have seen throughout holds together when we turn from idealized models to codes of behavior promulgated by the higher religions, and particularly in the conclusions that Christianity and Buddhism reach.

One need not comment that the ethical systems of Christianity and Buddhism revolve around the individual as the criterion for behavior. "Do unto others as you would have them do unto you" served as the Christian summary of ethical teaching for centuries. Wach explained that "self-restraint, temperance, contentment, patience, chastity, purity, humility, benevolence, liberality, reverence, gratitude, toleration, veracity, and righteousness are according to Tachibana, the virtues of a Buddhist of the Small Vehicle. In Mahayana Buddhism the six cardinal virtues culminate in wisdom (*prajna*) and love (*karuna*)."[26] All these many virtues, one might add, are individual qualities and hardly unique to the Buddhist tradition.

These ethical patterns do not seem radically different from any other set of ethics, however. H. Richard Niebuhr (1894–1962), an authority on Christian ethics and the history of Christian thought, made two profound comments on the efficacy of Christian ethics in his book *The Responsible Self:* "The situation of Christians then seems to be this: they cannot understand themselves or direct their actions or give form to their conduct without the use of the symbol Jesus Christ, but with the aid of that symbol only they never succeed in understanding themselves and their values or in giving shape to their conduct. And, furthermore, the problem of the adequacy, the revelatory value, of the symbols they associate with Jesus Christ is often as great as the problem of the revelatory value of the Christ symbol itself."[27]

And with a brutal frankness and honesty Niebuhr admitted that "in practice, Christians undertaking to act in some fashion in conformity with Christ find themselves doing something like what some others, conforming to other images, are doing. Identity of action there has not been; likeness, however, has often been present. (Christians have had no monopoly on humanitarianism or concern for those suffering deprivation; in reverence for life they have often been excelled by others.)"[28]

If the ethical standards and teachings of the two religions issue in behavior that is indistinguishable from the behavior of people who do not subscribe to the same set of teachings, what real difference do the teachings of Christianity and Buddhism make in the world of human affairs? If the teachings and behavior are not the essential difference between these two religions and other religions, particularly tribal religions, what makes them either ultimate expressions of religious reality or deserving of the appellation "higher" religions? If we consider the matter carefully, we will observe that the so-called "higher" or "world" religions receive that characterization because there are *more* people in the cultural traditions that follow these religions, not because they are "higher," "better," or more capable of providing a direction for the *oikumenē*.

An examination of the higher religions thus brings us to a point of diminishing returns. We are still attempting to discover the basis for understanding the human individual in a religious context. Both Christianity and Buddhism are incomplete in their analysis of religious reality because each took only a portion of the possible experiences of our species and, using the individual as a point of reference, explored the possible interpretations of experience, arriving at a simplistic ethic that was indistinguishable in performance from the behavior of nonbelievers. We still have the remaining category of human religious traditions to explore, the traditions that did not attempt to eliminate the intuitive apprehension and human emotions from their understanding of religious perceptions.

XV. Tribal Religious Realities

I suggested earlier that the original religious perception of reality becomes transformed over a period of time into philosophies and theologies, which purport to give a logical and analytical explanation of ultimate reality. These explanations, of course, have eliminated the human emotions and intuitive insights of the original experience and in their place have substituted a systematic rendering of human knowledge concerning the natural world. From this process of analysis have come the respective divisions of the natural world into spiritual and material, eternal and ephemeral, this-worldly and other-worldly, and absolute space and time dimensions. Not all societies and traditions reprocessed their religious experiences however, and we must turn to those traditions, which scholars have labeled "primitive," in order to see wherein the differences lie.

Primitive people do not differentiate their world of experience into two realms that oppose or complement each other. They seem to maintain a consistent understanding of the unity of all experience. "Among the primitives," according to Joachim Wach, "there is no clear distinction between the notions of spiritual and material, psychical and physical."[1] Rather than seeking underlying causes or substances, primitives report the nature and intensity of their experience. Carl Jung clarified this approach to experience somewhat when he wrote that "thanks to our one-sided emphasis on so-called natural causes, we have learned to differentiate what is subjective and psychic from what is objective and 'natural.' For primitive man, on the contrary, the psychic and the objective coalesce in the external world. In the face of something extraordinary it is not he who is astonished, but rather the thing that is astonishing."[2]

The traditional picture that Western thinkers have painted of primitive peoples is one of fear, superstition, and ignorance, the intense desire to come to grips with natural forces, and a tendency to attribute powers and intentions to the unusual acts of nature. Jung's suggestion that the astonishment occurs in the objective world rather than in the observer would seem to indicate that primitives have a rather keen sense of observation and are intensely aware of the nature of the physical world in which they live, constantly encountering the unique in everything they meet. Such an attitude is indeterminate, not absolute, and would seem to transcend fear and superstition. At the very minimum, the fact that the astonishment occurs in the objective world means that the identity of the primitive in a personal sense is preserved from destructive psychic disruptions.

But we must not consider the life of the primitive one series of astonishing events after another. Primitive peoples rapidly become accustomed to the apparent periodic movements of nature, and it is the unusual that attracts them. Carl Jung cautioned that "primitive man's belief in an arbitrary power does not arise out of thin air, as was always supposed, but is grounded in experience. The grouping of chance occurrences justifies what we call his superstition, for there is a real measure of probability that unusual events will coincide in time and place. We must not forget that our experience is apt to leave us in the lurch here. Our observation is inadequate because our point of view leads us to overlook these matters."[3] The first step in understanding the alternative world view of primitive peoples, therefore, is to recognize that they do not derive their beliefs out of "thin air" but that all beliefs and institutions derive from experience.

Although Jung warned that we tend to overlook unusual coincidences and relationships that primitive peoples discern, we must recognize that primitive peoples exist on the same planet as we do and therefore have the same basic types of daily experiences as we do. Their insights into the nature of reality, therefore, while occasionally more specific or emotional, or even more intuitive, than ours, refer to the same external reality. Their failure or refusal to differentiate subjective from objective, spiritual from material, seems to form the basic difference that separates them from us. Thus when we examine their system of beliefs, their myths, or their social and political organizations, we must remember that some things that have utmost importance for primitive peoples can be found within the Western scheme of knowledge but perhaps in a differentiated form that makes it difficult to identify properly.

Thus it is with the most common feature of primitive awareness of the world—the feeling or belief that the universe is energized by a pervading power. Scholars have traditionally called the presence of this power *mana*, following Polynesian beliefs, but we find it among tribal peoples, particularly American Indian tribes, as *wakan, orenda,* or *manitou.* Regardless of the technical term used, there is general agreement that a substantial number of primitive peoples recognize the existence of a power in the universe that affects and influences them. "The mana theory maintains that there is something like a widely distributed power in the external world that produces all those extraordinary effects," Carl Jung explained. And he suggested that "everything that exists acts, otherwise it would not *be*. It can *be* only by virtue of its inherent energy. Being is a field of force. The primitive idea of mana, as you can see, has in it the beginnings of a crude theory of energy."[4]

It would be comforting, of course, to claim that primitive peoples derived the principles of modern-energy theory from their religious experiences thousands of years before Western scientists formulated their complicated explanations, but it is not necessary to be extravagant. It is sufficient to note that the observations and experiences of primitive peoples were so acute that they were able to recognize a basic phenomenon of the natural world religiously rather than scientifically. They felt power but did not measure it. Today we measure power but are unable to feel it except on extremely rare occasions. We conclude that energy forms the basic constituent of the universe through experimentation, and the existence of energy is truly a conclusion of scientific experimentation. For primitive peoples, on the other hand, the presence of energy and power is the starting point of their analyses and understanding of the natural world. It is their cornerstone for further exploration.

Western thinkers continually misinterpret the recognition of power by primitive peoples as if it were a conclusion they had reached rather than a beginning they were making. Thus Paul Tillich wrote that "the conception of nature that we find earliest in history, so far as we have knowledge of it, is the magical-sacramental conception. According to it, everything is filled with a sort of material energy which gives to things and to parts of things, even to the body and the parts of the body, a sacral power. The word 'sacral' in this context, however, does not signify something in opposition to the profane. Indeed, at this phase of cultural development the distinction between the sacred and the profane is not a fundamental one."[5] Such an explanation is incorrect because it is phrased in the traditional language of Western thinkers, which separates spiritual and material into two distinct aspects of reality. Primitive peoples refuse to make such distinctions. We are not dealing, therefore, with a conception of nature in the same way that Western thinkers conceive of things, but with a simple recognition of the force-field that seems to constitute the natural world.

The implications of understanding the proper sense in which primitive peoples experienced the natural world is important because it bears directly on the manner in which they understand themselves. Ernst Cassirer, writing of the attitudes of primitive peoples, maintained that for them "nature becomes one great society, the *society of life*. Man is not endowed with outstanding rank in this society. He is a part of it but he is in no respect higher than any other member."[6] All species, all forms of life, have equal status before the presence of the universal power to which all are subject. The religious requirement for all life-forms is thus harmony, and this requirement holds for every species, ours included. Then natural world has a great bond that brings together all living entities, each species gaining an identity and meaning as it forms a part of the complex whole. If ever there were a truly evolutionary theological position, primitive peoples would represent it.

Primitive peoples somehow maintain this attitude toward the world and toward other life-forms. As long as the bond of life is respected, all species have value and meaning, emotions and intuitions remain a constant factor of experience, and harmony is maintained. The elimination of emotional intensity and intuitive insights into the world, which is accomplished by the great "world" religions, twists this basic apprehension of reality. "No religion could ever think of cutting or even loosening the bond between nature and man," Ernst Cassirer wrote. "But in the great ethical religions this bond is tied and fastened in a new sense. . . . Nature is not, as in polytheistic religions, the great and benign mother, the divine lap from which all life originates. It is conceived as the sphere of law and lawfulness."[7]

The great innovation of the world religions is to reduce natural events to a sequence containing some form of predictability, to introduce the conception of law and regularity into the natural world. Such an innovation is wholly artificial and may be understood by primitive peoples as the original sin. Certainly the acquisition of knowledge is understood in Genesis as the original sin, and it is ironic that in attempting to refine religious experiences into a more precise understanding that the great world religions commit the sin that alienates our species from the rest of the natural world. Paul Tillich noted that the primitive understanding of reality changes "when the system of powers is replaced by the correlation of self and world, of subjectivity and objectivity. Man becomes an epistemological, legal, and moral center, and things become objects of his knowledge, his work, and his use."[8] This point of departure separates primitive people from the rest of the human species; it distinguishes civilized from primitive, and unleashes the energies of our species on a path of conquest of the rest of nature, which has now been reduced to the status of an object.

It is curious that Tillich would support the tendency of the great world religions to reduce the natural world to an objective status, thereby artificially elevating our species above other life forms. Granted that we seek knowledge continually; knowledge is more than the ability to deal with theories. The curiosity arises because Tillich suggested that the "man who transforms the world into a universal machine serving his purposes has to adapt himself to the laws of the machine. The mechanized world of things draws man into itself and makes him a cog, driven by the mechanical necessities of the whole. *The personality that deprives nature of its power in order to elevate itself above it becomes a powerless part of its own creation.*"[9] It would appear, therefore, that organizing and systematizing religious experiences into reliable and predictable knowledge is a major theological transgression and a movement away from intimate understanding of our place in the world in an epistemological sense.

Arnold Toynbee described the severance of the bond of nature and our species in different terms than did Cassirer, and Toynbee's analysis gives us insight into the problems created by the expansion and sophistication of the great world religions. "The worship of Nature tends to unite the members of different communities because it is not self-centered," Toynbee maintained, "it is the worship of a power in whose presence all human beings have the identical experience of being made aware of their own human weakness." In contrast to the unifying effect which nature has on human communities, Toynbee suggested that "the worship of parochial communities tends to set their respective members at variance because this religion is an expression of self-centredness; because self-centredness is the source of all strife; and because the collective ego is a more dangerous object of worship than the individual ego is."[10]

The characteristic that purports to save members of world religions, while conceived on an idealistic and precise basis, is the very thing that destroys the members thereof—concentrating on the self to the exclusion of the world. Perhaps the best illustration we can find is the comparative status that primitive peoples and adherents of world religions enjoy vis-à-vis each other. Joachim Wach wrote that "in most primitive religions a strong tie binds the members of a tribal cult together, and on the level of great religions, spiritual brotherhood surpasses physical ties between brothers. A 'father or mother in God,' a 'brother or sister in God,' may be closer to us than our physical parents and relatives."[11] This claim may have a certain validity for specific individuals, but on the larger scale it does not appear to be operative. Wach himself noted that "whatever the prevailing mood, the religious association takes precedence over all other forms of fellowship. Religious loyalty, in theory at least, outranks any other loyalty everywhere except in the modern Western world."[12] The result of the teachings of the world religions, which center on the care and salvation of the individual, is, of course, the creation of the solitary individual, apart from any community of concern.

Most adherents of world religions would dispute the accusation that their tradition isolates individuals; yet their teachings appear designed to break the traditional ties that have bound communities together. "In order to create a new and profound spiritual brotherhood based on the principles enunciated by the new faith," Wach explained, "old bonds have to be broken. This break of sociological ties becomes one of the marks of the willingness to begin a new life. To become a disciple of the Buddha means to leave parents and relatives, wife and child, home and property and all else, as flamingos leave their lakes."[13] Theoretically, at least, the new community, which is formed according to the principles of the new faith, is superior to the sociological, family, and community ties, which are severed in the primitive community. The product, again, is not what the world religions claim it to be. "Modern Western man is all too prone to think of the solitary individual first and last," Wach wrote, "yet the study of primitive religions shows that, individual experiences notwithstanding, religion is generally a group affair."[14]

The attraction of the world religions appears to be their knowledge and idealism, their precise manner of articulating answers to perennial human questions about life, death, and meaning, and their ability to preach and teach methods of living that will enable people to survive in a world that often seems hostile. But clarity in articulating beliefs is not necessarily a benefit. Carl Jung suggested that "it is not ethical principles, however lofty, or creeds, however orthodox, that lay the foundations for the freedom and autonomy of the individual, but simply and solely the empirical awareness, the incontrovertible experience of an intensely personal, reciprocal relationship between man and an extramundane authority which acts as the counterpoise to the 'world' and its 'reason.' "[15] The great bond of experience with nature, no matter how vaguely defined, incorporates the emotional and intuitive dimension of our lives much better than do the precise creeds, doctrines, and dogmas of the great world religions and as such provides us with continuing meaning as long as we treat our apprehension of the great mystery with respect.

The first and great difference between primitive religious thought and the world religions, therefore, is that primitive peoples maintain a sense of mystery through their bond with nature; the world religions sever the relationship and attempt to establish a new, more comprehensible one. Foremost among the religious leaders who fought the great natural bond between our species and the other life-forms and processes of nature were the Hebrew prophets, with their constant warfare against the Baals. "The significance of prophetic criticism," Paul Tillich wrote, "lies in the fact that it dissolves the primitive unity between the holy and the real. To the prophets the holy is primarily a demand. . . . Nature as such is deprived of its sacred character and becomes profane. Immediate intercourse with nature no longer possesses religious significance."[16] In this criticism, therefore, we have a reductionism that severs the holy from its origin and makes it an intellectual ethical requirement. A demand can only originate in a system of duties and responsibilities, a legalism and can only produce another legal system and more duties and responsibilities. The collective ego of the new community, which becomes the object of worship, be it the Christian church or whatever, must itself be given structure and a means of operation, and religion becomes a group of humans examining their own beliefs rather than continuing to fulfill a role in the great process of nature.

Primitive relationships with nature have been subjected to criticism from many points of view. They are regarded as remnants of former days when our species had no scientific understanding of the natural world. Tillich defined primitve relationships with nature as "objectification" and suggested that "the objectification of the divine in time and space and in anthropomorphic conceptions, which takes place in myth, is disrupted by prophetic religion, regarded as inadequate by mysticism and dismissed as unworthy and absurd by philosophical religion."[17] Tillich's statement poses important questions for understanding primitive perceptions of religions and, ultimately, natural reality. Our first task is to examine the suggestion that primitive peoples in fact do objectify the divine in time and space.

We have suggested earlier that the major difference between Christianity and Buddhism is that one absolutizes time and human affairs and the other absolutizes natural processes, and ultimately space. By contrast, primitive peoples maintain the unity of space-time and refuse to use either concept as their analytical tool for understanding the world. Ernst Cassirer, writing about the society of natural life that characterizes primitive perceptions of nature, said that "we find the same principle—that of the solidarity and unbroken unity of life—if we pass from space to time. It holds not only in the order of simultaneity but also in the order of succession."[18] Like the modern physicist, the primitive holds the unity of experience in a continuum that transcends traditional Western divisions of space and time.

But there is an additional parallel between primitive peoples' perception of experiences and the theories of modern physics: space may conceivably have priority over time in that time occurs within space and must give way, at least conceptually, to spatial recognitions. "A native thinker makes the penetrating comment," Claude Levi-Strauss notes, "that 'all sacred things must have their place. . . .' It could even be said that being in their place is what makes them sacred for if they were taken out of their place, even in thought, the entire order of the universe would be destroyed. Sacred objects therefore contribute to the maintenance of order in the universe by occupying the places allocated to them."[19] Far from objectifying the sacred in time and space here is a recognition that religious perceptions in fact occur in the natural world and go a substantial distance in giving it structure. We have not only the recognition that a divine energy pervades the natural world but that it is able to reveal itself in particular objects and places. To deny this possibility would be to deny the possibility of an ultimate sense of reality itself. But it is important to note that primitives are dealing with recognitions, not beliefs that have an intellectual content; and recognitions, like perceptions, involve the totality of personality.

Tillich himself admitted that "the holy appears only in special places, in special contexts." But instead of recognizing that the preservation of memories concerning the appearance of the holy is the first stage in structuring the world view of the primitive, that is, the holy mountain, the sacred river or lake, the point of emergence from the underworld, Tillich argued that "the concentration of the sacramental in special places, in special rites, is the expression of man's ambiguous situation."[20] It is difficult to understand why recognizing sacred places and rites creates ambiguity. Primitive peoples are certainly not confused about the places and rites they consider sacred, for these form the basis of their community and provide an identity that incorporates rather than transcends the space-time dimensions. Ambiguity would only seem to appear if one wished to universalize the sacred nature of experience, thereby, in effect, lifting the sacred from its context of the natural world and holding it in one's mind as a set of concepts. Ambiguity only appears when one attempts to control the appearance of divinity and establish regular guidelines for any relationship that might ensue with divinity.

Whenever we begin to discuss the role of time and space for primitive peoples, we become embroiled in controversy because Western thinkers have traditionally separated space and time, unconsciously we might suggest, always considering them homogenous entities in their own right. Thus it is important to clarify the primitive perceptions of space and time so that we can be sure we understand the manner in which primitive peoples perceive experiences. "Primitive thought is not only incapable of thinking of a system of space," Ernst Cassirer wrote, "it cannot even conceive a scheme of space." And, he continued, "Its concrete space cannot be brought into a *schematic* shape. Ethnology shows us that primitive tribes usually are gifted with an extraordinarily sharp perception of space. A native of these tribes has an eye for all the nicest details of his environment."[21] The primitive easily comprehends the places of his or her experience, but he or she does not abstract from them a scheme of space in a Euclidian or Newtonian sense. The primitive person is thus in direct immediate relationship with his or her environment but fails to extend abstract principles continuously to conceive of "endless" dimensional existence. In view of our discussion of the conceptions of space-time in modern physics, it would appear that primitive peoples, in their religious perceptions of the natural world, coincide with the contemporary conceptual understanding of the world.

This view of primitive peoples provides them with an understanding of the natural world that immediately incorporates all aspects of experience. Thus primitive descriptions of events contain all elements of knowledge that Western scientists have traditionally extracted and organized into distinct academic disciplines. Whenever scholars have attempted to return to the primitive perception and illustrate the wholistic understanding contained in primitive mythologies, they have had to bring in the primitive perception of space as a means of demonstrating their thesis. Thus Claude Levi-Strauss suggests that there is a symmetry between anthropology and history in primitive thought-forms, making the two disciplines parallel, interwoven developments. Levi-Strauss encounters difficulty with his academic colleagues in advocating this position, and he complains that "this symmetry between history and anthropology seems to be rejected by philosophers who implicitly or explicitly deny that distribution in space and succession in time afford equivalent perspectives. In their eyes some special prestige seems to attach to the temporal dimension, as if a diachrony were to establish a kind of intelligibility not merely superior to that provided by a synchrony, but above all more specifically human."[22]

When we admit the equivalency of temporal and spatial dimensions as perspectives for understanding, we can answer the accusations of the prophets, the mystics, and the expositors of philosophical religion. Perceptions of experience articulated in predominantly spatial terms incorporate the immediacy of the situation without including prior causations and future projections as part of the original experience. Thus the immediate event is passed forward as it occurred, without editorial reordering, and primitive peoples preserve "chunks" of experience, not interpretive patterns of activity. Rather than being a demeaning manner of understanding, which fails to comprehend cause and effect and temporality, the primitive form of apprehension may be more sophisticated. Marshall McLuhan comments on this possibility in *Understanding Media,* suggesting that although "our ideas of cause and effect in the literate West have long been in the form of things in sequence and succession," such a way of understanding the world is "an idea that strikes any tribal or auditory culture as quite ridiculous, and *one that has lost its prime place in our own new physics and biology.*"[23]

We conclude that primitive peoples' perceptions of reality, particularly their religious experiences and awareness of divinity, occupy a far different place in their lives than do the conceptions of the world religions, their experiences, and theologies, philosophies, doctrines, dogmas, and creeds. Primitive peoples preserve their experiences fairly intact, understand them as a manifestation of the unity of the natural world, and are content to recognize these experiences as the baseline of reality. World religions take the raw data of religious experience and systematize elements of it, using either the temporal or the spatial dimension as a framework, and attempt to project meaning into the unexamined remainder of human experience. Ethics becomes an abstract set of propositions attempting to relate individuals to one another in the world religions, while kinship duties, customs, and responsibilities, often patterned after relationships in the natural world, parallel the ethical considerations of religion in the primitive peoples. Primitive peoples always have a concrete reference—the natural world—and the adherents of the world religions continually deal with abstract and ideal situations on an intellectual plane. "Who is my neighbor?" becomes a question of great debate in the tradition of the world religions, and the face of the neighbor changes continually as new data about people becomes available. Such a question is not even within the world view of primitives. They know precisely who their relatives are and what their responsibilities toward them entail.

As we attempt to devise a new metaphysics for our time, we face the question of integrating social existence around a new set of questions and beliefs that have planetary application and can transcend the parochial historical, racial, geographical, economic, and religious traditions. The vision once held out by the world religions—the equality of every person before the deity and in human society, peace and prosperity, and a universal brotherhood of life—are usually cited by adherents of the great world religions as a partial justification of their existence and as benchmarks of intellectual accomplishments that distinguish them from primitive peoples. As ideals, these goals are admirable, but are the doctrines, beliefs, and ethical systems of the great world religions capable of bringing about such conditions? Judging by their historical performance we would conclude no.

Can the primitive peoples do better? Paul Radin (1883–1959), an American anthropologist who studied many different primitive peoples, suggested that if asked "to state briefly and succiently what are the outstanding positive features of aboriginal civilization, I, for one, would have no hesitation in answering that there are three: the respect for the individual, irrespective of age or sex; the amazing degree of social and political integration achieved by them; and the existence there of a concept of personal security which transcends all governmental forms and all tribal and group interests and conflicts."[24] Insofar as it is possible to conceive three attributes of a society that we would like to emulate, these characteristics of primitive peoples look appealing. Primitive peoples, in their system of social organization, were hardly unsophisticated, and they do not deserve the scorn that Western thinkers, philosophers and theologians especially, have heaped upon them. If they did not construct massive scientific technologies and immense bureaucracies, neither did they create the isolated individual helplessly gripped by supraindividual forces.

But how can we incorporate the primitive modes of perception, both religious and secular, into our understanding of the world, especially in a world now emerging from the Darwinian-Newtonian era of scientific absolutism? Quite obviously we cannot return to the primitive forms of religion that once dominated the world view of small tribal groups. The modern tendencies to discover a guru or medicine man as a spiritual teacher all collapse of their own inadequacies. Efforts of tribal peoples to retribalize and return to their original posture toward the world collapse in the face of an affluent technology that rips them apart. We live in a modern, electronic age in which blood sacrifices, ceremonies, and even kinship ties cannot withstand the future shock of a rapidly changing style of life.

Our task in searching for a new metaphysics is not one of picking and choosing from a variety of applicants those elements of any human tradition that are either very appealing or that seem to describe reality in properly respectable terms. The major accusation that can be made against Christianity is that it is a conglomerate, a syncretism of divergent views, held together by faith and the expenditure of intellectual energy—I believe, therefore what I believe is true. Thus we cannot suggest that there is anything we can "borrow" from primitive peoples in the way of a view of the world, ceremonies, beliefs, customs, or traditions. We face the future immediately, and while we can be aware of the sound basis for primitive beliefs and customs, we can never return to them or take them up, expecting them to save us.

It is not necessary, however, to do so. Our examination of the *oikumenē* indicates that the most fruitful avenues of development today are directing us toward a new type of social existence that parallels primitive peoples', perhaps incorporates some of their insights or unconsciously adopts some of their techniques, but which will be fully modern and capable of providing a meaningful existence. The importance of these movements for primitive peoples is that as modern industrial society becomes aware of new ways of structuring its understanding of the world, economic and political decisions will begin to reflect a more comprehensive and intelligent view of the world and of our species, thereby taking the pressure, in a political and economic sense, away from the surviving primitive and tribal peoples.

Aside from recognizing that primitive religious perceptions affirmed a divine and universal power or energy inherent in the world of experience, what can we learn from the primitive tradition that would be relevant today? We have suggested that primitive myths and traditions contain a memory of historic events from which we can extract, for the benefit of various disciplines, additional knowledge concerning the history of our planet. Indeed, one of the chief characteristics of primitive mythology is that it originates in the prehistoric period prior to the invention of writing and alphabets and has the potential of enabling us to extend our knowledge of human affairs to that dimly understood time.

There are two substantial issues raised by the literal use of primitive myths to describe unusual planetary-wide happenings. Much of the material in myths, legends, and traditions deals with catastrophes and disasters on a scale nearly inconceivable to modern minds. Can we accept a literal rendering of these stories when we do not observe the same processes at work in the physical world today? Mingled with these stories of catastrophes are themes concerning the actions of gods and goddesses, similar in many respects to the ancient astronomical knowledge, that is, the gods and goddesses who play important roles in the stories of catastrophes, not coincidentally, also represent planets, suggesting that the stories recount an astral catastrophe in our solar system. Do we interpret these dramas of the gods literally or as religious themes of some moral importance?

Since the myths and legends of both primitive peoples and the distant ancestors of our present Western industrial nations had such a uniformity of concern about catastrophes, and feared the influence of heavenly bodies in their affairs, we must examine the basis upon which it may be possible to derive important knowledge from these stories.

XVI. The Traumatic Planetary Past

Ernst Cassirer wrote that "in the first mythological explanations of the universe we always find a primitive *anthropology* side by side with a primitive *cosmology*. The question of the origin of the world is inextricably interwoven with the question of the origin of man."[1] We have already suggested that primitive traditions contained a unified reporting of experiences and that from this raw data scholars are able to discern elements of information that can be understood as historical, theological, anthropological, and scientific. Indeed, Levi-Strauss contended that experiences and knowledge could be articulated spatially as well as temporally, expanding the arena we would ordinarily allow for the interpretation of materials.

Cassirer felt that "religion does not destroy these first mythological explanations. On the contrary, it preserves the mythological cosmology and anthropology by giving them new shape and new depth."[2] Precisely how new shape and depth are added to the original perception Cassirer never made quite clear. "Myth," he insisted, "is an offspring of emotion and its emotional background imbues all its productions with its own specific color."[3] And he defended the accuracy of the primitive perception, remarking that "primitive man by no means lacks the ability to grasp the empirical differences of things. But in his conception of nature and life all these differences are obliterated by a stronger feeling: the deep conviction of a fundamental and indelible *solidarity of life* that bridges over the multiplicity and variety of its single forms."[4]

Affirming the solidarity of life would seem to preclude reshaping the experience, and the discovery of emotion within the mythological form of exposition would testify that Cassirer, Levi-Strauss, Jung, and other scholars encounter the preserved memories of real experiences rather than the intellectual speculations of our long-departed ancestors. The old vision of myths as symbolic representations of mental realities and well-reasoned truths must be abandoned, and the contention that myths are parabolic means of conveying some greater reality no longer appears suitable as a means of understanding how primitive peoples understood the world and why they chose to preserve their experiences in this form.

Claude Levi-Strauss appears to agree with Cassirer, for he also sees myth as the product of a reshaping process: "Mythical thought for its part is imprisoned in the events and experiences which it never tires of ordering and re-ordering in its search to find them a meaning."[5] This attitude, while welcome as a buttress against the idea that primitive accounts simply reflect superstition, overlooks the actual content of the material. Myths rarely come to a decisive conclusion, which would indicate that the primitive peoples sought to reorder their memories to provide themselves with a meaning transcending the immediacy of the event. If we are speaking of the memories of events, as even Levi-Strauss would maintain, then we cannot seriously contend that the sequence of action is radically changed, since any alteration of the sequence would be objectionable to the listeners and would not materially add to any meaning that people might derive from reviewing the event.

Another objection can be raised regarding the probable reshaping of the contents of a primitive account of events. Carl Jung noted that "generally it is one of the shrewdest and wiliest men of the tribe who is entrusted with the observation of meteorological evidence." And of this sage Jung remarked that "his knowledge must suffice to explain all unusual occurences, and his art to combat them. He is the scholar, the specialist, the expert on chance, and at the same time the keeper of the archives of the tribe's traditional lore."[6] Such a responsibility is not likely to encourage any extensive editorial activity, since one would only occupy that position as long as the accuracy of interpretations remained relatively high. Extensive editorializing would make the knowledge less than secure and, being unreliable, would soon bring great embarrassment to the keeper of the tribal lore. Hence, we can conclude that the content of primitive myths remains fairly consistent throughout the duration of its existence until it is finally recorded by Western peoples encountering the tribe, or by the tribe itself when it acquires the art of writing.

Perhaps the most accurate description of the method of preserving primitive traditions is given by Claude Levi-Strauss when he notes that the elements of mythical thought "lie half-way between percepts and concepts. It would be impossible to separate percepts from the concrete situations in which they appeared, while recourse to concepts would require that thought could, at least provisionally, put its projects (to use Husserl's expression) 'in brackets.'"[7] But a linguistic form that is "half-way" between concepts and percepts would appear to combine the best elements of each into a consistent whole, communicating not simply the structure of events, but the emotional dimension as well.

Identifying both subjective and objective realities of myth creates a dilemma in interpretation. Is the fundamental meaning to be ascribed to the story subjective, and hence a mental or verbal reality? Or is it objective, hence literal, and descriptive of a unique and planet-wide event? Claude Levi-Strauss, facing this problem, describes the dilemma facing those who would attempt to interpret the traditions of primitive peoples:

> On the one hand it would seem that in the course of a myth anything is likely to happen. There is no logic, no continuity. *Any characteristic can be attributed to any subject;* every conceivable relation can be found. With myth, everything becomes possible. *But on the other hand, this apparent arbitrariness is belied by the astounding similarity between myths collected in widely different regions.* Therefore the problem: If the content of a myth is contingent, how are we going to explain the fact that myths throughout the world are so similar?[8]

If we concede the arbitrary nature of myth-formation, we are faced with the similarity of story lines. We eliminate this dilemma only by admitting an objective aspect to the story lines of myth and by attempting to discover the events which the different myths seem to describe.

With this admission we have traditionally entered the realm of religious thinking, and, more specifically, of fundamentalist religious thinking. A long-standing trait of Western religious thinkers, and an attitude against which scientists have long rebelled, has been the massing of myths to demonstrate the literal truth of religious beliefs. Much early work in the field of the history of religions was drawing the similarities of myths found in different parts of the world into a series of parallels designed to demonstrate the literal truth and religious superiority of the Christian Scriptures. Flood stories were not taken to be indications of a planetary disaster but as proof that the Bible was literally true and therefore to be believed in toto. Occasionally, similarities which did not support the literal truth of the Christian faith were discovered. They were explained as crafty devices scattered about the world by the devil to confuse the faithful.

Obviously our knowledge of the world could not make much progress under these restrictive conditions. Faith became a means of cutting off debate, and the great test of credibility occurred when evolutionary biologists clashed with religious fundamentalists over the origin of life-forms on our planet. Typically, scientific thinkers, having freed themselves from religious intolerance, promptly adopted absolute standards of truth of their own, rejecting religious myths as having any relationship to physical events. Myths and legends were then seen as fragments of the human evolutionary journey from superstition to enlightenment. Psychologists and sociologists saw them as "symbolic," "parabolic," and "poetic" expressions of intellectual propositions, but not as the remnant memories of a time in our planet's history before we were able to record our experiences.

The discussion between science and religion has remained open in this century, but the participants have rarely communicated, preferring rather to criticize either the superstition or godlessness of the other. Scientists largely adopted a snobbish attitude toward religious thinkers. But one must also blame the theologians, who sought to bolster the faith of their followers and save them from scientific skepticism. The articulation of issues and the identification of points of conflict have not been made sufficiently clear to attract the serious attentions of flexible minds on either side. But since the conflict between the uniformitarians and the catastrophists seems to be escalating, it is well within the scope of our metaphysical inquiry to determine how the battle wages. We shall look at the respective schools and thinkers who presently advocate the inclusion of planetary catastrophes as part of our knowledge of the earth and, by extension, of the solar system.

Christian fundamentalists, as we have noted, have continued their struggle to prove the literal truth of the Old Testament. George McCready Price, a Seventh Day Adventist, published several books that sought to show the effects of the Biblical Flood as they could be found in geological formations around the world. In *Evolutionary Geology and the New Catastrophism* (1926) and *The New Geology* (1923), Price attempted to demonstrate the existence of a planetary flood comparable to that described in Genesis and, of course, identical to the Noachian flood, without suggesting any cause of such a widespread catastrophe, preferring, most probably, to rely on the Hebrew deity as the causative agent. Alfred M. Rehwinkel, a Missouri Synod Lutheran, published *The Flood* in 1951 and placed his major emphasis on the literature of different peoples around the globe that gave testimony to the existence of a flood. Like Price, Rehwinkel failed to produce any causative agent, and his book is littered with admonitions to fundamentalists to remain true to the faith. Insofar as Rehwinkel relied upon the oral traditions and myths of human societies, his book has value in demonstrating the planetary scope of the disaster. Other minor writers of Christian commitment have occasionally produced books, usually demonstrating the literal truth of the Flood, which appears to be the major event that Christians feel they must relate to modern science. From our point of view, the great fallacy of these efforts is that the writers are not committed to discovering truth but rather see their task as justifying Christian beliefs. Only if religion can be reduced to the intellectual assent to a set of propositions concerning events in our planet's past can these books be seriously considered. They reduce the traditions of non-Christian peoples to mere extraneous witnesses to the validity of the Christian faith in a tangential sense.

A much more sophisticated effort has recently been made by Donald Wesley Patten in his book *The Biblical Flood and the Ice Epoch* (1966). While obviously a Christian, Patten has learned well the futility of attacking straw persons by the citation of biblical verses, and his book is a well-reasoned, well-documented presentation that deserves discussion among scientists. Unlike his predecessors, who failed to suggest a cause for the Flood, Patten makes numerous suggestions regarding extraterrestrial agents that might have been responsible. His critique of orthodox interpretations of the ice ages is devastating, since he uses the mathematical approach to the accumulation of ice, its spread, and the effects that might be anticipated had the Flood been derived from precipitation alone. Patten draws on the myths of non-Christian peoples less often than any other writer dealing with catastrophe, and his determination to meet scientific theories with scientific objections makes his work critical to any serious consideration of the history of the planet.

The last significant attempt by Christian-oriented writers to join issue with scientists is a series of symposium essays on Creation, published by Baker Book House in Grand Rapids, Michigan. The series consists of five volumes, four of which are edited by Donald Patten, and contain a number of his essays as well as essays by other fundamentalist thinkers. For the most part the selections vary from rather devotional and admonishing efforts to rather sophisticated attempts to deal with specific topics that modern secular scientists fail to confront adequately. If these essays indicate anything, it is that the subject of catastrophism can no longer be swept under the academic rug by Newtonian-Darwinian oriented scientists. We have too many facts available to us today that do not correspond to uniformitarian theories of the evolution of the solar system as a benign and seemingly endless, uneventful procession of cosmic time. The major flaw in this series, as in all books dealing with catastrophes and that are written by Western religious thinkers, is the assumption that geologic evidence and the testimony of primitive peoples to planetary catastrophes verify only the Christian faith and somehow give it a religious superiority over all other traditions.

Secular advocates of catastrophe generally present a much more palatable picture, since they do not have conversion to the Christian faith as a hidden agenda, and they appear to be seeking the truth of our planet's past for the sake of their own peace of mind as well as for our edification. Hugh Fox, in *Gods of the Cataclysm,* concentrates on the possibility of a world culture that embraced major portions of the planet prior to the catastrophe postulated by Patten. The book is erratic, and it is unscholarly in the sense that it adopts the popular format of citing evidence and then claiming proof in the previous citation. It attempts to deal with complexities of culture that cannot easily be summarized. Yet Fox has tremendous intuitive insights into possible connections among primitive and ancient peoples that seem to lead into new avenues of thought. While Fox's book would be more at home with newer speculations concerning pre-Columbian expeditions to the New World, which Barry Fell in *America B.C.* and Cyrus Gordon in *Before Columbus* suggest, Fox's work must be considered from the mythological point of view as describing planetary experiences of tremendous scope that forever changed the nature of human societies.

A much less speculative, and less courageous, book is Derek V. Ager's treatise *The Nature of the Stratigraphical Record* (1973). Ager, an avowed evolutionist and a professional geologist, reviews the stratigraphic record that geologists have compiled and concludes that catastrophes must be considered in any future exposition of geologic principles. He cites the widespread nature of some geological formations, demonstrating that traditional uniformitarian interpretations of how sediments were formed are hardly in keeping with what we presently know about geologic processes. Particularly devastating is his assertion that hurricanes can lay down a layer of sediment, or remove same, within a few hours. Thus, measuring the thickness of formations and hypothesizing the barely perceptible accumulation of deposits in view of this fact is basically absurd. Ager's flaw is his extreme conservatism, which, when paraphrased, would read "the only record we have is catastrophic, but let's continue to advocate the same geologic time scale even though we know it's fallacious."

In the field of history the great classic is Claude Shaeffer's study on the civilizations of the Near East. Examining the archeological excavations of the major centers of political life in the Asia Minor-Mediterranean area, Schaeffer demonstrated that in approximately 1500 B.C. Troy, the Egyptian cities, Huyuk, Tarsus, Ugarit, Byblos, and environs suffered a natural catastrophe of great severity. His *Stratigraphie comparee et chronologie de l'Asie Occidentale*, developed primarily on the basis of the similarity in the archeological reports, was the first introduction of a geographical dimension into Near Eastern archeology in the sense that the common occurrences of disaster were shown to have regional significance rather than being only local disturbances of minor importance.

The major advocate of a catastrophic interpretation of planetary history, however, is Dr. Immanuel Velikovsky, whose books *Worlds in Collision* (1950), *Ages in Chaos* (1952), *Earth in Upheaval* (1955), *Oedipus and Akhnaton* (1960), and *Peoples of the Sea* (1977), challenged the organization and interpretation of human knowledge in nearly every field. Velikovsky took as his point of departure the Exodus, as described in the Old Testament, and began the tedious task of coordinating ancient texts that might throw light on the literal nature of this event. But he refused to advocate the literal nature of the Exodus as a proof of the validity of the Hebrew-Jewish religious tradition, preferring instead to discover the agent that caused the parting of the Red Sea and the spectacular natural phenomena described in the Old Testament, with the subsequent intent of learning whether such an event was possible in terms of physical science.

The thesis was controversial to say the least. Scientists, who should have been accustomed to advocates of catastrophism, went into a tizzy, unfairly attacked Velikovsky personally instead of giving a critical analysis to his theories, and sought a textbook boycott against his original publisher, Macmillian, even before the book was published. *Worlds in Collision* became an instant bestseller, but Macmillian had to transfer the rights to it to Doubleday to escape the wrath of the scientific establishment. The rage of the scientists has not abated in the nearly three decades since publication of the book. Be it noted that one of Velikovsky's chief critic's, Harlow Shapley, a prominent astronomer, was not only wrong in his criticism of Velikovsky, but ended his career as one of the remaining advocates of the discredited idea that no cosmic dust occupied interplanetary space, an idea that was promptly abandoned with the onset of space flights. Velikovsky's other major scientific critics have largely been discredited in their theories or have silently adopted some of his views.

Rather than reply hysterically in kind to the treatment which the scientific establishment accorded him, Velikovsky casually offered verification of the thesis of *Worlds in Collision* by showing in *Ages in Chaos* that it held up exceedingly well when viewed primarily from a historical point of view. He further demonstrated in *Earth in Upheaval* that his thesis could be supported by reference to geological reports alone, since his critics had suggested that he depended too much upon ancient myths in his previous books. *Earth in Upheaval* showed beyond question (to those who would read it) that the planet had been shaken severely by some unusual incidents during recent geological time and that a uniformitarian interpretation of geological events did not fit the actual findings of geologists in many instances. *Oedipus and Akhnaton* and *Peoples of the Sea* conclude his present published works on the reconstruction of Near Eastern history. In *Oedipus and Akhnaton,* Velikovsky carefully examined the legends of Oedipus and correlated them with excavation reports made by Howard Carter during the digs in the Valley of the Kings in Egypt which resulted in the discovery of Tutankhamen's tomb. He made an excellent case for the identification of Oedipus with the historical Akhnaton.

The emotional outburst generated by Velikovsky's books was comparable to the furor that accompanies great revolutionary theories. It was reminiscent of Harvey's discovery of the circulation of the blood, Pasteur's discovery of germs, and the Copernican controversy over the shape of the solar system. While Velikovsky has suffered great personal abuse from intolerant opponents, he has had the satisfaction of seeing his predictions come true and his opponents' objections to his theory overrruled by subsequent discoveries. In recent years a groundswell of support has been building on his behalf. The Student Forum for Academic Freedom, a group centered at Lewis and Clark College in Portland, Oregon, devoted a series of issues of their journal *Pensee* to discussion of Velikovsky's ideas. Edited by Stephen Talbott, the journal was able to print ten issues before rising printing costs and general overhead forced its demise. The Student Forum for Academic Freedom also helped to plan a number of symposium presentations on Velikovsky's theories and a selection of the better articles published in *Pensee* is now available in hard cover under the title, *Velikovsky Reconsidered.*

In 1963 the *American Behavioral Scientist* printed a special issue that discussed the implications of scientific behavior that greeted Velikovsky. Alfred de Grazia edited the special issue which was also printed as a hardback book entitled *The Velikovsky Affair*. The selections printed in this book deal more with the attitude of scientists toward new and radical departures from orthodox beliefs than with verification of Velikovsky's major theses. Quite recently another journal, *Kronos,* has begun publishing on a regular basis articles dealing with the implications of the theory of catastrophe for the interpretation of human knowledge.

Since 1950 a substantial number of Velikovsky's predictions about the nature of the universe and the proper sequence of ancient history, put forth originally as a means for other scholars to check the validity of this theory, have been proven correct. In 1972 *Pensee* published a list of the predictions made first by Velikovsky which had been verified at that date. The list is worth reprinting because it demonstrates the comprehensive nature of the catastrophic theory and indicates the very broad scope of Velikovsky's interests and capabilities. Since that original listing of predictions additional verifications have come at such a rate as to make any updating of the list a full-time task in itself. It may well be that we shall someday view Velikovsky as one of the great minds of human history.

The list, then, of predictions concerning the physical universe that had been verified by 1972 is as follows:

Electromagnetism and the Sun.
  Space is not a vacuum; and electromagnetism plays a fundamental role in our solar system and the entire universe.
  The sun is an electrically charged body.

Venus.
  Venus originated in a violent disruption of Jupiter.
  Venus is hot.
  The Venetic atmosphere contains—besides carbon dioxide—carbohydrates and hydrocarbons.
  Venus was in near collision with earth.
  Venus may have an anomalous rotation.

Comets and Meteorites.
  A large comet was in collision with Earth.
  Many comets are of recent origin (historical times) and are the result of disruptions on planets.
  Some cometary tails and also some meteorites contain hydrocarbons.
  Some meteorites contain argon and neon.

Jupiter.
  Jupiter emits radio noises.
  Jupiter—a dark star.
  Part of the ammonia- and methane-rich Jovian atmosphere was converted into hydrocarbons by means of electrical discharges when it became Venus' trailing part.

Mars.

Mars has been subjected to stress, heating and bubbling activity in recent times.

Mars must have localized areas of strong radioactivity (due to interplanetary discharges).

Mars must have changed its orbit and its rotational momentum.

The Moon.

The moon has been subjected to heating (or liquefaction) and bubbling activity in recent times.

The majority of the lunar craters resulted from the collapse of large bubbles.

Evidence of petroleum hydrocarbons will be found in the moon.

Hydrocarbons on the lunar surface must have been mostly converted to carbides.

Lunar rocks will reveal remanent magnetism, despite the fact that the moon itself has an exceedingly weak magnetic field.

Moonquakes must be very numerous (not necessarily strong.).

Lunar rocks will be found to contain excessive inclusions of argon and neon from an extraneous source; on the basis of potassium-argon dating the age of the moon will be calculated as older than the solar system itself.

Localized spots of excessively strong radioactivity exist on the lunar surface.

A strong thermal gradient under the surface, due to disturbance in lunar motion will be found.

Thermoluminescence of lunar cores will show a thermal process in historical times.

The Earth.

The Earth has a magnetosphere. It reaches at least as far as the moon.

There have been many sudden reversals in the Earth's magnetic polarity, and they were caused by interplanetary discharges.

There have been shifts in the direction of the Earth's astronomical axis and in the position of the geographical pole.

Changes in the length of the day could have been caused in the past by electromagnetic interactions.

Some of Earth's petroleum deposits are of recent date and extraterrestrial origin.

The Earth's climate has undergone radical change as recently as the Bronze Age. Human settlements will be discovered "on the Kolyma or Lena Rivers flowing into the Arctic Ocean."

The last (Wisconsin) glacial period ended not 35,000 years ago but much later, and a more recent glacial advance occurred 3,400 years ago.

Ancient History.

Entire civilizations were overthrown by violent catastrophes in the Near East during historical times.

The Minoan B script writings unearthed on Crete and in the Peloponnesus are Greek.

Mesoamerican culture is several centuries older than the date assigned to it in traditional historical chronology.[9]

We still do not have all the findings from our space probes, but Velikovsky's predictions of what we shall discover seem destined to be verified many times in the future. The listing of verifications of Velikovsky's historical predictions will fill several volumes when Egyptian chronology is finally correlated properly with the histories of other civilizations. Scholars following up Velikovsky's interpretation of Near Eastern history report that his revised chronology resolves innumerable disputes that had been impossible with the traditional Near Eastern chronology.

Quite obviously, in this theory we are not dealing with generalities or with a casual reinterpretation of ancient myths that happen to fit a new scheme of things. Serious readers of Velikovsky's books discover continually that he opens doors that had previously been dogmatically shut to them. The capability of the theory to provide a meaningful interpretation of ancient history while simultaneously predicting phenomena of a cosmic nature is a good indication that Velikovsky has resolved a major problem in integrating separate fields of study into one comprehensive world view. The importance of his theory is that we can now derive a history of our solar system, partially from our scientific experiments and partially from accounts of ancient and primitive peoples, pushing backwards in time our knowledge of both the universe and ourselves. The problem of creation and the origin of life still remains an important question. But we can now eliminate many accounts formerly considered speculative or religious and place them quite properly within the context of our reliable knowledge of the natural world.

Velikovsky's theory suddenly made interdisciplinary studies respectable. New fields of endeavor such as geomythology and archeoastronomy are now opening up, and creative minds, unhampered by dogmatic considerations, are examining the knowledge of physical events, whether in the geological or astronomical field, which are preserved for us in the myths and legends of ancient and primitive peoples. Few scholars have given Velikovsky his just credit. More often they downgrade his thought while paraphrasing some of his better insights. In the field of geomythology, for example, Dorothy Vitaliano discusses the possiblility of myths' describing the occurrence of natural events (*Legends of the Earth*, [1973]). On page 262 Vitaliano ridicules Velikovsky's account of the Exodus and then promptly paraphrases Velikovsky's account on the following pages. She ends her discussion of the Exodus by attributing the separation of the waters to a strong wind, apparently oblivious to the description given in Exodus of all the phenomena accompanying the passage through the waters.

Why, we may well ask, did Velikovsky, of all the advocates of catastrophism, become the target of scientific outrage? In his preface to *Worlds in Collision,* Velikovsky himself suggested the probable answer:

> Harmony or stability in the celestial and terrestrial spheres is the point of departure of the present-day concept of the world as expressed in the celestial mechanics of Newton and the theory of evolution of Darwin. If these two men of science are sacrosanct, this book is a heresy.[10]

And heresy is what many scientists cried when they heard Velikovsky's thesis. Few critics defended either Newton or Darwin directly, since even they had intellectually passed beyond the theories of these men. But the attitude that Newton and Darwin communicated—the homogenous nature of existence, the uniform and uneventful passage of time, and eventually the idea that by projecting our present observations of nature backward into an infinite regression of cosmic time we could understand the world and its processes—formed the world view of scientists, which they did not wish to surrender. A substantial number of theories had been constructed on the basis of the uniform passage of time and the uniformity of cosmic processes, and the introduction of catastrophes, which had the effect of shortening the time span required to accomplish changes, coupled with the realization that infinite projections did not bring certain knowledge, proved too traumatic for most scientists.

The knowledge of the world had changed since the days of Newton and Darwin, but the assumptions upon which they had based their understandings had not changed. By introducing common-sense questions into different areas of knowledge, or what passed for knowledge, Velikovsky leveled the critique of knowledge that Revel had suggested as the necessary step for our species to take to achieve maturity. Many scientists, content in their isolated specialities, refused to take any additional steps to seek a comprehensive picture of the world, fearful, perhaps, that integrating their specialty into a new view of the world would deprive them of the aura of authority that Western civilization had lately given its scientists.

Some objections that Velikovsky raised to the interpretation of phenomena could hardly be countered by orthodox views. In discussing the creation of coal, for example, in *Earth in Upheaval,* Velikovsky noted:

> Seams of coal are sometimes fifty or more feet thick. No forest could make such a layer of coal; it is estimated that it would take a twelve-foot layer of peat deposit to make a layer of coal one foot thick; and twelve feet of peat deposit would require plant remains a hundred and twenty feet high. How tall and thick must a forest be, then, in order to create a seam of coal not one foot thick but fifty? The plant remains must be six thousand feet thick. In some places there must have been fifty to a hundred successive huge forests, one replacing the other, since so many seams of coal are formed.[11]

As Patten showed in his treatment of the formation of the glacial sheet, all Velikovsky had to do to raise a question about the validity of the orthodox theory of coal formation was to demonstrate mathematically the tremendous amount of material needed to produce the effects that are part of our common knowledge. To his credit, Wilfrid Francis, a world famous authority on the formation of coal, wrote in a letter to the editors of *Pensee* the following statement:

> In relation to the modes of formation of coals, I have found that Velikovsky has quoted from the works of many authorities of considerable scientific standing, particularly from the work of some German and English authorities of the 19th and 20th centuries. Much of the evidence presented by these authorities I have checked and found to be satisfactory! So much so, that I agree large scale accumulations of coal-forming debris have frequently been formed by diastrophic (or catastrophic) occurrences in past geological periods, and that, as a result of metamorphic changes, these now appear as mature coals, or, occasionally, as special accumulations of modified land and sea organic fossil products, including amber, jet, fusain, hard coals and cannel coals. I believe that this has occurred more often and on a much greater scale than was visualized by the earlier protagonists of the "drift" theory of coal formation; but acceptance of this conclusion by no means excludes the formation of many deposits by more "peaceful" processes, usually described as *"in situ"* formations.[12]

What can be said in summary concerning primitive accounts of catastrophic events in our planet's past, the theory of catastrophe in general, and Velikovsky's work in particular? Perhaps the first thing is that primitive traditions were not figments of primitive imaginations, no matter how sincere we may credit the primitive peoples in their efforts to explain the universe. Where Cassirer, Jung, and Levi-Strauss explain myths as an intellectual creation designed to account for natural processes or human reactions to human problems, we can transcend their complicated interpretations to recognize that our species has generally been fairly practical in its approach to the natural world. We have not cringed before winds and rain storms; we were not afraid of the orderly procession of the sun and moon; and we recognized in the unusual events of nature a reality that transcended mere mechanical explanations. In recognizing that primitive myths and the oral traditions of tribal peoples contain memories of past events, we give them a respectable status. These people preserved a knowledge of the history of our planet, and our recognition of this accomplishment enhances their sense of pride in traditions and cultural values.

The second implication of recognizing the general theory of catastrophe is that by accepting the thesis we will no longer have to complicate our understanding of natural processes. Rather than spinning elaborate yarns concerning the gradual disappearance of the dinosaur and its reemergence as oil millions of years later, we can skip the academic fantasies and proceed immediately to investigate the energy resources of our planet based upon the recognition that we have received petroleum and fossil fuels in unique and discernible ways, making it easier, perhaps, to discover new supplies of these necessities in places yet unsuspected.

Finally, with respect to the works of Immanuel Velikovsky and other catastrophists, we can begin to give serious attention to their outlines of planetary history. According the ancient sources a respect that is due them and analyzing the manner in which they phrased their memories of catastrophic events can bring us additional insight into the beliefs and capabilities of our own species at a relatively early time in our history. We can, perhaps, settle the old anthropological debate between independent invention and diffusion; we can give more intelligent attention to the many ruins of ancient civilizations, relying less upon scholarly fantasies and more upon a recognition that our species has always been immensely practical and has not emerged from a superstitious past. We can rephrase the questions concerning the origin of species and try to derive new rules for interpreting the phenomenon of life as we have experienced it and as we have seen it recorded in planetary catastrophes.

History has now become something more than the recounting of the experiences of certain civilizations, which learned at an early age to record their experiences in a written language. It now encompasses the history of our solar system and perhaps even the history of the universe. The massive accumulation of data which we now have concerning primitive and ancient peoples can be used to extend backward in time our knowledge of human existence. When we have eliminated the need to classify ancient traditions as "myths," we can see more clearly our ultimate relationship with the universe. When we begin to accept a new picture of cosmic life, we will have finally achieved the maturity that Teilhard understood to be our destiny.

Our proposed new metaphysic, therefore, must be grounded in the most comprehensive and integrated historical perspective we can discover. Incorporating the physical history of our planet with our own history, the merging of the history of *kosmos* and *oikumenē* is the most important step we can take to bring our various fields of knowledge together into one coherent whole. Revel's suggestion that only through a critique of culture and its components and a critique of civilization-as-sanction can we achieve the proper perspective is partially satisfied with this integration of subject fields. But the task of our generation is yet unfulfilled, since we have a responsibility to project a new kind of investigatory technique that can build on the outline we have now sketched. In the concluding chapters we will see how we can accelerate the types of changes that would be most constructive in this respect.

XVII. Theologians and Scientists

In most human cultures religious and scientific leaders have shared two traits: They have pretended to be the sole repository of knowledge, and they have been damn smug about it. The average citizen has traditionally deferred to these two groups and allowed them a semblance of authority in matters of faith and knowledge. Thus theologians and scientists have become the source of truth and have been responsible for its transmission. But while these two groups have been the source and authority for truth, they have rarely been the initiators of it. The truth they have protected has nearly always been obsolete, framed in outmoded concepts, and defended zealously against heresy. Truth, under these conditions, has become a matter of authority rather than inquiry. The sin of abusing authority falls equally on science and religion; for every Galileo that can be cited, there stands a Velikovsky.

The present time is no exception to the above-stated rule. In January 1975 a group of Christian theologians gathered at Hartford Seminary Foundation to discuss their concern that modern thought was eroding the pristine concepts of Christian theology. Feeling that there was too much emphasis on social action, the theologians sought to reaffirm the transcendence of God and issued a statement entitled "An Appeal for Theological Affirmation." This appeal listed thirteen themes and characterized them as "pervasive," "superficially attractive," and "false and debilitating" to the church's life and work. Beneath the generalities was a desire to snuff out heresy wherever it might be found.

The thirteen themes are as follows:

Theme 1: Modern thought is superior to all past forms of understanding reality, and is therefore normative for Christian faith and life.

Theme 2: Religious statements are totally independent of reasonable discourse.

Theme 3: Religious language refers to human experience and nothing else, God being humanity's noblest creation.

Theme 4: Jesus can only be understood in terms of contemporary models of humanity.

Theme 5: All religions are equally valid: the choice among them is not a matter of conviction about truth but only of personal preference or life-style.

Theme 6: To realize one's potential and to be true to oneself is the whole meaning of salvation.

Theme 7: Since what is human is good, evil can adequately be understood as failure to realize human potential.

Theme 8: The sole purpose of worship is to promote individual self-realization and human community.

Theme 9: Institutions and historical traditions are oppressive and inimical to our being truly human; liberation from them is required for authentic existence and authentic religion.

Theme 10: The world must set the agenda for the Church. Social, political and economic programs to improve the quality of life are ultimately normative for the Church's mission in the world.

Theme 11: An emphasis on God's transcendence is at least a hindrance to, and perhaps incompatible with, Christian social concern and action.

Theme 12: The struggle for a better humanity will bring about the Kingdom of God.

Theme 13: The question of hope beyond death is irrelevant or at best marginal to the Christian understanding of human fulfillment.[1]

Publication of the affirmation naturally caused a great sensation in Christian theological circles. There had always been an uneasy truce between social activists and conservative pietists concerning the transcendence and immanence of God, and the sudden attack on activism and the belief in immanence seemed unwarranted. Interest in the statement increased in the months following its publication, and a larger group was convened in May at the National Council of Churches' headquarters at 475 Riverside Drive to discuss the positions taken by the signers of the affirmation. During the interim, rumors had filtered through eastern religious circles that Harvey Cox, secular-city advocate and social activist, was the target of the affirmation.

Harvey Cox attended the May conference to see if indeed he had been the intended victim of the theological barbs. Although the Hartford statement itself was righteously indignant at those who held modern beliefs that tended to erode the faith, the May meeting in New York dissolved into a council of timid sloganeers, unwilling to deal with Cox's alleged heresies and unable to refine their concept of heresy. Queried by Cox about the absence of women and minority groups at the second meeting, Richard Neuhaus lamely offered the excuse that women and blacks had been excluded because those persons invited had to be able to deal with "ideas." The theologians promised, however, to publish a book of essays outlining the dire peril in which Christianity found itself in the twentieth century, and then they retired. Harvey Cox, smiling and content at his victory, chortled at the sudden collapse of discussions concerning his alleged heresies.[2]

Cox immediately busied himself with creating another group of religious leaders, primarily social activists, and they gathered in Boston to devise a response to the Hartford Affirmation. On January 6, Epiphany in the Christian festival year, they issued a "Boston Affirmation," which, considering that the group had a year to respond to the challenge of Hartford, was incredibly wide of the mark in answering the complaints of the Hartford group. Among the theses expounded by the Boston Affirmation are:

Creation: God brings into being all resources, all life, all genuine meanings.
Fall: Humanity is estranged from the source of life.
Exodus and Covenant: God delivers from oppression and chaos. God chooses strangers, servants, and outcasts to be witnessses and to become a community of righteousness and mercy.
Prophecy: In compassion God speaks to the human community through prophets.
Wisdom: The cultural insights and memories of many people and ages illuminate the human condition.
The New Covenant: God is known to us in Jesus Christ.
Church Traditions: God calls those who trust the power of suffering love to form into communities of celebration, care and involvement.
Present Witnesses: The question today is whether the heritage of this past can be sustained, preserved and extended into the future. Society as presently structured, piety as presently practiced, and the churches as presently preoccupied evoke profound doubts about the prospects. Yet we are surrounded by a cloud of witnesses who prophetically exemplify or discern the activity of God. The transforming reality of God's reign is found today.[3]

And then a shopping list of social problems was appended, giving evidence that American society and Christianity were not exactly in good shape.

Only if the world was in imminent danger of being overwhelmed by an invasion of straw people did these two "affirmations" of faith have any relevance. Framed in the most general terms, the two statements failed to clarify, illuminate, or project any encompassing vision of reality. Their definitions of faith and articulation of problem areas were phrased in such general terms that many a non-Christian would have gladly affirmed the propositions they advanced. Like many another media event of our age, the release of the two affirmations generated excitement, a sense of movement and commitment, and a sense of status for the theologians involved. But in retrospect, the affirmations hardly began a Copernican, or even Lutheran, revolution in theological thought. They have begun to look like the desperate efforts of a selected group of theologians to reassert a semblance of authority without which religious institutions in the West have traditionally been powerless.

Science is an overly broad designation for millions of specialists who teach, experiment, and write about the nature of our physical world and the social and other institutions that our species has created within that world. In the last several centuries scientists have come to occupy a place in Western civilization comparable to the priests and autocratic rulers of the ancient Near Eastern civilizations. Experts in specific fields seem able to project an aura of authority in subject areas where they have little knowledge and experience. But the saving grace of the scientists, when viewed from a longer temporal perspective, is that theories, while dogmatically defended during a certain generation of scientists, must withstand the assaults of succeeding generations of thinkers. Unlike religious truths, which may continually be asserted by authorities, scientific truths are always subject to reversal.

A case in point is the present popularity of the geological theory of plate tectonics, the idea that continents float on the crust of the earth and wander over the globe. Originally advanced by the geologist Alfred Wegener in successive editions of his book *The Origin of Continents and Oceans,* issued between 1915 and 1929, the theory was regarded as totally discredited by 1952 and was relegated to the file of bizarre but interesting ideas. As additional studies on various aspects of geology accumulated, evidence tended to show that Wegener's theory had some substance. By the mid-1960s a new generation of geologists had adopted it as the probable description of massive continental-wide geologic processes. While such verification is unusual, most original thinkers having to wait for their death for vindication, plate tectonics' success does indicate that time, not authority, is the ultimate arbiter of scientific truth.

Thus it was all the more puzzling to discover that a group of 186 scientists, including 18 Nobel Prize winners, had issued a statement in September 1975 blasting what they called "the pretentious claims of astrological charlatans." The statement of the scientists was released in a special issue of *The Humanist* magazine. The scientists noted that "we are especially disturbed by the continued uncritical dissemination of astrological charts, forecasts, and horoscopes by the media and by otherwise reputable newspapers, magazines and book publishers."[4] The statement was originally drafted by Bart J. Bok, former president of the American Astronomical Society and professor emeritus at the University of Arizona, who carefully omitted the fact that a number of past greats of science had been devoted astrologers including Galileo, Kepler, and Sir Isaac Newton.

In a separate article in *The Humanist* Bok wrote: "It is deplorable that so many newspapers now print this daily nonsense." And in describing the influence of astrology over the populace, Bok sketched out the sequence of events that he felt to be debilitating to the human mind. "At the start the regular reading [of horoscopes] is sort of a fun game, but it often ends up as a mighty serious business," he warned ominously. "The steady and ready availability of astrological predictions can over many years have insidious influences on a person's personal judgment."[5] Phrased in such a foreboding manner, Bok's warning was reminiscent of J. Edgar Hoover's dark warnings against communism in the 1950s; the reader became convinced that danger existed, yet the precise nature of the misfortune never became clear.

The basis for scientific concern, apparently, was the assertion that science had found no verification of astrological principles. Believing that astrology was part of the magical world view of ancient peoples who had no concept of the vast distances between the earth and the stars and planets, the scientists suggested that "these distances can and have been calculated, [and] we can see how infinitesimally small are the gravitational and other effects produced by the distant planets and the far more distant stars. It is simply a mistake to imagine that the forces exerted by stars and planets at the moment of birth can in any way shape our futures."[6] Like the divine theologians of Hartford and Boston, the scientists devised a confused definition of their opponents' position and then promptly dispatched the straw person with great and dramatic authoritative effect, leaving the impression among the uninitiated and casual readers that they had "disproved" astrology.

Among the notables who signed the statement on astrology were Sir Francis Crick, well-known biologist and winner of the Nobel Prize; Linus Pauling, professor of chemistry at Stanford University and another Nobel Prize winnner; George Wald, prize-winning biologist from Harvard University; and Sir Peter Medawar of the Medical Research Council of Middlesex, England. It was not evident from the statement whether the biologists and chemists regarded themselves as professionally competent to issue an authoritative statement on astrology, a field of study somewhat tangent to their own fields of expertise, although by no means irrelevant to them personally and professionally if it were shown to be a serious field of study.

This attack on astrology was apparently the first of a series of efforts to be made by scientists subscribing to the desire to drive superstition and ignorance from our midst. In the spring of 1976 *The Humanist* announced the formation of a Committee to Scientifically Investigate Claims of Paranormal and Other Phenomena. Again a very unusual group of scientists, this time twenty-five in number, banded together to express concern about "a rising tide of superstition and uncritical acceptance of paranormal phenomena."[7] They announced plans to expand a newsletter into a journal, *The Zetetic,* and use that as a vehicle to investigate psychic healing, psychokinesis, immortality, reincarnation, Kirlian photography, orgone energy, psychic surgery, faith healing, astrology, UFOs, dianetics, poltergeists, psychics and sensitives such as Edgar Cayce, Jean Dixon, and Uri Geller, and the ancient astronaut theories. Apparently, every phenomenon that cannot be properly explained by modern scientific theories will come under scrutiny.

The task that *The Humanist* scientists propose would boggle the average mind, since it involves the accumulation of material on nearly every dissident theory in a number of fields and the systematic investigation of phenomena which may not all fit together in any present explanation of our experiences. From the tone of the announcement, however, there is an indication that these scientists are not intent upon an objective investigation of the data but intend to discredit belief in this great variety of subjects. According to a *New York Times* article, committee members expressed a fear that Western civilization may be "overwhelmed by irrationalism, subjectivism and obscurantism." The scientists, apparently, were worried about the degree to which "parascientific, pseudoscientific and plainly fraudulent beliefs and theories gain acceptance among the public."[8] It is thus for our benefit, not theirs, that this committee desires to toil in the vineyards of current belief.

The degree to which this impartial committee proposed to operate was discussed in a letter sent on June 11, 1976, to Geller and published in the July/August issue of *The Humanist,* with the warning that if Geller chose not to answer their offer to investigate him within forty-five days they would deem his lack of response as a refusal and would inform the news media of his failure to appear before the committee. It is strange that these scientists would choose Uri Geller of all people to be the subject of their first investigation. Geller has already spent some time being tested at the Stanford Research Institute, and that group is not exactly the bastion of superstition in the modern world. And Geller has done some tests with British scientists along the same lines. While we do not yet understand the phenomenon that sometimes appears to accompany this young man, we have no assurance that a command performance before a committee which threatens to attack him in the news media will shed any light on the subject. Certainly *The Humanist's* record to date would lead an impartial observer to believe that we are now seeing the emergence of efforts to control our thoughts and beliefs by a small, determined group of scientists, apparently volunteers in the effort to keep us thinking right.

It is distressing to see both scientists and theologians on the attack against mythical and real ideas when there has not been a corresponding aggressive effort on the part of anyone to call their respective disciplines to account. Our species has never lacked volunteers in the fight to control the minds of people, but it seems strange that this rather sedate time of intellectual activity would call forth such vehement expressions of alarm from the members of two of humankind's oldest professions. Instead of demonstrating a willingness to critically analyze culture and our conception of civilization, which Jean François Revel suggested as necessary to enable the Western nations to transcend their current difficulties, we see representatives of the two major intellectual traditions of the West reassert their authority and demand of our times an unqualified allegiance to doctrines and beliefs derived in former days.

The voices we have traditionally identifed as having responsibility to search for and expound truth seem to have fallen by the wayside. Rather than engaging in a restless quest for meaning, they spend their time preserving and isolating various theories and doctrines, concerned for the purity of expression rather than the potential for growth. A careful examination of the history of Western civilizations would reveal that this situation has always existed. We need only turn to the Hebrew prophetic tradition to see that the major theological expressions of the Hebrew-Judaic-Christian-Islamic religious heritage have always originated outside the institutional and social forms of the day. The great Protestant Reformation, the founding of the Catholic orders, and the expansion of pentecostal and fundamentalist churches in the United States are all evidences that religious rennovations are generally regarded as heretical in their generation.

All too often major scientific developments are not the result of established, responsible scientists, but the work of the maverick, the outsider, the original mind that cannot dwell in the hallowed institutions and groves of academe. In recent years the scientific establishment has nourished the image of a penitent Galileo standing before the Pope; a lonely scientist, the seeker of truth persecuted by the forces of established intolerance and ignorance. But what of the lonely, shunned, and discredited Harvey attempting to prove to colleagues his theory of the circulation of blood? What of Pasteur attempting to show that germs are largely responsible for human illnesses? What of the refusal of archeologists and anthropologists to accept the Folsom point until one of their own had made the same discovery?

Scientific progress has as often been made by the amateur as by the professional. Breaking the code of Linear B, the insoluble language of Crete, was not accomplished by a professional linguist but by Michael Ventris, an English architect. In the throes of confusion in modern physics, after the disappointing experiments to prove the existence of the ether surrounding the earth, an obscure patent office clerk named Albert Einstein advanced an interpretation of the phenomenon that became known as the theory of relativity. Professional archeologists scoffed at Heinrich Schliemann, a German business-man who had childhood dreams of uncovering the city of Troy, until he demonstrated the reality of Homeric legends. Silas Newcomb, one of the greatest mathematicians in American history, proved beyond a mathematical doubt that it was impossible for an airplane to fly; in the same year, the Wright Brothers took off at Kittyhawk, North Carolina. Other examples could be mentioned, but the point would remain the same—scientific progress is not the exclusive province of the professional scientist but a corporate social venture of inquiring minds.

If we cannot rely upon the professional scientist or theologian to give us direction, where can we turn for guidance in bringing meaning into our lives? In asking this question we must remember that the traditional division of experience into subjective and objective, and the corresponding division of the world into the physical world, or *kosmos,* and the social world, the *oikumenē* are no longer epistemological boundaries that we should respect. Our task is rather to transcend these ancient limitations and arrive at new understandings that incorporate the insights that can be obtained in each area. Let us turn first to the world of human affairs, the *oikumenē.*

In the world of human social, political, and technological institutions, the nature of rapid change makes it imperative that we perceive patterns rather than conceptually identify them. "The serious artist," Marshall McLuhan writes, "is the only person able to encounter technology with impunity, just because he is an expert aware of the changes in sense perception."[9] And McLuhan notes that "our specialist and fragmented civilization of center-margin structure is suddenly experiencing an instantaneous reassembling of all its mechanized bits into an organic whole."[10] In this situation it will be the generalist who will survive and give leadership, not the specialist. The old distinctions between professional and amateur, which used to distinguish those who had knowledge from those who dabbled in scattered bits of information, no longer holds. The true seeker of wisdom, the true philosopher, the inquiring mind, will provide leadership in the coming generation, not the expert who brings only specialization and myopic vision to the problems.

Ruth Nanda Ashen, in an introduction to Werner Heisenberg's *Across the Frontiers,* summarized the emergence of new ideas in science as indicating a new sense of unity. "For underlying the new ideas," she wrote, "including those of modern physics, is a unifying order, but it is not causality; it is purpose, and not the purpose of the universe and of man, but the purpose *in* the universe and *in* man."[11] Such a conception transcends the old idea that Mother Nature, a disguised reemergence of the old image of God, is carefully planning out the order of reality. Rather we now must discern a unifying order that encompasses all individual fields of knowledge and presents a comprehensive vision of reality. In a scientific sense also we must become generalists, not specialists, in order to bring meaning into our experiments and investigations of physical reality.

Robert Ardrey, one of the more energetic generalists in our day, describes us as a species lacking a religion. "We are members of societies lacking common bodies of assumption,"[12] he continues. His solution to our problem is the merging of the two isolated strands of intellectual thought, religion and science, in a new philosophy:

> What we lack is an evolutionary philosophy. For too long the philosopher has been the univited guest at our table. For too long in contemporary life the philosopher has remained a weird and somewhat embarrassing eccentric to whom we give Christmas baskets. And if we are a people lacking a philosophy, this must be a reason why. As our knowledge grows, so does our understanding diminish.[13]

Clearly now the objections raised by theologians and the distress demonstrated by the scientists, let alone the popular discussion of the ancient astronaut theories, indicates that we face a conflict between the specialists and the new generalists. The situation does not call for antagonisms on the part of the general public against the specialists. Certainly no hard and fast guidelines can be drawn that would separate scientists and theologians from the rest of society. In the concluding chapters we will discuss some hopeful aspects of the present theological and scientific dilemma, indicating if only temporarily, what may be the productive lines of thought for the future.

XVIII. The Future of Theology

The Western world view has been fragmented for nearly a century as a result of the conflict over the Book of Genesis and evolution. For the most part, scientists have pretended that religion is not a serious part of human life but rather represents the vestiges of ancient superstitions, which we, for the most part, have outgrown. Religion is too often viewed by scientists as a subgrouping of psychology or psychoanalysis, and hence, at best, is seen as a crutch for people who have not yet been brought into a state of intellectual enlightenment. With this attitude fairly prevalent in the scientific community, theologians have tended to take an interdisciplinary approach when they have tried to communicate on an intellectual basis with scientists about the place of religion in human society.

Pierre Teilhard de Chardin's book *The Phenomenon of Man* represented an effort to bring religion and science together, and if Robert Ardrey wanted an evolutionary philosophy, he might have considered Teilhard's major work as a response, albeit in anticipation, of his suggestion. But Teilhard's philosophy, while in tune with the major premises acceptable to biologists and paleontologists, made few substantial overtures to modern physics, which seems to dominate scientific concern in this generation. Thus in attempting to attach conceptions of energy to his general biological outline, Teilhard seemed to incorporate the quantum phenomenon in the evolutionary scheme, running into difficulty thereafter when he attempted to pull his entire vision together, since his thought ultimately produced a monism of mentality.

In his major work *Christian Faith and Natural Science*, Karl Heim tended to absolutize spatial considerations of modern physics to the exclusion, or deemphasis, of the temporal and transformational aspects. "The rift between belief and natural science," Heim maintained, "can today be bridged, and mutual comprehension established, only if it is possible to transpose the concept of space, which has acquired a position of primary significance in modern physics, in a higher connotation to the world-picture of belief." [1] Working from this premise, and in terms of the total picture of modern theories in physics, Heim was not avoiding a theological-scientific confrontation by any means. He transformed Kantian conceptions of space into a modern rephrasing of the problem of knowledge, concluding that "the structure of space has its origin neither in the subject nor in the object but always in the *relation* which arises between a particular subject and a particular object whenever they encounter one another." [2]

Quite obviously, physical reality defined in relationships in the sense of an organic event is well within the conceptual boundaries of modern physics and has great relevance to theology if we proceed from the premise that religion is concerned with the relationship of the individual and the deity. Once we have accepted the reality of this relationship, we can proceed beyond Euclidian conceptions of space, using the non-Euclidian geometries of Bolyai and Lobachevski, to describe the possibility of other spaces in which divinity could be present, capable of intruding, on its own initiative, into spaces mathematically and geometrically inferior. The probable common-sense meaning of this complicated manner of using non-Euclidian spaces as a location of divinity is that the supraspaces in which religious reality exists are always tangent, in an ultimate sense, to any spatial realities that may exist at our level of awareness and apprehension.

This conception of the universe resolves a great many theological problems since it easily transcends the old argument, one we have seen in an unsophisticated form in the Hartford and Boston Affirmations, between the transcendence and immanence of divinity. The difficulty with Heim's conception of the universe, when it is translated into theological-scientific terms, is that it is extremely hard to visualize and conceptualize, eliminating the picture of space-time, which religious doctrines have traditionally embraced, and making religious sensitivities more a matter of proper mathematical conception than devotional attitudes. If this sacrifice of easily used descriptive images is worth the price of clarifying articles of the faith, Heim has succeeded in eliminating the cultural contexts of which Bultmann complained when he began his effort to "de-mythologize" the Christian message. Absolutizing non-Euclidian spaces enabled Heim to easily resolve the problem of making relevation an event in space-time while releasing it from chronologies and places which have been objectionable to other thinkers.

Ian Barbour, discussing Karl Heim's effort to bring science and religion together, feels that "for Heim 'spaces' tend to be equated with different perspectives on the same events." This objection would have weight only if we insist on bringing the reality of other spaces into the causal, chronological sequence of our own understanding of time, reducing the different "spaces" of self, world, and God to one system of reference. Barbour summarizes his commentary on Heim's system by suggesting that "as Heim uses the concept of spaces, then, God's action seems to occur, as it does for others in this second major group, in the transformation of personal interpretive perspectives, rather than in the control of events in nature." [3] Such an objection, raised within the context of traditional Christian assertions that God "acts" in natural and historic events, would seem to indicate that Barbour feels that Heim's treatment of nature is not ultimately dealing with entities that we experience.

Of more importance in our discussion is Heim's effort to describe the changes in our conception of nature, since these ideas tend to show his orientation toward nature as a whole. This set of conceptions is important because it indicates the extent to which Heim released himself from specifically Christian presuppositions concerning nature and the physical world. Heim had a tendency to project from the basis of the experiences of our species to a description of the nature of other entities and their experiences. Thus in discussing modern physics, Heim wrote:

> ... since atomic physics has resolved the rigidity of lifeless matter into infinitesimal spaces in which elemental particles execute purposeful movements at enormous velocities like living individuals, the last possible reason has been eliminated for regarding the inorganic world as an unconscious inanimate mass. Once again we are simply being naïvely presumptuous if we suppose that because these worlds in which the electrons and protons circle, infinitesimally small as they are according to human standards, have nothing in common in shape or size with a human body, it follows that the inner life too of these unimaginably tiny beings is negligible in comparison with all the joys and sorrows, struggles and defeats, which a human soul experiences. [4]

Such a conception is powerful, to say the least, and would meet with approval by Teilhard as an effort to link the various levels of organic, and even inorganic, existence. But it illustrates a tendency of Karl Heim to comprehend the nature of the physical universe as a mirror, in miniature to be sure, of the experiences of our species rather than as things in themselves.

Heim drew these parallels whenever he had to confront the practical task of relating other life-forms to our own. Thus when he described the possible relationships that can be used to understand the unity of life, he proposed that the actions of some plants and animals, when viewed in a process of changing the rate of observation through photography, act amazingly like ourselves:

> The growth of flowers has been filmed and it has been shown that if we look at the development of a flowering plant through the time-lens, reducing each day to one second, then the process is reminiscent of the respiratory movements of a human being. [5]

And following this example Heim compared a creeper climbing a wall to a drowning man grasping and clinging to a rescuing plank. This tendency to portray the unity of life through examples familiar to our species continues the traditional Christian propensity to cast an understanding of the physical and biological world in our own image. It therefore fundamentally precludes the question of our relationship to the rest of the world. In this conception our species is still determinative, and we stand above nature, not as an equal part of it with other species.

These objections border on the trivial when compared with the efforts of other theologians to confront the problem of bringing science and religion into a contemporary dialogue concerning the reality of the world. Certainly Heim's thinking is original, and his suggestion that space be given at least a logical primacy over time indicates a dramatic breakthrough in the ability of theologians to deal with difficult conceptual problems raised by the findings of modern science. Substantial but more practical theologies can well emerge out of Heim's thinking, and if we reexamine Tillich's difficulty in understanding how the holy places of the physical world can exist and yet are illustrative of our ambiguous situation, we can understand how far Heim brought contemporary theological thinking with his concentration of space and spaces.

There remain, however, numerous practical problems, which neither Teilhard nor Heim attempted to handle, and these problems, for the most part, are those numerous questions that arise in the minds of sincere laypersons who attempt to understand how they can reconcile their understanding of modern science, even though it remains at a fairly unsophisticated level, with the emotional and personal experiences they tend to relate to religious thinking and traditions. For the most part nonprofessional people tend to phrase their questions in common-sense language, which acts as a shorthand to otherwise complicated questions. Any theology that seeks to relate its particular insights to the world in which we live must deal with practical and simple questions as well as with very complicated systems of analysis that adequately treat scientific notions with the respect to which they are entitled.

Ian Barbour, who was conspicuous by his absence at the Hartford and Boston Affirmation parties, is one of the most exciting theologians today because he does not avoid the difficult questions. Although some of his answers appear to follow uninspired and traditional Christian responses, he gives every indication of being capable of changing his mind when presented with new evidence or a new way of structuring questions. His writings are thus extremely provocative in a theological sense. Such an attitude toward his material automatically raises his work above the level of discussion exemplified by the Hartford and Boston Affirmations. For example, attempting to interrelate science and religion, Barbour poses the question: "If the same world is the subject of scientific regularities and of providential action, do we not have to show how natural and divine causality can be conceived to coexist?" Posing such a difficult question directly enables him to suggest a direct answer:

We can agree that the "language of grace" drawn from man's redemption in Christ, must remain central in Christian theology; *but in the discussion of God's action in nature this need not prevent us from employing categories of thought that can be related to the terms in which the scientist describes the world.*[6]

The above quotation illustrates the basic orientation that Barbour brings to the discussion of science and religion. Theological concepts can be discussed in traditional theological language, according to Barbour, but precise boundary lines can also be established to channel the discussion according to the most constructive lines of thought. When we begin to describe the relationship of deity and the world of nature, we must gain insights from the findings of science concerning the probable structures and processes of the world. To call Barbour a process theologian, therefore, is beside the point, since he appears to be a new generalist, choosing the most fruitful epistemological tools to begin to bring science and religion together. If he has a fault in attempting to perform this feat, it is perhaps in not recognizing the value of his own insights. Describing scientific assumptions, he suggests "that the orderliness of nature is *an implicit assumption* of science. Clearly it is not a formal presupposition or a logical premise, and it is never mentioned in scientific research itself; it is simply taken for granted in the scientific community and in the culture of which it is a part." [7]

If the existence of God is a matter of religious faith, then the assumption of orderliness is a matter of scientific faith, and Barbour's clear task should be to challenge scientific orthodoxy on this point in the same manner that scientists challenge religious orthodoxy on its contentions. But Barbour fails to take advantage of his own perceptions, emphasizing that we can have two complementary perspectives on the single world of experience by creating a new related language that is compatible with both scientific and religious assertions. In the overall scheme of this effort he tries to derive two contrasting perspectives on the world, arguing that "in emphasizing two contrasting *perspectives* on one reality, rather than two *aspects* of one reality, the argument has moved from God's control of nature to the interpretative perspective of the observer. The interpretation, not the events, becomes religiously significant." [8]

This shift in emphasis allows Barbour to remove the difficult theological task of "proving" the specific activity of God at any one historical event, and it enables him to open theological analysis to revelations of many kinds, at many historical and cultural crises, in many places, without being forced into preexisting categories of interpretation. Admittedly this shift involves Barbour in practical difficulties with conservative and less sophisticated theologians who tend to view revelation as occurring only within the Christian context, but the new basis for analysis allows Barbour to make room for scientific discoveries and theories that a more rigid theological interpretation prohibits.

In placing the emphasis on the interpretation of events, we must not, however, deny the physical reality of the events themselves. The primitve and ancient traditions concerning the activities of the deity may be cast as a religious

explanation of unusual events. After we have extracted the religious interpretations from those events, we are still left with the physical reality that caused
them to be regarded as unusual and that inspired primitive peoples to describe
their causative factors as the activities of deity. The "two perspectives" that
Barbour purports to have achieved are in reality a separation of the different
manner in which we ascribe causative factors to events of the natural world, and
they come together in the event itself. We can therefore retain the religious
meanings of events in a continuous substantial manner while changing our
understanding of the mechanisms that science would use to describe the manner
in which they took place. Velikovsky's treatment of the Exodus, for example, as
both a religious significant event and a physical planetary incident capable of
being dissected using the concepts of history, physics, geology, and other sciences
is compatible with Barbour's new methodology.

Barbour continually returns to the question of nature. He writes: "We *seek a
theology of nature*. Such a theology must take the findings of science into account
when it considers the relation of God and man to nature, even though it derives
its fundamental ideas elsewhere." [9] But he depends too much on the theory of
evolution to structure some of his questions. "At this point," Barbour continues,
"the evolutionary and indeterminate character of cosmic history is relevant, and
is acknowledged in the theological reflections of Birch and Teilhard." [10] But do
we have to project theological questions into an infinite evolutionary past?
Barbour himself raises this question:

> Most contemporary theological works say very little about nature. Discussions of
> providence, for example, refer extensively to God's activity in history but are silent
> about his activity in nature. What, then, was God's role in the long stretches of cosmic
> time before man's appearance? Is a sharp distinction between history and nature
> tenable, if nature itself has a history and if man is rooted in nature? [11]

In a practical sense, the educated person who desires to integrate scientific
knowledge with religious beliefs is bothered by this question. There is, very
simply, no good answer to it as long as the question is phrased as if the
particular activity our species discerns or intuits regarding the deity is taken to
be descriptive of God's essence rather than as an interpretation of our
experiences. Barbour's solution, that we are dealing with two perspectives on an
event, is very helpful, since obviously we cannot project a possible activity for
God during the time when we were not around to participate in the event.

Barbour returns to this question, however, in another context. His willingness to seek relationships of different dimensions, pulling a widely divergent
knowledge of science and religion into a common intellectual context, is one of
the strengths in his work. He warns against the traditional Western tendency to
conceive religion as being predominantly mental, suggesting that "if Christianity is radically interiorized, nature is left devoid of meaning, and the stretches of
cosmic history before man's appearance are unrelated to God." [12] Returning the
question of religious activity to a foundation in the natural world thus enables

us to keep a broad perspective on our place as a part of nature rather than allowing us to wander away, "de-mythologizing" our descriptions of experience, in the manner of Bultmann.

The theology of nature that Ian Barbour proposes, as opposed to traditional "natural theology," is "an attempt to view the natural order in the framework of theological ideas derived primarily from the interpretation of historical revelation and religious experience." [13] But, we might add, he does so with a plentiful amount of both theory and data from the scientific world which enables us to ground any theological statements in the collective historical experiences of our species. "If one is to subscribe to a Christian world-view," Barbour writes, "it must make more sense of all the available evidence than any other world-view." [14] There would seem to be no way, therefore, that Barbour would not in the future confront the religious traditions of the primitive peoples and attempt to reconcile both their religious insights and their collective memories of planetary events with Western religious and scientific knowledge.

The importance of Barbour's present efforts to derive a satisfactory synthesis of science and religion is his insistence that we are basically dealing with one world of experience and that in some manner, perhaps not even known to us at present, everything must stand in a comfortable and coherent relationship with everything else. "The fabric of interlocking religious belief must also be contextually tested," he argues, adding that "ideas of God, self, society and nature are not independent." [15] They are not, of course, independent, but they are certainly isolated into small complexes of belief, which may not necessarily coalesce using the present Western method of integrating knowledge. Barbour's thinking illustrates that problem, for he continues to act as if a complementary development of science and religion, held by faith in an intellectual tension, is capable of providing an intelligent and futuristic view of the meaning of human life.

In *Myths, Models and Paradigms,* Ian Barbour begins to let scientific methodology exert too much influence on him. Anxious to provide a solid foundation for future theological inquiry, he relies heavily on contemporary interpretations of the structure of theories, and he suggests that religious thinking could profit by understanding theory-origination procedures. "Broadly speaking," he writes, "a model is a symbolic representation of selected aspects of the behaviour of a complex system for particular purposes. It is an imaginative tool for ordering experience, rather than a description of the world." [16] When we deal with scientific theories, this situation is indeed true, since scientists are attempting to make the data conform to their assumption that nature is orderly. They therefore select data to fit their present conception of orderliness. Depending upon their other presuppositions, such as the unreliability of ancient traditions, the idea that cosmic time can be projected infinitely and homogeneti-cally backward toward a point of cosmic origin, and the idea that our species as a rule seeks an intellectual interpretation of phenomena, scientists then interpret their findings according to a logical framework. But, if their "selected aspects" are incomplete, if they overlook important data because of the tendency to seek orderliness prematurely, then, of course, the conclusions are wrong. That Western science, for the most part, still conceives the natural processes to be mechanical in operation, should be a warning to Barbour that basing theological expositions on a methodology derived from science is to exclude those very factors—emotions and intuitions—which the Western religious traditions have always excluded with destructive results.

If one assumes, however, that we do discover a model through which theological ideas can be systematically articulated, Barbour sees the theological task quite properly as one of organic growth. "The most that one can expect of any set of beliefs is that it will make more sense of all the available evidence than alternative beliefs," he argues. "The choice is not between religion and science, but between theism, pantheism and naturalism, let us say, as each is expressed in a particular historical tradition." But, Barbour warns, "no basic beliefs are capable of demonstrable proof. A set of beliefs must be considered as an organic network of interrelated ideas." [17] Barbour could immensely profit, therefore, from an investigation of the non-Western religious traditions, particularly from the so-called primitve or tribal traditions that do not see religion as a set of beliefs but as a series of reports on events which they have experienced over the course of historical time.

It may be that at this stage of his intellectual development Ian Barbour is poised on the brink of such an investigation. He certainly hints that a vast area of alternative data is available if we look beyond the area of cognitive claims which have traditionally formed the substance of Western religious and scientific thought. "Before analysing criteria for cognitive claims," he writes in *Myths, Models and Paradigms*, ". . . we should look for a moment at possible criteria for non-cognitive functions. One such criterion is the ability of a religious tradition to *fulfill social and psychological needs.* Desirable social goals might include group unity, community stability and social harmony. Among psychological goals are self-understanding, maturity, and integration of personality." [18] These noncognitive functions, as we have previously learned from Radin, are the characteristics of primitve societies.

That Barbour is approaching a major breakthrough in leaving the exclusivity of the Christian tradition to move out into the larger world of religious experiences of all social traditions represented by our species is apparent in his expansion of noncognitive functions idea. "At the theoretical level, coherence among ethical values is supported by beliefs about the nature of reality and the destiny of man. More significantly, at the practical level, motivation to sustain action is a product of personal transformation and reorientation as well as commitment to a worldview. Religious beliefs can be judged by the ethical norms they uphold and their effectiveness in motivating ethical action." [19] Ethical actions, and indeed ethics themselves, derive from world view, and the Christian ethics, which concentrates on the individual, falls short of the mark in that it does not correspond to any conceivable world view that can be identified by modern science. Barbour will resolve his present difficulties in the future when he recognizes the fallacy of misplaced concreteness as a theological shortcoming as well as a scientific misunderstanding. The individual is not the absolute point of reference for either religious or scientifc analysis; the group is.

We come, then, to Barbour's understanding of the traditional Christian model for God: "In biblical theology the central model for God is a human person." [20] This is the fundamental point of departure that exists between those religions of the Hebraic-Islamic-Christian tradition and the religions of the rest of our species. The religious tradition that derives its geographical orgin from the Near East always casts its conception of deity in quasi-human terms, expanding human qualities infinitely in those theologies that emphasize omnipotence, ominscience, eternality, and creativity, and playing down the other qualities of which our species is not particularly proud—vengeance, egotism, and other excesses. Now other religious traditions have cast their image of deity in human terms. Certainly American Indians—with their stories of the Grandfathers, the Corn Mothers, and the Transformers—have used human conceptions to express religious experiences. On the whole, however, they have preserved the same dimension of aloofness for their deities as we have. The Near Eastern religions have not maintained this distinction. Instead they have elaborated on every aspect of deity that could be placed in a system of analysis and exposition. Their religions thus comprehend primarily the *knowledge* of the image of God, and this knowledge is transformed into creeds, doctrines, and dogmas, and religion eventually becomes a cognitive exercise rather than an experience.

The world of human institutions, particularly in the United States, is undergoing rapid and profound change. The age of the specialist is over, and the generalist must consume an increasing amount of material in order to make sense of the world. Ian Barbour's theology offers the best present hope of understanding how to integrate the religious and scientific aspects of our life. Rather than coming before the theological public to demand that immanence or transcendence be emphasized, Barbour faces the difficult problem of communicating with scientists, on the one hand, and seeking a means of bringing their insights into correspondence with our deepest religious feelings and experiences. In theology Barbour suggests that "we need new symbols of transcendence which do not imply priority in space and time; we have tended to spatialize and temporalize God, putting him outside, alongside, or before the world." [21] If this is Barbour's understanding of the present theological task, then we are in good hands.

Is the present task either theological or scientific, however, in view of the present tendency of both institutions and knowledge to coalesce? Barbour's efforts should properly be considered to be metaphysical, since he seeks a synthesis of understanding by making the unusual but proper connections between presently disconnected areas of interest. In his own words "systematic connectedness is sought among areas of inquiry usually considered in isolation. Insofar as it succeeds, the power of such a conceptual synthesis lies in its ability to integrate and illuminate a wide range of experience—in science, history, art, ethics, religion, and so forth." [22] Such an inquiry, according to Ian Barbour, is a metaphysical one, and an examination of his present corpus of works would indicate that he is one of the leading metaphysicians of our generation.

What then of religion? Perhaps the best description of the manner in which we will come to understand the religious experience in the future was given by Carl Jung in his essay "The Meaning of Self-Knowledge":

> What does lie within our reach, however, is the change in individuals who have, or create for themselves, an opportunity to influence others of like mind. I do not mean by persuading or preaching—I am thinking, rather, of the well-known fact that anyone who has insight into his own actions, and has thus found access to the unconscious, involuntarily exercises an influence on his environment. The deepening and broadening of his conciousness produce the kind of effect which the primitves call "mana." It is an unintentional influence on the unconscious of others, a sort of unconscious prestige, and its effect lasts only so long as it is not disturbed by conscious intention. [23]

This state of existence would seem to provide the final synthesis we seek. It certainly describes the charismatic religious figure all societies have experienced. And the well-informed generalist, sincere and determined to make sense out of the present world, would seem to fulfill this archetype. We can conclude, therefore, that religion in the future will become an important force in the affairs of our species, that it will transcend doctrines, dogmas, and creeds, and become something we are, rather than something we believe. Theology and philosophy may well coalesce into their former unity, and we may become seekers and lovers of truth.

XIX. The Transformation of Science

Part of the wonder of modern life is the rapid expansion of knowledge. We double the amount of knowledge almost every decade, and Kenneth Boulding, internationally respected economist and futurist, has observed that "as far as many statistical series related to activities of mankind are concerned, the date that divides human history into two equal parts is well within living memory."[1] For the most part the knowledge we are continuing to gather is specific—measurements, experiments, and investigations. Archeological digs, space probes, and controlled experiments characterize our present quest for knowledge. As Robert Ardrey has pointed out, we have banished the philosopher from the tables of knowledge; little is being done today to pull the mass of information and knowledge together and bring it into a simplified, coherent whole.

One of the phenomena of our search for knowledge today is the development of interdisciplinary studies. We began by crossing some fields that appeared related, such as biology and chemistry, astronomy and physics, geology and physics, to form respectively biochemistry, astrophysics, and geophysics. But with the increase of knowledge in every field and the indications that some difficult problems can be resolved better by combining fields, we are now in the process of combining previously unrelated fields into new and exciting areas of fruitful research. Geomythology, the combination of the principles of geology with the oral traditions and myths of primitive peoples to determine the extent of geological disruptions in historical times, or during such times as these events would be the subject of human eyewitness accounts, is a new science that shows promise. Archaeoastronomy—the effort to derive the astronomical knowledge of ancient peoples from their monuments, oral traditions, and other remnants of culture—has come a long way, particularly with the studies of Gerald Hawkins who showed that the ancient British ruin of Stonehenge had all the characteristics of a computer for determing the solstices. When placed in a modern scientific context, this new effort to show the relevance of the knowledge of non-Western and primitive peoples can only serve to broaden the base of our total knowledge of the world and bring increasing respect for those non-Western societies of long ago.

One of the major problems that now confronts science, and, indeed, all of our efforts to make sense of the mass of material that we have available, is the manner in which various fields of knowledge can be properly combined. Scientists have long suspected that our knowledge will eventually be unified, but exactly how this process will come about has puzzled them. They continually find new relationships between existing fields of knowledge, but no general theory has yet emerged that can adequately combine all our knowledge into one consistent framework of interpretation. Werner Heisenberg, for example, explained the problems of conception that face physicists who attempt to combine closely related fields to physics:

> It is very difficult to see how concepts like perception, function of an organ, affection could be a part of the coherent set of the concepts of quantum theory combined with the concept of history. On the other hand, these concepts are necessary for a complete description of life, even if for the moment we exclude mankind as presenting new problems beyond biology. Therefore, it will probably be necessary for an understanding of life to go beyond quantum theory and to construct a new coherent set of concepts, to which physics and chemistry may belong as "limiting cases."[2]

One of the problems in establishing a basis for understanding life, it would appear, is to find the proper method of reintroducing the human emotions and intuitions, which were originally squeezed out of experiences to form an abstract general knowledge. We thus appear to be coming full circle in our quest for reliable information.

R. G. Collingwood, attempting to make a meaningful relationship between historical knowledge and scientific knowledge, writes of the value of generalization, noting that in natural science, the data "are given by perception, and perceiving is not understanding. The raw material of natural science is therefore 'mere particulars,' observed but not understood, and, taken in their perceived particularity, unintelligible. *It is therefore a genuine advance in knowledge to discover something intelligible in the relations between general types of them.*"[3] The path to a coalescence of knowledge, it would appear, involves establishing relationships between general types of particulars. And speaking of the acceptance of a scientific theory, Ian Barbour remarks that "a theory is valued if it accurately accounts for known observations and yields precise predictions of future measurements. The scientist is particularly impressed if it explains a variety of types of phenomena and, above all, if it leads to the discovery of novel phenomena not previously anticipated."[4]

If Collingwood and Barbour are correct in their assessment of the nature of scientific advances and the acceptance of theories by the scientific establishment, and if Heisenberg has accurately assessed the difficulty of combining emotional functions and the knowledge of physical science, we must begin to look for a system that has the largest possible combination of factors and fields of knowledge to consider for our general interpretation of the world. In this respect the knowledge of primitive peoples may prove helpful since it does combine the emotions and intuitions with a memory of physical events experienced on our planet. The difficulty with this solution is that our present knowledge far outstrips any conceivable descriptions we could derive from the primitive traditions. At best they can form a prehistoric foreword to our present knowledge.

Yet this suggestion is a step in the right direction. R. G. Collingwood writes that:

> There is only one hypothesis on which natural processes could be regarded as ultimately historical in character: namely, that these processes are in reality processes of action determined by a thought which is their own inner side. This would imply that natural events are expressions of thoughts, whether the thoughts of God, or of angelic or demonic finite intelligences, or of minds somewhat like our own inhabiting the organic and inorganic bodies of nature as our minds inhabit our bodies. Setting aside mere flights of metaphysical fancy, such an hypothesis could claim our serious attention only if it led to a better understanding of the natural world.[5]

Collingwood's requirement has been met, since the physicists understand our knowledge of the physical world as limited primarily by our mental ability to conceive of interpretations of phenomena. Indeed, Leon Brunschvicg finds that "twentieth-century science has liberated history, which was enslaved by the philosophy of history to an illusory imitation of the philosophy of nature—an imitation which we know to be illusory *because twentieth-century science itself has taken the form of a history.*"[6] Our eventual unification of knowledge, therefore, will be the application of historical requirements to natural science and the introduction of the physical sciences to the interpretation of history.

It is important to recognize that this combination of factors, this coalescing of social and physical sciences, appears to be the proper direction to take in order to combine all aspects of knowledge into one coherent scheme of interpretation. It is important because one system of interpretation which has survived from ancient times contains a combination of physical and social sciences, extends far backward into our species' past, and survives today as an important influence, although presently under attack. That system, of course, is astrology, which combines a knowledge of the universe and particularly astronomy with a knowledge of human emotions and personality types. Astrology seems to have originated remotely enough in the past of our species to have shown an amazing resiliency and persistence in spite of the efforts by religious and scientific establishments to extinguish it. It would be well, therefore, to inspect more closely the complaints lodged against astrology by Bart J. Bok and others and attempt to discern the nature of their objections.

Bart J. Bok wrote a companion article in *The Humanist* that was published with the "Objections to Astrology," signed by the 186 scientists. Bok described astrology as a "pseudoscience," and said: "All I can do is state clearly and unequivocally that modern concepts of astronomy and space physics give no support—better said, negative support—to the tenets of astrology."[7] Attempting to trace astrology backward, Bok wrote that "it was only natural that early civilizations would consider the stars and planets in the heavens as awesome evidence of supernatural powers that could magically affect their lives."[8] He suggested that while people were relatively unsophisticated—even to the time of Newton—there were good reasons for exploring astrology; what reasons, exactly, he did not state. Bok's major objection to astrology, however, was based on his understanding of the results of modern astronomy, to wit:

> . . . all this changed when the first measurements were made of the distances to the sun, planets, and stars and when the masses of these objects were determined. The foundations of astrology began to crumble when we came to realize how vanishingly small are the forces exerted by the celestial objects on things and people on earth— and how very small are the amounts of radiation associated with them received on earth. The only perceptible and observable effects evident to all of us are produced by the tidal forces caused by the gravity of the moon and sun. To assume that the sun, moon, and planets would exert special critical forces upon a baby at birth—forces that would control the future life of the infant—seems to run counter to common sense.[9]

Bok elaborated on this theme—that the force that could be exerted by the stars and planets is negligible—twice in his article, and it is instructive to repeat his warnings in order to clarify exactly how he interprets the tenets of astrology.

> I should mention here that these forces—according to astrology, critically effective only at the precise moment of birth—can hardly be gravitational or radiative in nature. The known forces that the planets exert on a child at the time of birth are unbelievably small. The gravitational forces at birth produced by the doctor and nurse and by the furniture in the delivery room far outweigh the celestial forces. And the stars are so far away from the sun and earth that their gravitational, magnetic, and other effects are negligible.[10]

It is clear from these two examples that Bok restricts astrological interpretations of the influence of the stars to mechanical forces that can be measured directly. It is doubtful that many competent astrologers would agree with Bok on this point or that they would insist that a mechanical force comparable to gravity or magnetism directly affects anyone, astrologically or not. We shall return to this point presently.

Bok recommends another article in the same issue, "Astrology: Magic or

Science" by Lawrence E. Jerome, as the proper analysis of the origins of astrology; so we shall review Jerome's article also. "Astrology is false," Jerome wrote, "because it is a system of magic, based on the magical 'principle of correspondences.' "[11] And then he proceeded to show that primitive peoples development of the idea of magic was responsible for astrology. But he appeared to lack a precise idea of the primitive person, for he wrote: "Prehistoric man had been used to watching the comings and goings of the heavenly bodies, and *when the magical world picture arose with the advent of civilization,* astrology was a natural consequence."[12] It is difficult to determine exactly how Jerome conceived early civilizations or where he derived his knowledge of ancient societies, for he suggested that priests of the state religions used astrology "to keep the citizens in line, convincing them that only by working for the good of the state could they keep the 'powers of nature' in check."[13]

Jerome never did discuss the errors of correspondences in any adequate manner. He referred the readers to Richard Cavendish's book *The Black Arts,* Jack Lindsay's *Origins of Astrology,* and his own article "Astrology and Modern Science: A Critical Analysis," published in the journal *Leonardo* in 1973. The only examples of the correspondences that Jerome gave are noteworthy in their vagueness: "Thus, Pisces (the Fish) is called a water sign, red Mars is associated with war, quick and elusive Mercury governs the metal quicksilver (mercury), planets in opposition are in disharmony, and so on."[14] Such an analysis is hardly a criticism of correspondences that are erroneously placed together; it reads more like an incorrect and amateurish rendering of some phrases of astrological language from one who knew little about the subject.

The concept of "biological clocks" came under Jerome's attack, since some advocates or sympathizers of astrology had apparently recently claimed a possible correlation between astrology and the newly discovered phenomenon of internal tempos in organisms that appear to respond to cosmic rhythms. Jerome discussed the discovery in 1920 that the length of the day determines the time of flowering in plants and the 1950 discovery that "virtually all living organisms display some periodicity, ranging from twenty-four-hour activity cycles to year-long breeding cycles with precise seasonal timing."[15] And he mentioned such books as *The Cosmic Clocks* by Michel Gauquelin and *Astrological Birth Control* by Sheila Ostrander and Lynn Schroeder, which cite biological discoveries as evidence that the basic assumptions of astrology are true. But, Jerome noted, "such arguments are fallacious, since astrology is based on the magical 'principle of correspondences' and not on any supposed physical influences by the planets and stars."[16]

It is apparent from reading the "Objections to Astrology" by the 186 scientists, Bok's article on astrology, and Jerome's article that the scientists did not have their ducks lined up in a row, so to speak. For example, Jerome insists that astrology is in error because it is based on correspondences, an improper methodology, but he avoids the works of Gauquelin and Ostrander and Schroeder, which appear to favor some type of influence, by insisting that influence is not the basis for astrology. His colleague Bok, however, does not mention correspondences but suggests that astrology is based on some mechanical influences. The so-called scientific refutation of astrology admirably qualifies as an emotional outburst but hardly deals with the issue of the validity of astrology; so we remain curious about the vehemence of the attack. Perhaps it is symptomatic of an unconscious recognition by the scientists that they will soon have to deal responsibly with astrology and, like St. Paul before his conversion, are spending their emotional energy in resistance.

There are, to be sure, immense difficulties with astrology as it is presently constituted, and we will examine some of the problems, conceptually and factually, that presently inhibit us from coming to grips with this strange remnant from our species' past. First, however, we must correct some of the misconceptions that are contained in both Bok's and Jerome's objections. Jerome placed his heaviest emphasis on the idea that correspondences have a magical orgin and therefore cannot be regarded as valid in any way. Such an objection is simply not true. Correspondence is a very important analytical tool for connecting bodies of theory and data. Ian Barbour, writing in *Issues in Science and Religion,* tells us:

> The links between theoretical concepts and experimental observations have been termed "rules of correspondence," "epistemic correlations," or "coordinating definitions." For some concepts these *rules of correspondence* may be very direct and simple, as for example the association of "length" with the results of a particular measuring operation. For other concepts, such as "energy" or "neutron," rules of correspondence may be more complex.[17]

Far from being some aspect of magic, therefore, the idea of correspondence is a respectable way to interpret phenomena, and it is used by contemporary scientists. That ancient peoples may have also used such an epistemological methodology does not invalidate their results unless we have more information that they improperly used correspondences.

Bok seemed to rely upon an outdated concept of causality in his insistence that the forces exerted by the planets and stars do not have significant impact on human beings. He twice implied that scientists have measured the forces that stars and planets must produce here on earth and suggested that because of the vast distances involved they can exert no significant force. Now one of the important innovations that modern physics has made in its conception and interpretation of forces and distances is the abandonment of Newtonian ideas. Werner Heisenberg wrote:

> Newton had introduced a very new and strange hypothesis by assuming a force that acted over a long distance. Now in the theory of the fields of force one could come back to the older idea, that action is transferred from one point to a neighboring point, only by describing the behavior of the fields in terms of differential equations. This proved actually to be possible, and therefore the description of the electromagnetic fields as given by Maxwell's equations seemed a satisfactory solution to the problem of force. Here one had really changed the program given by Newtonian mechanics.[18]

In other words, modern physicists do not often speak of forces at a distance when dealing with situations on the stellar scale, and the idea that modern science has measured forces exerted by the stars and planets and found them to be negligible is not accurate. The best we can conclude is that of the forces measured to date we have not attempted to correlate in any manner the possible correspondences that might be suggested by astrology.

If we explore further the cautious manner in which the physicist phrases the interpretation of phenomena, we arrive at a wording suspiciously similar to astrological contentions of "influences" and "correspondences." Werner Heisenberg wrote about the objective description of nature by physicists:

> The whole objective description of nature in the Newtonian sense, in which determinate values are attributed to the defining elements of the system, such as position, velocity and energy, had to be abandoned in favor of a description of observation situations, in which only the probabilities of certain outcomes can be given. The words in which we allude to atomic phenomena *therefore became problematic*. It was possible to speak of waves or particles, and necessary to realize at the same time that this expedient by no means involved a dualistic description of the phenomena but rather an absolutely unitary one; the meaning of the old terms became somewhat blurred.[19]

This language hardly sounds reassuring in the manner in which Bok would have us believe that certainties exist. The probabilities of which physicists speak could very well be the "influences" or "tendencies" of personality, which astrologers describe, if transposed into a system for interpreting personal qualities instead of physical properties.

There are, to be sure, scientists who have an open mind toward astrology, and it is fruitful to discuss how they approach the matter. Lyall Watson, rather than dismissing astrology out of hand, makes an effort to simplify the issues of contention between the orthodox scientist and the astrologer in his book *Supernature.* "Astrology," he writes there, "is based upon the fundamental premise that celestial phenomena affect life and events on earth." And he warns that "no scientist, and certainly no biologist familiar with the latest work on weather and natural rhythms, can deny that this premise is proved."[20] "Earth and its life are affected by the cosmos," Watson maintains, "and there is room for argument only in the matter of degree. Astrologers make many claims that are still without foundation and may well be ill-conceived, but there is a growing body of evidence to show that some of it, at least, is true."[21]

One of the major processes observed by scientists, particularly by biologists, that seems to indicate a natural rhythm are the biological clocks, which Jerome decided did not support a valid claim of proof by astrology. Frank A. Brown, Jr., in an article published in the *American Scientist,* described the so-called "biological clocks." He did not connect his observations of natural rhythms of plants and animals with astrology, but he did outline the phenomena for examination by scientists. "It did not require a very long initial study to demonstrate beyond all reasonable doubt that living things, *even while in so-called constant conditions,"* Brown reported, "had access to outside information as to the time of day (or position of the sun), time of lunar day (or position of moon), time of lunar month, and even time of year."[22]

Brown's conclusions regarding the innate sense of time in plants and animals which appear to have some correspondence with the regular motions of the heavens, particularly the sun and moon, are worth noting at length:

> Collectively these facts provide incontrovertible evidence that even when we have thought we have excluded all forces influencing the living things, there is, nonetheless, cyclic information, unquestionably with all the natural periodicities of the atmosphere imbedded in it, still impressing itself upon the organism.[23]

And he continues:

> Clearly then, there must still be unidentified physical factors affecting life. It now seems reasonable to postulate that these latter factors are very important to the living things in the timing of their rhythmic processes, or, in other words, in the operation of their clocks and calendars.[24]

And Brown concluded his article by interpreting biological processes in terms familiar to us from modern physics and philosophy, using space and time dimensions:

> The demonstration that the physical environment of living things is organized *temporally* in terms of still unknown, subtle and highly pervasive forces, which the living organisms can resolve, encourages one to speculate that there may be some comparable subtle and pervasive *spatial* organization of the environment which is contributing at least in a small way towards accounting for geographical distributions or periodic migrations of organisms.[25]

Whether or not the suggestion that organisms organize themselves spatially supports astrological theories, Brown's speculations certainly can be integrated with both modern physics and Teilhard's and Ardrey's efforts to articulate a cohesive understanding of human life.

In one sense astrology does deal with spatial considerations, for it integrates the activities of the heavens, particularly the sun, moon, and planets, with human psychological propensities. If we understand astrological theories as a greatly expanded version of field theory in which human and astral elements become part of the general field under consideration, with nonphysical influences and correspondences the desired result, we have a novel situation of immense sophistication. We may be dealing, in this respect, with a solution to Heisenberg's puzzle of how to integrate physiological and psychological functions with the concepts of modern physics.

The immediate objection to this interpretation of astrological theory is that the ancients considered the planets and stars to be living divinities. But we are not absolutely certain that they considered them in this manner. With a certain degree of leeway (and since we have no firsthand knowledge of ancient conceptions of the stars and planets we can have this flexibility), we can say that their conceptions of the living nature of astral bodies is not radically different from some contemporary conceptions. Lyall Watson writes about the physical nature of the planets:

> It has now been shown that Venus and Saturn are also powerful sources of radio waves. At least part of the planetary effect may be due to the fact that each body leaves behind it in space a magnetospheric tail of disturbance like a long wake of disturbed water that takes time to settle. The tail that the earth drags behind it may be more than five million miles long. *So, far from being insignificant specks in space, it seems that the planets are more like territorial animals that leave behind them powerful marks whose influence lingers on long after they themselves have passed by.*[26]

Whether or not the ancients could discern these characteristics by their observations of the planets remains an unanswered question. Certainly any significant irregular activity or close approach of a planet to the earth might result in celestial phenomena in which the tails or magnetospheres would appear prominently.

A more fundamental question is raised by astrology, and neither proponents nor critics ever seem to reach it. How did the ancients arrive at their knowledge of astrology? Bok, of course, finds it natural that primitive peoples would consider the planets and stars as having supernatural powers and fear them. But such a statement illustrates a preconceived idea of primitive peoples and does not take into account the complexities of astronomical observation. The planets are barely visible most of the time, and it would take a very astute observer considerable time to discover the irregularities of the planets even if he or she had already determined a regularity to the heavens. A person would almost have to know what to look for in the sky in order to discern planetary orbits, and there would have to be impelling reasons to consider the heavens malevolent in the first place.

Scholars are not much help in answering the difficult question of how astronomical or astrological observations began. Ernst Cassirer, for example, explained the relationship between astrology and astronomy in an evolutionary manner:

> The first and essential aim of astronomy was to win an insight into the nature and activity of these powers in order to foresee and to evade their dangerous influences. Astronomy could not arise except in this mythical and magical shape—in the shape of *astrology*. It preserved this character for many thousands of years; in a certain sense it was still prevalent in the first centuries of our own age, in the culture of the Renaissance. Even Kepler, the real founder of our own scientific astronomy, had to struggle throughout his life with this problem. But finally this last step had to be made. Astronomy supersedes astrology; geometrical space takes the place of mythical and magical space.[27]

Notice that Cassirer assumes, without any basis whatsoever, that primitive peoples believed that the planets and stars had dangerous influences which they must escape. Such an idea could only come about through human experience. No group of people would assume without any reason whatsoever that tiny spots of light far away in the sky could have any relationship to them whatsoever.

It seems natural to assume that astrology arose first and then, over the course of centuries, was "de-mythologized," losing its superstitious aspect and its correspondence to human fate. But Giorgio de Santillana, writing in his famous study of astrological myths *Hamlet's Mill*, points out the obvious fact that "it is essential to recognize that, in the beginning, astrology presupposed an astronomy."[28] This sequence of development seems eminently reasonable. Before the sky can be divided into houses of the zodiac, it must be presumed to be, or observed to be, regular with respect to the Precession of the Equinoxes, or there is no way that horoscopes can be drawn in the manner in which we presently know them.

De Santillana suggests that "the theory about 'how the world began' seems to involve a breaking asunder of a harmony, a kind of cosmogonic 'original sin' whereby the circle of the ecliptic (with the Zodiac) was tilted up at an angle with respect to the equator."[29] If such a tilt occurred in the memory of our species, it would certainly signal that the heavens were not to be trusted and would have to be watched rigorously thereafter to forecast another disaster. The zodiac imagery, according to de Santillana, "stands, as the evidence develops, for an astronomical process, the secular shifting of the sun through the signs of the zodiac which determines world-ages, each numbering thousands of years. Each age brings a World Era, a Twilight of the Gods. Great structures collapse; pillars topple which supprted the great fabric; floods and cataclysms herald the shaping of a new world."[30]

We have, of course, heard all this imagery before in the oral traditions of primitive peoples and in the folklore and mythology of ancient civilizations. Generally it has been rejected by the Western tradition as symbolic language, mythological themes which represent psychoanalytic efforts to come to grips with the meaning of life. The tendency of Western thinkers has been to downgrade the importance of ancient texts, since no incidents they describe are observable today in natural processes, and since it is assumed that early peoples were ridden with unimaginably vivid fantasies. But the documents that describe ancient astrological observations do not have superstitious beliefs as their outstanding characteristics. "Now that documents of the earliest ages of writing are available," de Santillana writes, "one is struck with a wholly unexpected feature. Those first predecessors of ours, instead of indulging their whims with childlike freedom, behave like worried and doubting commentators: they always try an exegesis of a dimly understood tradition. They move among technical terms whose meaning is half lost to them, they deal with words which appear on this earliest horizon already 'tottering with age' as J. H. Breasted says, words soon to vanish from our ken. Long before poetry can begin, there were generations of strange scholiasts."[31] We cannot assume, therefore, like we always have, that these early records are deficient in sophistication.

So we can conclude that behind the ancient astrological system lies an astronomy of immense sophistication. Some people have raised doubts about the possibility of the ancients deriving their knowledge of the heavens through observation. But speaking of the discovery of the Precession of the Equinoxes, Giorgio de Santillana remarks that "it is said that it must have taken an almost modern instrumentation to detect the motion over the brief space of a century, and this is certainly correct. Nobody claims, however, that the discovery was deduced from observations during one century. And the shift of 1 degree in 72 years, piling up over centuries, will produce appreciable shifts in certain crucial positions if the observers have enough intentness of mind and know how to keep records."[32] On this point even de Santillana, our most astute modern mind on ancient astrological origins, falls into fantasy. What happened *before* people kept records? How was the knowledge passed on during those centuries? The question becomes critical, since Jean Sendy, commenting on de Santillana's explanation, objects: "In any case, seventy years is a long time. Assuming that our ancient observer begins his career at the precocious age of 10, by the time he is 80 his eyes will no longer be as sharp as they were in his youth, but he will have found disciples, and those disciples will in turn form disciples. After a few centuries the difference caused by the precession will be too large to go unnoticed; the birth of spring will be advanced by several days, five days in three centuries. But could observers without precise scientific writing have determined the existence of the precession on the basis of observations made by successive generations? It seems impossible that they could have accomplished such a feat."[33]

There we have the crux of the scientific and historical problem raised by astrology. How could our species have discovered the all important Precession of the Equinoxes if the only perceptible movement occurred but once in an average person's lifetime? Could a scholar, no matter how intelligent, pass along even a detailed map of the heavens sufficiently accurate to enable another person who had never seen a certain stellar complex to determine that in fact a shift had occurred? If each ancient astronomer had one chance, and one only, to view a certain alignment of the heavens, that person would naturally assume that the alignment he saw was correct. There would never be an opportunity to begin to determine irregularities without written and fairly accurate information to which one could refer for guidance. Before we blithely cast aside the idea of astrology or ancient astronomy, we should confront and resolve the very difficult question concerning the nature and degree of sophistication of knowledge possessed by ancient peoples about the world. If they were able to resolve the questions raised above, can we belittle their astrological knowledge as mere superstition, unworthy of our consideration?

Lyall Watson maintains in *Supernature* that "the basic tool of astrology is therefore a valid one and beyond dispute. Arguments arise only over the use of the tool, the way in which the horoscope is interpreted; but it is surprising how far science and astrology are in agreement. Astrologers begin their interpretation of the birth data by saying that things on earth are influenced by events outside. Scientists must agree. Astrology says that persons, events, and ideas are all influenced at the time of their origin by the prevailing cosmic conditions. Science, which spends a large amount of its time measuring the continual changes in the cosmic scene, must concede that this is possible."[34] Rather than believing they have disproved astrology, scientists would be well advised to sweep away their preconceptions about the degree of intellectual capability possessed by ancient peoples and begin to ask themselves the difficult questions concerning the insights about the physical world possessed by their ancestors, and more especially about the origins of astronomy, metallurgy, agriculture, weaving, and other special skills and knowledge, which the ancients handed down to us.

Carl Jung phrased this question in another manner, writing about the origin of the atomic theory: "But where did Democritus, or whoever first spoke of minimal constitutive elements, hear of atoms? This notion," he maintained, "had its origin in archetypal ideas, that is, in primordial images which were never reflections of physical events but are spontaneous products of the psychic factor. Despite the materialistic tendency to understand the psyche as mere reflection or imprint of physical and chemical processes, there is not a single proof of this hypothesis."[35] In denying the physical basis for knowledge, Jung posited the origin of ideas in the psyche, and this solution is probably the alternative that astrologers offer us. Giorgio de Santillana, discussing the nature of astrological knowledge, says that "its beginning has already been placed in the Neolithic, without setting limits in the past; let prehistoric archaeologists decide. The astronomical system seems to conceive of the Golden Age, the Saturnian Era, as already mythical, in the proper sense. One can then say that it took shape about 4000 B.C., that it lasted into protohistory and beyond."[36]

A proper rendering of our present body of scientific knowledge, therefore, would involve astrological knowledge. It would involve the various sciences, skills, and crafts of the ancients, and it would extend our present certain knowledge of history backward until at least 4000 B.C. Twentieth-century science, which has now, according to some commentators, achieved the status of a history, must be transformed into a body of knowledge whose framework of interpretation is basically historical rather than theoretical. As the various fields of knowledge begin to coalesce, we will discover that it is the introduction of a historical dimension into the interdisciplinary research and investigation that produces the most beneficial results.

XX. The Metaphysics of Modern Existence

We have reached the end of our survey. Jean-François Revel's suggestion that only in America could sufficient intellectual, political, economic, and moral leadership be generated to bring the rest of our species a new and overpowering vision of meaning for our time remains to be tested in the future paths our nation takes. We have merely suggested a possible alternative line of leveling a critique of culture with its component fields of knowledge and the assumption that underlies the belief in civilization-as-sanction. Proceeding on the theory that non-Western traditions have had a heavy emphasis on social and religious reality rather than on scientific knowledge and technical expertise, we sought to discover ways of incorporating the insights of their historical experiences into a cohesive way of approaching the knowledge and experience of the world.

Is the United States the scene of revolutionary change, at least in the fields of culture and civilization, that would justify Revel's optimism and confidence in us? We can, I believe, optimistically answer yes. Social and political movements in the United States remain healthy and vigorous, although they perhaps lack the energy partisans like to see in movements. The reactionary stance, which has been adopted by theologians and scientists, is also healthy, for although it shows that they fear the erosion of their status in our society, it also indicates that they have intuitively identified the fields they shall have to confront in the decades ahead.

We can pause a moment and examine in more general terms the trauma these two groups are feeling today. Theologians, it seems obvious, cannot bring themselves to confront the sophistication of the modern scientific world view or the knowledge that stands behind it. Speaking of theological doctrines that depend upon the transcendence or immanence of the deity is certainly outmoded today. Some theologians, to be sure, now speak of *transcendence* in a moral sense, but the world itself has represented spatial terms for such a period of time that it is easily misunderstood and cannot, like some other words, be resurrected. *Immanence* also seems to fall short of the mark and immediately reminds us of Schleiermacher's effort to speak to the cultured despisers of religion. Of present theologians, as we have suggested, only Ian Barbour and Karl Heim seem willing to do battle with modern scientific descriptions of the universe as they are now emerging from modern physics.

The Hartford and Boston theologians cannot be regarded as reactionaries in any prejorative sense, since they appear unaware of the complexity of knowledge that secular thinkers confront. They are extremely conservative rather than reactionary. They appear to be unwilling to open the question of religious reality for discussion, preferring rather to attempt to bolster traditional Christian doctrines by an exercise of the will. This defense, while admirable, is no more successful than the tribal peoples' attempting to reinstitute ceremonies that have long since been overtaken by historical events. In theology, truth must once again represent experience rather than an absolute or literal interpretation of a tradition. In the long and painful transitional period we face, theology must come to grips with how people think before it can attempt to direct the manner in which people act.

The presupposition of this book is that eventually, and we would hope in our lifetime, theology and philosophy will disappear as professions to be replaced by a general quest for reality on the part of everyone. The philosophical or theological search for certainty or proper exposition of doctrines and theories must be replaced by the emergence of wise people with a religious charisma who provide stability to their communities. Both religion and philosophy must come to reflect what people are rather than what they believe to be true. Before these professions disappear, however, their task must be to lead us in the search for a more mature understanding of our place in the universe. Theology and philosophy must aggressively act as critiquing disciplines that can correlate and synthesize the knowledge and experiences of our species and provide a comprehensive vision of what it means and has meant.

The scientific establishment seems to have taken exactly the opposite tack from theology. Rather than being frightened by the plentitude of modern knowledge, scientists seem to fear the knowledge of ancient peoples. Attaching themselves firmly to an evolutionary interpretation of the growth of human knowledge, they ridicule and degrade any suggestion that our ancestors had any real knowledge of their world. Astrology, which appears to be a rather sophisticated correspondence between the observed movement of stars and planets and human emotions and perceptions, is considered to be simply the remnant superstitions of another more primitive time. That such a system might very well represent a synthesis, using the universe as a "field" in our modern sense, of human knowledge at a particular time in history is hardly considered at all.

Scientists, but particularly astronomers, should look carefully at the ancients' knowledge of the stars. We have already pointed out the difficult time primitive peoples must have had in discerning the regularity of the Precession of the Equinoxes which is a prerequisite to any formation of zodiac houses or astrological knowledge. The same questions can be raised with respect to ancient knowledge of eclipses. How could any particular civilization, be it Chinese, Babylonian, Egyptian, or Mayan, devise sufficient knowledge about the movements of the sun and moon to predict eclipses when in order to establish the cycle of eclipses one must have a knowledge of the whole planet, since the same eclipse may not be visible from the same observation point in succeeding cycles? The knowledge of ancient peoples is thus not easily discarded by a careful thinker unless assumptions and presuppositions already have eliminated it from consideration.

The collective traditions of ancient and primitive peoples, then, present a barrier in the conceptualization processes of modern science that must be overcome. Scientists—particularly in the fields of astronomy, archeology, anthropology, and geology—must dispose of their assumptions and presuppositions about the ancient world and be willing to incorporate non-Western traditions. An important integration that must take place in the conceptual process is the realization that the history of our species and the history of our planet may share a significant number of events. This realization, of course, undercuts the present assumption that the universal movements, particularly those observed in our solar system, have been stable, continuous in their rate of development, and have occurred over a greatly extended period of time. Such a shift in perception will be difficult, but it will be necessary.

One common problem shared by scientists and theologians is that they must account for the origin of things. The great scientific revolution of the last century, in which evolution replaced divine creation, only substituted a rather pale "nature" for God but preserved the question of origins, which had been a perennial topic among Western intellectuals at all stages in the development of Western civilization. J. Z. Young, a biologist, writing in *Doubt and Certainty in Science,* remarks that:

> In the past we have continued to rely for our general views essentially on the medieval conception that the universe was created at some finite time in the past. But do we need to consider that the universe started at all? This may seem absurd until you realize how limited and arbitrary is our present view that there was a beginning. It is an unwarranted extension.[1]

Eliminating the idea that we must derive our knowledge of the universe from the imagined processes of its beginning and carry that conception into our interpretation of the life-forms of our planet and eventually into our interpretation of the experiences of our species is unnecessary at this time. It presumes that we can have a certain knowledge based either upon the divine revelation of the mechanics of creation or upon the projections backward into an infinite expanse of time those natural processes we observe and pretend to observe today.

Insofar as we can have reliable knowledge about the experiences of our species on the planet, we have only those direct observations that we make or that have come down to us in the various human traditions. Projections into either the past or the future that seek to make present observations the absolute standard for interpreting past or future events are unreliable. The same can be said for the extension of human attributes as reliable indicators of the psychic existence of other life-forms. Projecting a sense of emotions and mental properties to other life-forms may well give us insight but it gives only a temporary form of knowledge that must then be reframed in terms applicable to all forms of life.

Projections based upon planetary processes that attempt to explain the formation or activities of other heavenly and astral bodies assumes that the beginning had a continous, uniform, and homogenous aspect. In view of the many discontinuities we observe in our own solar system, we cannot make this assumption absolute. There may very well be startling similarities in the planets of our immediate celestial neighborhood, but a casual reading of an astronomy text is not comforting in this respect. We can only conclude that our own solar system is filled with unexplained mysteries. Again J. Z. Young offers helpful advice. Writing of the universe and solar system, he contends: "Here we find ourselves more baffled. We cannot properly comprehend the pattern of the stars. Our astronomers are working hard to find rules of brain action that shall make us able to do so, but in spite of their considerable discoveries I feel sure that they would agree that they have not yet found the really significant clue." [2]

There is a radical distinction, therefore, between accumulating data concerning our solar system and the universe which is based upon the viewpoint that we discern with our own planet as a reference point, and planetary, solar, and galactic activities considered as separate from our geocentric point of reference. The extension of space on a solar or galactic scale in terms of measurements of light years may, in the backward glance of another century, prove to have been primitive and egocentric. We must be prepared to adopt entirely new ways of thinking for each dimension of existence, perceived as a space-time unity, which we are able to observe and measure. Just as measurements at the subatomic level become exceedingly difficult as the concepts we use vanish and coalesce, so measurements on the solar and galactic scale may become increasingly useless in describing reality.

In the field of human affairs it will become important to eliminate evolutionary presuppositions from our thinking. Many social programs are based upon evolutionary principles; they assume that with proper motivation groups of people can be inspired to "better their lot." When this ideology combines with the already prevalent transfer of wealth-creating opportunities to government licensing and largess, we have the potential for a totalitarianism transcending anything experienced by ancient peoples. As American institutions transform themselves into organisms only remotely connected with their ideological and theoretical roots, we must make every effort to redirect those institutions back to their original mission, eliminating those incapable of doing so, and making all institutions more flexible.

Christopher Stone's suggestion that we now accord natural objects an equal status with other entities possessing legal rights must be implemented. Such a transformation would enable us to gain a proper perspective on our relationship with the natural world. This seminal conception of legal rights, which Stone has articulated, may well be the first sign of a new awareness of the metaphysical aspect of legal theory, triggering a whole series of explorations that could revolutionize our conception of society. Creative legal thinking, such as that demonstrated by Stone, might very well replace both theology and philosophy as the two disciplines that have the potential to exercise intellectual leadership in the decades ahead.

Marshall McLuhan visualizes our future as one in which we cease being gatherers of food and start becoming gatherers of information. He sees the specialist becoming obsolete and the generalist and synthesizer becoming increasingly important. Already we are seeing the development of interdisciplinary work that appears to be fruitful in explaining previously incomprehensible data. As more and more fields are brought together in an interdisciplinary sense, it will become apparent that our knowledge of the world does form a unity when properly perceived. Generalists and synthesizers will be forced to confront non-Western modes of thought and gather from these traditions more sophisticated ways of viewing materials and new ways of classifying phenomena. The emotional and intuitive side of knowledge will appear more valuable than the objective knowledge we now prize so highly.

The nature of all academic disciplines and professions should change radically. Specialists will discover that they are required to possess general knowledge as well as in-depth skills in their particular fields. We can look at this development as a pendulum moving between generalization and specialization, or we can observe that it is a vertical process of deepening knowledge while also broadening the base or context in which the information makes the greatest contribution to our understanding. The absolutism that has characterized Western fields of knowledge, which Alfred North Whitehead often characterized as "misplaced concreteness," will give way to a flexible and wise manner of conceiving situations and their probable alternatives.

What can be said, therefore, about the rather tedious task in which we have been engaged in this book? Does each individual have to struggle through the sophisticated thinking of Werner Heisenberg and encounter the immensely complicated psychological system of Carl Jung? Such a task would be impossible for the majority of our citizens and would prove tedious when developed in the classroom as a course in either philosophy or science. A transformation of the ideas of science, the work Ian Barbour is now performing, into a system of thought compatible with religion and other human-oriented subjects would consume most of our educational years, and the results would hardly be worth the effort.

If we consider the matter carefully, we shall discover that the problem is not one of making the educational process more complex and forcing people to delve into the sophisticated theories of modern physics, astronomy, or psychoanalysis. Rather the problem is that Western people have stepped out of the mainstream of our species' traditional way of recording and remembering experiences. Western thinkers have erected a series of absolute concepts, some dealing with the physical world, others describing the world of human affairs. As a consequence, Western people have been taught to think in a restricted manner. The whole development of modern science today would suggest that we are returning to the ancient manner of thinking in which all the contents of experience are integrated in a single descriptive language.

While we have certainly discussed new conceptions of space-time, of energy-matter transformation systems, of planetary history and cataclysmic events, such thinking does not require additonal effort on the part of Western people but less effort. The radical change must occur when Western thought-patterns eliminate unexamined assumptions and presuppositions concerning the nature of the world. When Western thinkers start confronting knowledge directly without feeling obliged to trace origins, to applaud our present efforts to gain information while rejecting past syntheses of knowledge, and to see the value in discontinuities as well as in uniformities, then we can bring about the unity of human knowledge. So the preliminary task in forming a metaphysics of modern existence is to eliminate old interpretations of data that already predispose us to understand certain things about the world and preclude us from considering other things.

The critique of culture that Revel suggested is not simply tidy housekeeping but a fundamental revolution in the manner in which we think. When this requirement is applied to the traditional Western manner of thinking, then the division of experience into *this-worldly* and *otherworldly* and *kosmos* and *oikumenē* vanish. We then directly confront events that can be analyzed from any number of standpoints and, depending upon the information desired, produce some intelligible information concerning the world. The importance of modern physics in this respect is that it is the first of the sciences to systematically reject the old divisions of subject-object in favor of the integrated event. The epistemology that emerges from modern physics is extremely compatible with the way in which many traditions think, speak, and derive both cultural values and rules for governing society.

Revel entitled his book *Without Marx or Jesus* to indicate that the two major traditions of the West were incapable of leading our species into the future. Both traditions carry too many assumptions regarding the nature of the world to be able to bring a clear vision to the vast amount of data that confronts us. As we enter upon a task of unifying our knowledge of the world, we cannot be confined to outmoded ways of ordering information, if that requires not disturbing traditional understandings of reality. Replacing Christian theological principles with scientific substitutes—nature for God, uniformitarianism for God's will, and so forth—and the further replacing the field of human affairs or scientific doctrines with Marxist political dogmas hardly solves the problem of understanding. Revel suggests, and it seems only reasonable to concur, that the next giant step our species must take is to achieve maturity. Making particular cultural traditions an absolute standard of truth, even with the best of intentions, falls short of this responsibility.

There is even a similarity of purpose and technique present in both science and the world of human affairs. Christopher Stone suggests that we attempt to take the new language of ecological concern outside the courthouse walls where it can become part of our everyday speech so that the radical change it represents will eventually become familiar to us and finally acceptable and part of our "common-sense" view of the world. Werner Heisenberg suggested basically the same thing. "We know that any understanding must be based finally upon the natural language because it is only there that we can be certain to touch reality, and hence we must be skeptical about any skepticism with regard to this natural language and its essential concepts. Therefore, we may use these concepts as they have been used at all times. In this way modern physics has perhaps opened the door to a wider outlook on the relation between the human mind and reality."[3]

Very early in the development of our species, two major departures in the manner of gaining knowledge occurred. In the East the tendency was to concentrate on the psychological aspect of human experience and to derive knowledge from tracing psychological moods into the interior of the self, searching for the center of existence. The result was the generation of the belief that the physical world was an illusion, *maya,* and the real meaning to existence was the casting aside of phenomena and the creation of a self devoid of personal characteristics, thus eliminating the pain of life by denying it an ultimate status in experience and understanding.

Western peoples took the opposite approach. Searching for the ultimate physical substance that constituted the world, Western peoples produced an incredibly complex technology that could manipulate the physical universe in a variety of ways. But the result meant a reduction of the psychological to a phenomenon of the peculiar interaction of atoms and molecules. While the East remained in physical poverty, the West created a spiritual vacuum, coming eventually to believe that only the physical was real.

Today we seek to expand our knowledge of the world, and the signposts point to a reconciliation of the two approaches to experience. Western science must now reintegrate human emotions and intuitions into its interpretation of phenomena; Eastern peoples must confront the physical world and the effects of technology. We shall understand as these traditionally opposing views seek a unity that the world of historical experiences is far more mysterious and eventful than we had previously suspected. In the re-creation of metaphysics as a continuing search for meaning which incorporates all aspects of science and historical experience, we can hasten the time when we will come to an integrated conception of how our species came to be, what it has accomplished, and where it can expect to go in the millennia ahead. Our next immediate task is the unification of human knowledge.

Appendix: The Emerging Dissident Literature

In recent years a number of books have dealt with alternative explanations to some of modern science's most cherished beliefs. In general one could relate these books by saying that they are, in one way or another, challenging the tendency of scientists and historians to interpret data in a uniformitarian manner. Recognition of severe and planet-wide catastrophes during some part of earth history is now emerging, and while the proponents of this view are not generally well regarded by the orthodox scientific establishment, they do raise important questions.

Often a reader is excited at the prospect of seeing the world from a different light, but he or she has no place to find further readings that would direct the investigation. Some of the sources I have mentioned in this book deserve careful and thorough reading themselves. I have decided to give more information on them so that the reader can follow up on this general theme of catastrophism.

The best book currently in print that questions the theoretical basis for evolution is Norman MacBeth's *Darwin Retried*. MacBeth was seriously ill for several years and, to take his mind off his problems, began reading books on evolution. This avocation became a decade-long search for assurance and led MacBeth to raise a number of important questions regarding the validity of evolution. One of the startling revelations of his book concerns *eohippus,* the tiny proto-horse of the evolutionary chart. It seems that this ancestry has not been proven by the discovery of any series of remains but was created to demonstrate evolutionary principles. MacBeth points out that nearly every evolutionary family tree has all the known specimens on the branches of the tree and the missing ancestors and descendants are always those that would make the series realistic—missing links so to speak.

MacBeth, being an attorney, applies common rules of evidence to the arguments favoring evolution and concludes that the theory rests on a curious logic. It's not that evolution has been proven correct. Rather, the other theories, particularly divine creation, are not acceptable; so evolution wins by default. But as MacBeth accurately contends, the error of some theories does not validate a favorite theory.

A rather oblique attack on uniformitarianism in geology is Derek V. Ager's excellent book *The Nature of the Stratigraphical Record.* Citing the wide geographical spread of some sedimentary formations, Ager suggests that we are dealing with more than the minute erosion of mountains lasting millions of years when we look at the stratigraphic record. He recounts the damage done by hurricanes and tidal waves, noting that they can accumulate or destroy sediments of tens of feet in a matter of hours, and suggests that if we measure geological time according to uniform processes of erosion we are leaving out the most important building and eroding forces we presently observe—violent storms. His conclusion, therefore, is that the geologic record tells us more about catastrophes than about geological uniformities.

Ager states emphatically that he is an evolutionist, and he expresses his sense of foreboding that any religious fundamentalist might seize upon his explanation of geological catastrophes as evidence of the literal truth of Genesis. But almost every cite of index fossils in the book contains the curious explanation that these fossils appear suddenly, without ancestors and without descendants, leading one to believe that while evolution is a nice general theory that purports to explain biological phenomena, it is extremely difficult to demonstrate with specific examples. Such incongruities should have alerted Ager to the implications of his theory, for when geological uniformitarianism departs, biological evolutionary theories will collapse also. Ager endorses the orthodox geological time scale that measures the Permian era at forty million years, the Eocene at ten million, and so forth. But Ager does not answer how we measure time this precisely when we are only looking at the catastrophic record in the stratigraphy of our planet.

The Biblical Flood and the Ice Epoch by Donald W. Patten is surprising. Patten is a Christian fundamentalist, but his writing lacks the dogmatic rigidity characteristic of such a breed and presents a scientific, intelligent, and highly intuitive account of the great Flood. Prooftexts are missing. Patten suggests that the Biblical Flood was a result of the intrusion into the earth's gravitational-magnetic field of an astral visitor, Mercury, for a year's duration, creating a major crisis, dumping most of our present water on the planet, building our youngest mountain chains, and changing the effect of our life processes by removing a protective layer of clouds by precipitation.

Patten's theory of glaciation seems to account for phenomena that geologists presently cannot bring together. He places major emphasis on the observed rules of meteorology and climate that we have available to us making an excellent case for the idea that the glaciers could not have been formed by the actions of winds and precipitation of the oceans alone. His theory of mountain building is as impressive. It links two major belts of mountains—the trans-Pacific rim which circles that ocean, and the Alpine-Himalayan belt which crosses the Europe-Asia land mass—with the visit and gravitational pull of Mercury. The frozen violence that we see recorded in these mountain chains certainly makes Patten's theory seem possible and, indeed, probable.

Climate and the Affairs of Men by Nels Winkless III and Iben Browning is an effort to defuse Velikovsky's catastrophism (at least the jacket cover implies this goal). This book illustrates the peril of edging toward catastrophism rather than adopting it. Winkless and Browning suggest that geological eras are opened and closed by catastrophic events—probably the collision of the earth with asteroids. They consider the orthodox belief in fourteen major mountain-building periods as evidence that the earth has sustained fourteen hits from outer space bodies in its history. Obviously this interpretation strains credibility. Velikovsky himself only suggests the occurrence of two catastrophes—dating each—and attributes disruptions on the earth to the activities of electromagnetic conflict between the earth and Mars and Venus. *Climate and the Affairs of Men,* while attempting to be orthodox, results in a theory of solar collisions so bizarre as to make Velikovsky sedate by comparison.

The geological counterpart ot the above-named book is probably Dorothy Vitaliano's *Legends of the Earth,* mentioned earlier in the text. She attempts to show that some spectacular volcanic explosions were probably observed and described by members of our species, but she rejects the idea that anything extraterrestrial was involved. Her explanations of myths, therefore, are hardly credible for the astute reader. She does develop an excellent bibliography and makes a concerted effort to cover many myths and geologic oddities, and this scholarly gathering of data makes the book valuable but not definitive.

Hamlet's Mill, another book already mentioned in the text, deals with the probable astronomical and astrological knowledge of the ancients as seen through myths, particularly myths that revolve about the Precession of the Equinoxes and the changing of polar stars. Some challenging ideas are presented that indicate the extent to which scholars have refused to credit ancient peoples with a sophisticated knowledge and concern about the stars and their movements. *Hamlet's Mill* is absolutely essential for any effort at synthesizing our knowledge of the ancient peoples and modern astronomy and may well prove to be a landmark study of the thinking of ancient peoples.

Lawrence LeShan has written *The Medium, the Mystic, and the Physicist,* which presents, with respect to the field of psychology and religious experience, what I have tried to present in this book with respect to the conceptualization process. That is, he links diverse descriptions of states of feeling to show a consistency, in the same manner I have tried to develop the thesis that real knowledge of reality must be primarily a matter of perception and a careful handling of the process of deriving concepts of knowledge from those perceptions. I regard our books as dealing with the same matter from different approaches and feel that they are complementary in many ways. Whether the religious experiences of the American Indian can rest comfortably within LeShan's psychological-physical context is a question I have not yet given proper attention. I will.

Two good books discuss the implication of Immanuel Velikovsky's theory— *Velikovsky Reconsidered* by the editors of *Pensee*, and *The Velikovsky Affair*. Two newsletter and quarterly publications also deal with this theory. *Kronos* is a scholarly quarterly that emphasizes mythology, psychology, and the humanistic side of the theory and its implications. (Address: KRONOS, co/Dr. Robert Hewson, Department of History, Glassboro State College, Glassboro, N.J. 08028.) The *Research Communications Network*, successor to *Pensee*, coordinates information on all phases of the catastrophic theories now being advanced. It brings articles and books to the attention of its subscribers so that they can continue to pursue the subject in the latest publications. The service is worth the money for a serious reader. (Address: *Research Communications Network*, P.O. Box 414, Portland, Ore. 97207)

Velikovsky Reconsidered consists of a series of essays, originally published in *Pensee*, that bear directly on Velikovsky's theory of catastrophism and discuss the implications of it for a reordering of our world view. Bill Mullen's excellent essay "The Center Holds" gives a broad perspective on how the specifics of the theory have been received, the implications of some of the corollaries that must inevitably result, and an appraisal of the present situtation.

The Velikovsky Affair is a hardback printing of the special issue of the *American Behavioral Scientist*, which dealt with the reception of Velikovsky's theory by the scientific establishment. Some selections deal with verifying parts of the theory; others recount the probing of the situation by *Harper's* reporter Eric Larrabee; and the remainder of the articles attempt to discover why Velikovsky should have been subjected to such personal abuse by the leading astronomers when his book was released. On the whole it is not pleasant reading for anyone who believes that scientists are objectively looking for facts and theories in an effort to extend human knowledge, since it chronicles the treatment of our modern Galileo, persecuted by science instead of religion.

There are probably a great many more books dealing with the emerging heresy of catastrophism which I have not yet seen or read. However, to do my part in keeping this important discussion on track, I thought it would be good to give a more complete and informal discussion of the books which have been important in my own thinking on this matter.

Bibliography

BOOKS

American Friends Service Committee. *Uncommon Controversy*. Seattle, Wash.: University of Washington Press, 1970.

Ardrey, Robert. *African Genesis*. New York: Dell Publishing Co., 1967.

———. *The Hunting Hypothesis*. New York: Atheneum, 1976.

———. *The Social Contract*. New York: Atheneum, 1970.

———. *The Territorial Imperative*. New York: Dell Publishing Co., 1966.

Barbour, Ian. *Issues in Science and Religion*. New York: Prentice-Hall, 1966.

———. *Myths, Models and Paradigms*. New York: Harper & Row, 1974.

Bateson, Gregory. *Steps to an Ecology of Mind*. New York: Ballantine Books, 1972.

Cassirer, Ernst. *An Essay on Man*. New Haven, Conn.: Yale University Press, 1944.

Collingwood, R. G. *The Idea of History*. New York: Oxford University Press, 1946.

De Grazia, Alfred, ed. *The Velikovsky Affair*. New Hyde Park, N.Y.: University Books, 1966.

De Santillana, Giorgio, and von Dechend, Hertha. *Hamlet's Mill*. Boston, Mass.: Gambit Inc., 1969.

Eliade, Mircea, and Kitagawa, Joseph. *The History of Religions: Essays in Methodology*. Chicago: University of Chicago Press, 1959.

Ferré, Frederick. *Language, Logic and God*. New York: Harper Torchbooks, 1961.

Gauquelin, Michel. *The Cosmic Clocks*. New York: Avon Books, 1969.

Hall, Edward T. *The Silent Language*. New York: Doubleday & Co., 1959.

Heim, Karl. *Christian Faith and Natural Science*. New York: Harper Torchbooks, 1953.

Heisenberg, Werner. *Across the Frontiers*. New York: Harper & Row, 1974.

————. *The Physicist's Conception of Nature*. New York: Harcourt, Brace & Co., 1958.

————. *Physics and Beyond*. New York: Harper & Row, 1971.

————. *Physics and Philosophy*. New York: Harper Torchbooks, 1958.

Jung, C. G. *The Structure and Dynamics of the Psyche*. Collected Works, vol. 8. Princeton, N.J.: Princeton University Press, 1969.

————. *The Archetypes and the Collective Unconscious*. Collected Works, vol. 9, part 1. Princeton, N.J.: Princeton University Press, 1959.

————. *Aion: Researches into the Phenomenology of the Self*. Collected Works, vol. 9, part 2. Princeton, N.J.: Princeton University Press, 1959.

————. *Civilization in Transition*. Collected Works, vol. 10. Princeton, N.J.: Princeton University Press, 1970.

————. *Psychology and Religion: East and West*. Collected Works, vol. 11. Princeton, N.J.: Princeton University Press, 1958.

————. *The Spirit in Man, Art, and Literature*. Collected Works, vol. 15. Princeton, N.J.: Princeton University Press, 1966.

Klibansky, Raymond, and Paton, H. J., eds. *Philosophy and History: The Ernst Cassirer Festschrift*. New York: Harper Torchbooks, 1963.

Leopold, Aldo. *A Sand County Almanac*. New York: Ballantine Books, 1970.

Levi-Strauss, Claude. *The Savage Mind*. Chicago: University of Chicago Press, 1966.

————. *Structural Anthropology*. New York: Basic Books, 1963.

Lovejoy, Arthur O. *The Great Chain of Being*. New York: Harper Torchbooks, 1936, 1960.

Mazlish, Bruce, ed. *Psychoanalysis and History*. New York: Grosset's Universal Library, 1971.

McLuhan, Marshall. *Understanding Media: The Extensions of Man*. New York: McGraw-Hill Publishing Co., 1965.

Neumann, Erich. *The Origins and History of Consciousness*. 2 vols. New York: Harper Torchbooks, 1962.

Niebuhr, H. Richard. *The Responsible Self*. New York: Harper & Row, 1963.

Pelikan, Jaroslav, ed. *Twentieth Century Theology in the Making*. 3 vols. Translated by R. A. Wilson. New York: Harper & Row, 1969, 1970.

Radin, Paul. *The World of Primitive Man*. New York: Grove Press, 1953.

Revel, Jean François. *Without Marx or Jesus*. New York: Doubleday & Co., 1970.

Sax, Joseph. *Water Law, Planning, and Policy*. New York: Bobbs-Merrill Co., 1968.

Schweitzer, Albert. *The Quest of the Historical Jesus*. New York: Macmillan Co., 1961.

Sendy, Jean. *The Coming of the Gods*. New York: Berkeley Medallion Books, 1970.

Slater, Philip. *Earthwalk*. Garden City, N.Y.: Anchor Press, 1974.

Söderblum, Nathan. *The Living God*. Boston: Beacon Press, 1962.

Stone, Christopher. *Should Trees Have Standing?* New York: Discus Books, 1975.

Teilhard de Chardin, Pierre. *The Phenomenon of Man*. New York: Harper Torchbooks, 1971.

Tillich, Paul. *Christianity and the Encounter of the World Religions*. New York: Columbia University Press, 1963.

————. *The Protestant Era*. Abridged ed. Chicago: University of Chicago Press, 1957.

Toffler, Alvin. *Future Shock*. New York: Random House, 1970.

Velikovsky, Immanuel. *Ages in Chaos*. New York: Doubleday & Co., 1952.

————. *Earth in Upheaval*. New York: Doubleday & Co., 1955.

————. *Oedipus and Akhnaton.* New York: Doubleday & Co., 1960.

————. *Worlds in Collision.* New York: Doubleday & Co., 1950.

Wach, Joachim. *The Comparative Study of Religions.* New York: Columbia University Press, 1961.

————. *Types of Religious Experience.* Chicago: University of Chicago Press, 1951.

Watson, Lyall. *Supernature.* New York: Bantam Books, 1974.

Werner, Heinz. *Comparative Psychology of Mental Development.* Rev. ed. Chicago: Follett, 1948.

Whitehead, Alfred North. *Adventures of Ideas.* New York: New American Library, 1933.

Young, J. Z. *Doubt and Certainty in Science.* New York: Oxford University Press, 1950.

ARTICLES

Bok, Bart J. "A Critical Look at Astrology." *The Humanist,* September-October 1975, pp. 6-9.

"The Boston Affirmation." *Christianity and Crisis,* 16 February 1976, pp. 23-27.

Brown, Frank A., Jr. "The Rhythmic Nature of Animals and Plants." *American Scientist* 47:147-68.

Daedalus. *Religion in America,* Winter 1967.

Ferté, Thomas. "A Record of Success." *Pensee,* Student Academic Freedom Forum, May 1972, pp. 11-15, 23.

Francis, Wilfrid. "Letter to the Editor." *Pensee,* Student Academic Freedom Forum, Fall 1972, p. 21.

Jerome, Lawrence E. "Astrology: Magic or Science." *The Humanist,* September-October 1975, pp. 10-16.

"Objections to Astrology." A Statement by 186 Leading Scientists, *The Humanist,* September-October 1975, pp. 4-5.

"The Neuhaus-Coffin-Cox Debate." *Christian Century,* 4 June 1975.

"Open Letter from Curtis Fuller to Dr. Paul Kurtz." *Fate Magazine,* October 1976, pp. 7-19.

Reich, Charles. "The New Property." *The Yale Law Journal* 73:733-87.

Salt River Water Users' Association v. *Kovacovich,* 3 Ariz. App. 28, 411 P. 2d. 201 (1966).

BIBLIOGRAPHY OF THE EMERGING DISSIDENT LITERATURE

Ager, Derek. *The Nature of the Stratigraphical Record.* New York: John Wiley & Sons, 1973.

De Grazia, Alfred. *The Velikovsky Affair.* New Hyde Park, N.Y.: University Books, 1966.

De Santillana, Giorgio, and von Dechend, Hertha. *Hamlet's Mill.* Boston, Mass.: Gambit Inc., 1969.

Kronos, A Journal of Interdisciplinary Synthesis. Glassboro State College, Glassboro, N.J. 08028.

LeShan, Lawrence. *The Medium, the Mystic, and the Physicist.* New York: Ballantine, 1974.

MacBeth, Norman. *Darwin Retried.* Boston, Mass.: Gambit Inc., 1971.

Patten, Donald Wesley. *The Biblical Flood and the Ice Epoch.* Seattle, Wash.: Pacific Meridian, 1966.

Research Communications Network. P.O. Box 414, Portland, Oregon 97207.

Velikovsky Reconsidered. By the editors of *Pensee.* Garden City, N.Y.: Doubleday & Co., 1976.

Vitaliano, Dorothy B. *Legends of the Earth.* Bloomington, Ind.: Indiana University Press, 1973.

Winkless, Nels, III, and Browning, Iben. *Climate and the Affairs of Men.* New York, Harper's Magazine Press, 1975.

Notes

NOTES FOR CHAPTER 1

1. Revel, *Without Marx or Jesus*, p. 253.
2. Ibid., p. 79.
3. Ibid., p. 81.
4. Ibid., p. 173.
5. Ibid., pp. 9–11.
6. Ibid., p. 14.
7. Ibid., p. 107.
8. Teilhard de Chardin, *The Phenomenon of Man*, p. 212. Italics mine.
9. Heisenberg, *The Physicist's Conception of Nature*, p. 67.
10. Slater, *Earthwalk*, p. 38.

NOTES FOR CHAPTER 2

1. Barbour, *Issues in Science and Religion*, p. 262.
2. Ibid.
3. Heisenberg, *The Physicist's Conception of Nature*, p. 52.
4. Barbour, *Issues in Science and Religion*, pp. 4–5.
5. Leon Brunschvicg, "History and Philosophy," in Klibansky and Paton, eds., *Philosophy and History: The Ernst Cassirer Festschrift*, p. 32–33.
6. Heisenberg, *The Physicist's Conception of Nature*, p. 64.
7. Tillich, *The Protestant Era*, p. 217. Italics mine.
8. Barbour, *Myths, Models and Paradigms*, p. 145.
9. Paul Tillich, "Philosophy," in Pelikan, ed., *Twentieth Century Theology in the Making*, vol. 2, p. 255.

10. Heinz Heimsoeth, "The Modern Period up to the Middle of the Eighteenth Century," in Pelikan, ed., *Twentieth Century Theology in the Making*, vol. 2, p. 270.
11. Ferré, *Language, Logic, and God*, p. 161.
12. Ibid.

NOTES FOR CHAPTER 3

1. Lovejoy, *The Great Chain of Being*, p. 25.
2. Bateson, *Steps to an Ecology of Mind*, p. 462.
3. Tillich, *The Protestant Era*, p. 20.
4. Ibid., pp. 26–27.
5. Ibid., p. 120.
6. Cassirer, *An Essay on Man*, p. 83.
7. Johan Huizinga, "A Definition of the Concept of History," in Klibansky and Patton, eds., *Philosophy and History: The Ernst Cassirer Festschrift*, p. 5.
8. Cassirer, *An Essay on Man*, p. 100. Italics mine.
9. Ferré, *Language, Logic and God*, pp. 160–61. Italics mine.
10. Heim, *Christian Faith and Natural Science*, p. 204.
11. Wach, *The Comparative Study of Religions*, p. 139. Italics mine.
12. Ibid., p. 121. Italics mine.
13. Söderblum, *The Living God*, pp. 231–32.
14. American Friends Service Committee, *Uncommon Controversy*, p. 31.
15. Quoted in Söderblum, *The Living God*, p. 315. Italics mine.
16. Söderblum, *The Living God*, p. 386.
17. Barbour, *Issues in Science and Religion*, p. 5.
18. Collingwood, *The Idea of History*, p. 31.

NOTES FOR CHAPTER 4

1. Heisenberg, *The Physicist's Conception of Nature*, p. 11.
2. Barbour, *Issues in Science and Religion*, pp. 157–58.
3. Heisenberg, *Physics and Beyond*, p. 40.
4. Heisenberg, *The Physicist's Conception of Nature*, pp. 19–20.
5. Barbour, *Issues in Science and Religion*, p. 297. Italics mine.
6. Whitehead, *Adventures of Ideas*, p. 161.
7. Tillich, *The Protestant Era*, p. 9.
8. Ibid.
9. Heisenberg, *The Physicist's Conception of Nature*, p. 84.
10. Heim, *Christian Faith and Natural Science*, p. 26.
11. Heisenberg, *The Physicist's Conception of Nature*, pp. 28–29.
12. Ibid.
13. Ibid., p. 29.
14. Barbour, *Issues in Science and Religion*, p. 182.
15. Heisenberg, *Physics and Philosophy*, p. 164.
16. Ibid., p. 66.

17. Ibid.
18. Heim, *Christian Faith and Natural Science;* p. 135.
19. Heisenberg, *Physics and Philosophy,* p. 115.
20. Barbour, *Issues in Science and Religion,* p. 297.
21. Heisenberg, *The Physicist's Conception of Nature,* p. 24.
22. Heisenberg, *Across the Frontiers,* p. 115.
23. Heisenberg, *The Physicist's Conception of Nature,* p. 46.
24. Heisenberg, *Physics and Philosophy,* p. 63.
25. Heisenberg, *Across the Frontiers,* p. 22.
26. Heisenberg, *Physics and Philosophy,* p. 12.
27. Ibid., p. 88.
28. Barbour, *Issues in Science and Religion,* p. 297.
29. Ibid., p. 253.
30. Heisenberg, *The Physicist's Conception of Nature,* p. 24.
31. Barbour, *Issues in Science and Religion,* p. 289.
32. Heisenberg, *The Physicist's Conception of Nature,* p. 105.

NOTES FOR CHAPTER 5

1. Psalm 8:6–8, KJV.
2. Barbour, *Issues in Science and Religion,* p. 22.
3. Bateson, *Steps to an Ecology of Mind,* p. 427.
4. Barbour, *Issues in Science and Religion,* p. 83.
5. Cassirer, *An Essay on Man,* p. 20.
6. Levi-Strauss, *Structural Anthropology,* p. 3.
7. Teilhard de Chardin, *The Phenomenon of Man,* p. 13.
8. Ibid.
9. Ibid.
10. Ibid., p. 65.
11. Ibid.
12. Watson, *Supernature,* p. 35.
13. Teilhard de Chardin, *The Phenomenon of Man,* p. 65.
14. Ibid., p. 40.
15. Ibid., p. 41.
16. Ibid., pp. 45–46.
17. Ibid., p. 49.
18. Ibid., p. 151.
19. Ibid., p. 146.
20. Ibid., p. 186.
21. Ibid., pp. 209–210.
22. Ibid., p. 271.
23. Ibid., p. 294.

NOTES FOR CHAPTER 6

1. Teilhard de Chardin, *The Phenomenon of Man,* p. 45.
2. Ibid., p. 263.

3. Ibid., p. 89.
4. Etienne Gilson, "Concerning Christian Philosophy," in Klibansky and Paton, eds., *Philosophy and History: The Ernst Cassirer Festschrift*, p. 74.
5. Cassirer, *An Essay on Man*, p. 224.
6. Bateson, *Steps to an Ecology of Mind*, p. 451.
7. Ibid., p. 346.
8. Ardrey, *The Hunting Hypothesis*, p. 201.
9. Barbour, *Issues in Science and Religion*, p. 397.
10. Ardrey, *The Hunting Hypothesis*, p. 192.
11. Ibid., p. 120.
12. Ibid., p. 81.
13. Ibid., p. 201.
14. Heisenberg, *Physics and Beyond*, p. 114.
15. Teilhard de Chardin, *The Phenomenon of Man*, p. 89.
16. Ardrey, *African Genesis*, p. 225.
17. Ardrey, *The Social Contract*, p. 347.

NOTES FOR CHAPTER 7

1. Teilhard de Chardin, *The Phenomenon of Man*, p. 83.
2. Brown, Frank A., Jr., "The Rhythmic Nature of Animals and Plants," *American Scientist*, Volume 47, June 1959, p. 157.
3. Ibid., p. 159.
4. Ibid., p. 166.
5. Ibid., p. 168.
6. Levi-Strauss, *Structural Anthropology*, p. 59.
7. Ibid.
8. Teilhard de Chardin, *The Phenomenon of Man*, p. 69.
9. Ardrey, *African Genesis*, p. 59.
10. Ibid., p. 12.
11. Ibid., p. 19. Italics mine.
12. Ibid., p. 47.
13. Ibid., pp. 57–58.
14. Ibid., pp. 53–54.
15. Ibid., p. 92.
16. Ibid., p. 91.
17. Ibid., p. 105.
18. Ibid., p. 107.
19. Ardrey, *The Social Contract*, p. 3.
20. Ardrey, *African Genesis*, p. 135.
21. Ibid., p. 120.
22. Ibid., p. 21.
23. Ibid., p. 348.
24. Ibid., p. 350.
25. Ardrey, *The Hunting Hypothesis*, p. 26.
26. Ibid., p. 11. Italics in the original.
27. Ibid., p. 61.

28. Ibid., p. 28.
29. Ibid.
30. Ibid, 92.
31. Ibid.
32. Ardrey, *African Genesis*, p. 149.
33. Ibid., p. 333.
34. Ardrey, *The Hunting Hypothesis*, p. 104.
35. Ardrey, *African Genesis.*, p. 41.

NOTES FOR CHAPTER 8

1. Heim, *Christian Faith and Natural Science*, p. 101.
2. Watson, *Supernature*, p. 3.
3. Ibid., p. 114.
4. Bateson, *Steps to an Ecology of Mind*, pp. 417–18.
5. Ibid., p. 452.
6. Ibid., p. 470.
7. Ardrey, *African Genesis*, p. 87.
8. Cassirer, *An Essay on Man*, pp. 115–16.
9. Bateson, *Steps to an Ecology of Mind*, p. 367.
10. Ibid., pp. 412–13.
11. Hall, *The Silent Language*, p. 62.
12. Teilhard de Chardin, *The Phenomenon of Man*, p. 165. Italics mine.
13. Ibid.
14. Ardrey, *African Genesis*, p. 19.
15. Ardrey, *The Hunting Hypothesis*, p. 128.
16. Ardrey, *African Genesis*, p. 135.
17. Jung, "The Psychological Aspects of the Kore," in *The Archetypes and the Collective Unconscious*, Collected Works, Volume 9, part 1, p. 188.
18. Ardrey, *African Genesis*, p. 127.
19. Ibid., pp. 128–29.
20. Ibid., p. 129.
21. Barbour, *Issues in Science and Religion*, p. 409.
22. Ardrey, *African Genesis*, p. 127.
23. Ardrey, *The Hunting Hypothesis*, p. 8.
24. Ibid., p. 66.
25. Ardrey, *African Genesis*, pp. 137–138.
26. Ibid., p. 164.
27. Ardrey, *The Hunting Hypothesis*, p. 66.
28. Ibid., p. 120.
29. Ibid.
30. Ardrey, *The Social Contract*, p. 357.

NOTES FOR CHAPTER 9

1. Ardrey, *African Genesis*, p. 128.
2. Ibid., p. 21.

3. Jung, "The Concept of the Collective Unconscious," in *The Archetypes and the Collective Unconscious,* Collected Works, Volume 9, part 1, p. 43.
4. Ibid., p. 78.
5. Ibid.
6. Teilhard de Chardin, *The Phenomenon of Man,* p. 221.
7. Ardrey, *The Hunting Hypothesis,* p. 119.
8. Jung, "Psychology of the Child Archetype," in *The Archetypes and the Collective Unconscious,* Collected Works, Volume 9, part 1, p. 173.
9. Teilhard de Chardin, *The Phenomenon of Man,* p. 71.
10. Jung, "Conscious, Unconscious and Individuation," in *The Archetypes and the Collective Unconscious,* Collected Works, Volume 9, part 1, p. 279.
11. Ibid., "The Phenomenology of the Spirit in Fairytales," p. 224. Italics mine.
12. Ibid., "Archetypes of the Collective Unconscious," p. 40.
13. Ibid., p. 3.
14. Ibid., "The Concept of the Collective Unconscious," p. 42.
15. Ibid., "The Psychology of the Child Archetype," p. 160.
16. Ibid., "The Psychological Aspects of the Kore," p. 183.
17. Ibid., "On the Psychology of the Trickster-Figure," p. 264.
18. Ibid., "Archetypes of the Collective Unconscious," p. 38.
19. Jung, "The Fight with the Shadow," in *Civilization in Transition,* Collected Works, Volume 10, p. 218.
20. Jung, "Christ, A Symbol of the Self," in *Aion,* Collected Works, Volume 9, part 2, p. 71.
21. Jung, "The Concept of the Collective Unconscious," in *The Archetypes and the Collective Unconscious,* Collected Works, Volume 9, part 1, p. 43.
22. Jung, "The Ego," in *Aion,* Collected Works, Volume 9, part 2, p. 3.
23. Jung, "Conscious, Unconscious, and Individuation," in *The Archetypes and the Collective Unconscious,* Collected Works, Volume 9, part 1, p. 284.
24. Jung, "The Shadow," in *Aion,* Collected Works, Volume 9, part 2, p. 8.
25. Jung, "Archetypes of the Collective Unconscious," in *The Archetypes and the Collective Unconscious,* Collected Works, Volume 9, part 1, p. 31.
26. Jung, "The Syzygy: Anima and Animus," in *Aion,* Collected Works, Volume 9, part 2, p. 14.
27. Jung, "Archetypes of the Collective Unconscious," in *The Archetypes and the Collective Unconscious,* Collected Works, Volume 9, part 1, p. 35.
28. Ibid., "The Phenomenology of the Spirit in Fairytales," p. 222.
29. Ibid., "Positive Aspects of the Mother-Complex," p. 92.
30. Ibid., "The Mother Archetype," p. 82.
31. Ibid., "The Psychology of the Child Archetype," p. 164.
32. Ibid., p. 170.

NOTES FOR CHAPTER 10

1. Ardrey, *The Hunting Hypothesis,* p. 137.
2. Ardrey, *The Social Contract,* p. 345.
3. Heisenberg, *The Physicist's Conception of Nature,* pp. 16–17.
4. McLuhan, *Understanding Media: The Extensions of Man,* p. 145

5. Heisenberg, *The Physicist's Conception of Nature,* p. 17.
6. McLuhan, *Understanding Media: The Extensions of Man,* p. 43.
7. Toffler, *Future Shock,* p. 18.
8. McLuhan, *Understanding Media: The Extensions of Man,* p. 4.
9. Ibid., p. 255.
10. Toffler, *Future Shock,* p. 17.
11. McLuhan, *Understanding Media: The Extensions of Man,* p. 15.
12. Toffler, *Future Shock* pp. 311–12.
13. Ibid., p. 161.
14. McLuhan, *Understanding Media: The Extensions of Man,* p. 105.
15. Ibid., p. 124.
16. Werner, *Comparative Psychology of Mental Development,* p. 402.
17. McLuhan, *Understanding Media: The Extensions of Man,* p. 26.
18. Ibid., p. 53.
19. Ibid., p. 352.
20. Ibid., pp. 357–58.
21. Toffler, *Future Shock,* p. 283.
22. Ibid., p. 92.
23. Ibid., p. 107.
24. Slater, *Earthwalk,* p. 15.
25. Toffler, *Future Shock,* p. 139.
26. Ibid., pp. 139–40.
27. Ibid., pp. 413–14.
28. Ibid., p. 284.
29. McLuhan, *Understanding Media: The Extensions of Man,* p. 138.
30. Ibid., p. 352.
31. Ibid., p. 283.
32. Ibid., pp. 138–39.
33. Ibid., p. 70.

NOTES FOR CHAPTER 11

1. Ardrey, *The Hunting Hypothesis,* p. 170.
2. Neumann, *The Origins and History of Consciousness,* p. 184.
3. Teilhard de Chardin, *The Phenomenon of Man,* p. 262.
4. Wach, *The Comparative Study of Religions,* pp. 126–27.
5. Toffler, *Future Shock,* p. 266.
6. McLuhan, *Understanding Media: The Extensions of Man,* pp. 26–27.
7. Toynbee, *A Study of History,* p. 42.
8. Ibid., p. 39.
9. Johan Huizinga, "A Definition of the Concept of History," in Klibansky and Paton, eds., *Philosophy and History: The Ernst Cassirer Festschrift,* p. 7.
10. Bateson, *Steps to an Ecology of Mind,* p. 484.
11. Levi-Strauss, *The Savage Mind,* p. 117.
12. Toffler, *Future Shock,* p. 29.
13. Wach, *The Comparative Study of Religions,* p. 129.

14. Gerardus van der Leeuw, "The Connection between Religion and Philosophy in the History of Religion," in Pelikan, ed., *Twentieth Century Theology in the Making*, Volume 2, pp. 257–58.
15. Leon Brunschvicg, "History and Philosophy," in Klibansky and Paton, eds., *Philosophy and History: The Ernst Cassirer Festschrift*, p. 27.
16. Cassirer, *An Essay on Man*, pp. 96–97.
17. Neumann, *The Origins and History of Consciousness*, pp. 436–37. Italics mine.
18. Jung, "The Undiscovered Self," in *Civilization in Transition*, Collected Works, Volume 10, p. 252.
19. Hans Meyerhoff, "Freud and the Ambiguity of Culture," in Mazlish, ed., *Psychoanalysis and History*, p. 66.
20. Jung, "The Undiscovered Self," in *Civilization in Transition*, Collected Works, Volume 10, p. 252.
21. Ibid., pp. 252–53.
22. Revel, *Without Marx or Jesus*, p. 71.
23. Jung, "The Spiritual Problem of Modern Man," in *Civilization in Transition*, Collected Works, Volume 10, p. 81.

NOTES FOR CHAPTER 12

1. Reich, Charles, "The New Property," *Yale Law Journal*, V. 73, Number 5, April, 1964, p. 733.
2. Ibid., p. 738.
3. *Rocky Mountain News, Parade Magazine*, December 7, 1975, p. 7.
4. P.L. 91-230.
5. Reich, "The New Property," p. 745.
6. Ibid., p. 747.
7. Ibid., p. 758.
8. Ibid., p. 754.
9. Ibid., pp. 769–70.
10. Ibid., p. 773.
11. Ibid., p. 778.
12. Ibid.
13. Ibid., p. 785.

NOTES FOR CHAPTER 13

1. 3 Ariz. App. 28, 411 P. 2d. 201 (1966).
2. Leopold, *A Sand County Almanac*, p. 217.
3. 405 U.S. 727 (1972).
4. Volume 45, Number 2, 1972.
5. Stone, *Should Trees Have Standing?* p. 19.
6. Ibid., p. 21.
7. Slater, *Earthwalk*, pp. 184–85.
8. 354 F. 2d. 608 (1965).
9. Stone, *Should Trees Have Standing?* pp. 47–48.

10. Ibid., p. 62.
11. Ibid., p. 76.
12. Ibid., p. 88.
13. Ibid., p. 103.
14. Ibid., p. 101.

NOTES FOR CHAPTER 14

1. Tillich, *Christianity and the Encounter of the World Religions*, p. 63.
2. Wach, *Types of Religious Experience*, p. 65.
3. Toynbee, *An Historian's Approach to Religion*, p. 274.
4. Ibid., p. 19.
5. Tillich, *Christianity and the Encounter of the World Religions*, p. 64.
6. Barbour, *Issues in Science and Religion*, pp. 236–37.
7. Wach, *Types of Religious Experience*, p. 112.
8. Tillich, *Christianity and the Encounter of the World Religions*, p. 65.
9. Toynbee, *An Historian's Approach to Religion*, p. 93.
10. Söderblum, *The Living God*, p. 324.
11. Ibid., p. 151.
12. Wach, *Types of Religious Experience*, pp. 38–39.
13. Ibid., p. 65.
14. Gerardus van der Leeuw, "The Connections between Religion and Philosophy in the History of Religion," in Pelikan, ed., *Twentieth Century Theology in the Making*, Volume 2, p. 258.
15. Stcherbatsky, *The Conception of the Buddhist Nirvana*, p. 4.
16. Hermann Bauke, "The History of the Christological Doctrine," in Pelikan, ed., *Twentieth Century Theology in the Making*, Volume 2, p. 108.
17. Ibid., p. 109.
18. Gerardus van der Leeuw, "The Connections between Religion and Philosophy in the History of Religion," in Pelikan, ed., Twentieth Century Theology in the Making, Volume 2, p. 258.
19. Toynbee, *An Historian's Approach to Religion*, p. 128.
20. Bateson, *Steps to an Ecology of Mind*, p. 450–51.
21. Schweitzer, *The Quest of the Historical Jesus*, pp. 370–71.
22. Barbour, *Issues in Science and Religion*, p. 217.
23. Söderblum, *The Living God*, p. 160.
24. Wach, *The Comparative Study of Religions*, p. 117.
25. Ibid.
26. Ibid., p. 118.
27. Niebuhr, *The Responsible Self*, pp. 158–59.
28. Ibid., p. 168.

NOTES FOR CHAPTER 15

1. Wach, *The Comparative Study of Religions*, p. 93.
2. Jung, "Archaic Man," in *Civilization in Transition*, Collected Works, Volume 10, p. 63.

3. Ibid., p. 60.
4. Ibid., p. 69.
5. Tillich, *The Protestant Era*, pp. 99–100.
6. Cassirer, *An Essay on Man*, p. 83.
7. Ibid., p. 100.
8. Tillich, *The Protestant Era*, p. 120.
9. Ibid., p. 123. Italics mine.
10. Toynbee, *An Historian's Approach to Religion*, p 34.
11. Wach, *The Comparative Study of Religions*, p. 125.
12. Ibid., p. 139.
13. Ibid., p. 128.
14. Ibid., pp. 121–22.
15. Jung, "Religion as the Counterbalance to Mass-Mindedness," in *Civilization in Transition*, Collected Works, Volume 10, p. 258.
16. Tillich, *The Protestant Era*, p. 108.
17. Paul Tillich, "Myth and Religion," in Pelikan, ed., *Twentieth Century Theology in the Making*, Volume 2, p. 346.
18. Cassirer, *An Essay on Man*, p. 83.
19. Levi-Strauss, *The Savage Mind*, p. 10.
20. Tillich, *The Protestant Era*, p. 111.
21. Cassirer, *An Essay on Man*, p. 45.
22. Levi-Strauss, *The Savage Mind*, p. 256.
23. McLuhan, *Understanding Media; The Extensions of Man*, p. 86. Italics mine.
24. Radin, *The World of Primitive Man*, p. 11.

NOTES FOR CHAPTER 16

1. Cassirer, *An Essay on Man*, p. 3.
2. Ibid.
3. Ibid., p. 82.
4. Ibid.
5. Levi-Strauss, *The Savage Mind*, p. 22.
6. Jung, "Archaic Man," in *Civilization in Transition*, Collected Works, Volume 10, p. 59.
7. Levi-Strauss, *The Savage Mind*, p. 18.
8. Levi-Strauss, *Structural Anthropology*, p. 208. Italics mine.
9. Thomas Ferté, "A Record of Success," Pensée, Volume 2, No. 2, May 1972, pp. 11–15, 23.
10. Velikovsky, *Worlds in Collision*, p. vii.
11. Velikovsky, *Earth in Upheaval*, pp. 217–18.
12. Wilfrid Francis, "Letter to the Editor," Pensée, Volume 2, No. 3, Fall 1972, p. 21.

NOTES FOR CHAPTER 17

1. These thirteen themes were articulated in the document known as the Hartford Appeal for Theological Affirmation that was produced by the January 1975 meeting of eighteen theologians at the Hartford Seminary Foundation.

2. The *Christian Century*, 4 June 1975, pp. 563–64, reported the meeting substantially in this manner.
3. *Christianity and Crisis*, 16 February 1976, pp. 23–27.
4. Bart J. Bok, Lawrence E. Jerome and Paul Kurts, "Objections to Astrology," *The Humanist*, September/October 1975, p. 4.
5. Bart J. Bok, "A Critical Look at Astrology," *The Humanist*, September/October 1975, p. 8.
6. Bok, Jerome, and Kurtz, "Objections to Astrology," *The Humanist*, September/October 1975, p. 4.
7. *New York Times*, 1 May 1976, 26:1.
8. Ibid.
9. McLuhan, *Understanding Media: The Extensions of Man*, p. 18.
10. Ibid., p. 93.
11. Heisenberg, *Across the Frontiers*, p. xii.
12. Ardrey, *The Social Contract*, p. 363.
13. Ibid., p. 364.

NOTES FOR CHAPTER 18

1. Heim, *Christian Faith and Natural Science*, p. 126.
2. Ibid., p. 135.
3. Barbour, *Issues in Science and Religion*, p. 437.
4. Heim, *Christian Faith and Natural Science*, pp. 101–2.
5. Ibid., p. 88.
6. Barbour, *Issues in Science and Religion*, p. 425. Italics mine.
7. Ibid., p. 182.
8. Ibid., p. 430.
9. Ibid., p. 415.
10. Ibid.
11. Ibid., p. 5.
12. Ibid., p. 454.
13. Ibid., p. 5.
14. Ibid., p. 255.
15. Ibid., p. 253.
16. Barbour, *Myths, Models and Paradigms*, p. 6.
17. Ibid., p. 145.
18. Ibid., p. 142.
19. Ibid.
20. Barbour, *Issues in Science and Religion*, p. 217.
21. Ibid., p. 458.
22. Ibid., p. 262.
23. Jung, "The Meaning of Self-Knowledge," in *Civilization in Transition*, Collected Works, Volume 10, p. 303.

NOTES FOR CHAPTER 19

1. As quoted in Toffler, *Future Shock*, p. 15.

2. Heisenberg, *Physics and Philosophy*, p. 104.
3. Collingwood, *The Idea of History*, p. 222. Italics mine.
4. Barbour, *Myths, Models and Paradigms*, p. 92.
5. Collingwood, *The Idea of History*, p. 217.
6. Leon Brunschvicg, "History and Philosophy," in Klibansky and Paton, eds., *Philosophy and History: The Ernst Cassirer Festschrift*, p. 32.
7. Bok, "A Critical Look at Astrology," *The Humanist*, September/October 1975, p. 6.
8. Ibid., p. 7.
9. Ibid.
10. Ibid., pp. 8–9.
11. Lawrence E. Jerome, "Astrology: Magic or Science," *The Humanist*, September/-October 1975, p. 10.
12. Ibid., p. 11. Italics mine.
13. Ibid.
14. Ibid., p. 12.
15. Ibid., p. 14.
16. Ibid.
17. Barbour, *Issues in Science and Religion*, p. 140.
18. Heisenberg, *Physics and Philosophy*, p. 95.
19. Heisenberg, *Across the Frontiers*, p. 157. Italics mine.
20. Watson, *Supernature*, p. 50.
21. Ibid.
22. Frank A. Brown, Jr., "The Rhythmic Nature of Animals and Plants," *American Scientist*, Volume 47, June 1959, p. 161.
23. Ibid., p. 166.
24. Ibid., p. 168.
25. Ibid.
26. Watson, *Supernature*, p. 35. Italics mine.
27. Cassirer, *An Essay on Man*, p. 49.
28. De Santillana and von Dechend, *Hamlet's Mill*, p. 345.
29. Ibid., p. 5.
30. Ibid., p. 2.
31. Ibid., p. 119.
32. Ibid., p. 142.
33. Sendy, *The Coming of the Gods*, p. 206.
34. Watson, *Supernature*, p. 57.
35. Jung, "Concerning the Archetypes, With Special Reference to the Anima Concepts," in *The Archetypes and the Collective Unconscious*, Collected Works, Volume 9, part 1, p. 57.
36. De Santillana and von Dechend, *Hamlet's Mill*, p. 340.

NOTES FOR CHAPTER 20

1. Young, *Doubt and Certainty in Science*, p. 159.
2. Ibid., p. 162.
3. Heisenberg, *Physics and Philosophy*, pp. 201–2.